FIXING U.S. INTERNATIONAL TAXATION

Fixing U.S. International Taxation

Daniel N. Shaviro

OXFORD
UNIVERSITY PRESS

Oxford University Press is a department of the University of Oxford. It furthers the University's objective
of excellence in research, scholarship, and education by publishing worldwide.

Oxford   New York
Auckland   Cape Town   Dar es Salaam   Hong Kong   Karachi   Kuala Lumpur   Madrid
Melbourne   Mexico City   Nairobi   New Delhi   Shanghai   Taipei   Toronto

With offices in
Argentina   Austria   Brazil   Chile   Czech Republic   France   Greece   Guatemala   Hungary
Italy   Japan   Poland   Portugal   Singapore   South Korea   Switzerland   Thailand
Turkey   Ukraine   Vietnam

Oxford is a registered trade mark of Oxford University Press in the UK and certain other countries.

Published in the United States of America by
Oxford University Press
198 Madison Avenue, New York, NY 10016

Library of Congress Cataloging-in-Publication Data

Shaviro, Daniel N.
  Fixing U.S. international taxation / Daniel N. Shaviro.
    pages cm
  Includes bibliographical references and index.
  ISBN 978-0-19-935975-2 ((hardback) : alk. paper)
1. International business enterprises—Taxation—Law and legislation—United States.
2. Income tax—United States—Foreign income. 3. Corporations, American—Taxation—Law and
legislation—United States. 4. Investments, Foreign—Taxation—Law and legislation—
United States. 5. Double taxation—United States. I. Title. II. Title: Fixing United States
international taxation.

  KF6499.I57S53 2014
  343.7306'8—dc23

                                                                                2013026835

9 8 7 6 5 4 3 2 1

Printed in the United States of America on acid-free paper

Note to Readers
This publication is designed to provide accurate and authoritative information in regard to
the subject matter covered. It is based upon sources believed to be accurate and reliable and is
intended to be current as of the time it was written. It is sold with the understanding that the
publisher is not engaged in rendering legal, accounting, or other professional services. If legal
advice or other expert assistance is required, the services of a competent professional person
should be sought. Also, to confirm that the information has not been affected or changed by
recent developments, traditional legal research techniques should be used, including checking
primary sources where appropriate.

*(Based on the Declaration of Principles jointly adopted by a Committee of the
American Bar Association and a Committee of Publishers and Associations.)*

To My Wife, Patricia Ludwig

Contents

Acknowledgments

I AM GRATEFUL to Yariv Brauner, Edward Kleinbard, Yoram Margalioth, Fadi Shaheen, Stephen Shay, and five anonymous reviewers for their comments on earlier drafts of the manuscript.

1 Introduction and Overview

A. A Fork in the Road?

Yogi Berra once offered the advice, "When you come to a fork in the road, take it." He could almost have been speaking about the U.S. international tax rules, which govern how we tax cross-border or multinational investment. For "outbound" investment, or that earned abroad by U.S. companies, the U.S. rules, for almost a century, have muddled along in the netherworld between two sharply etched approaches that dominate the literature: each intuitively appealing but utterly inconsistent with the other.

The first approach is called *worldwide* or *residence-based* taxation. Under it, the U.S. rules would impose tax at the same rate on U.S. companies' foreign source income (FSI) as on their domestic income. The great apparent virtue of this approach is that it would prevent the companies from reducing their U.S. tax liability by investing (or reporting income) abroad rather than at home.

The second approach is called *source-based* or *territorial* taxation. Under it, the United States, recognizing that foreign companies pay no U.S. tax when they invest abroad, would extend this same U.S. tax exemption for FSI to its own companies. (This approach is therefore also called *exemption*). The great apparent virtue of this approach is that it would avoid placing U.S. companies under a competitive disadvantage, as compared to their foreign rivals, when they invest abroad.

How could one possibly object to either approach? Surely no one wants the U.S. tax rules to encourage our companies to invest (or report income) abroad rather than at home. That would seemingly be self-defeating. Yet surely no one wants U.S. firms to face competitive handicaps when they invest abroad. Whether one favors a "level playing field"—long one of tax policy's most powerful and popular (if trite) metaphors—or is actively rooting for "our" home team firms to "win" their contests on the road, imposing a tax handicap on U.S. firms seems self-defeating as well.

Unfortunately, however, we cannot follow both of these approaches at once. For example, if we tax U.S. company General Electric (GE) when it invests at home, and do not tax GE's global rival Siemens when it invests in Germany, we simply cannot tax GE's German income both at the U.S. domestic rate and at our zero tax rate for Siemens' German income. Rather, we must choose one or the other, or else compromise with something in the middle that fully satisfies neither approach.

In stating the dilemma this way, I have diverged from the prevailing custom in international tax policy debate, which is to compare *all* countries' taxes on a given investment, rather than just those imposed by a given country (such as the United States). My reasons for describing the problem this way, rather than in the conventional way, will become clear later in this chapter and throughout the book. But even if one takes account of all countries' taxes when checking for tax bias, the same problem arises unless everyone charges the same rate. Thus, suppose the U.S. tax rate is 35 percent, while that in Germany is only 20 percent. In these circumstances, the U.S. tax system could not match GE's overall global tax rate, when investing in Germany, both to the 35 percent rate that it would pay domestically, and to the 20 percent rate that Siemens was paying in Germany.

Accordingly, whether one looks just at U.S. taxes or at all countries' taxes (where their rates differ), one faces the same dilemma. Under either formulation, concern about GE's tax minimization incentives suggests imposing U.S. tax (or at least a make-up tax) on its German income, while concern about the GE vs. Siemens differential suggests that the U.S. exempt non-U.S. source income. Yet, however intuitively appealing we might find each approach, we cannot follow them both.

Reflecting the evident awkwardness of this dilemma, the U.S. rules, for almost a century, have been suspended in the middle between the worldwide and territorial poles, taxing U.S. companies' FSI, but at a greatly reduced effective rate compared to that which applies domestically. Opposing political forces, backed by the rival approaches' offsetting intuitive appeal, have long battled to a stalemate that not only satisfies neither side, but is absurdly dysfunctional due to its elaborate Rube Goldberg-style structure. Not merely unaesthetic (though surely that as well), this structure makes it inevitable that the planning and compliance costs the system induces will be "disproportionately high relative to their role in the activities of the corporation," and "extremely high relative to the revenue raised by the U.S. government on this income" (Blumenthal and Slemrod 1996, 48).

The years since this statement was made have only added to its truth, due to the development of all sorts of new tax planning tricks that empower U.S. companies to lower their U.S. (and foreign) tax obligations at the cost of extra paperwork and convoluted internal cash flow management. Making things worse still, all of this "costly tax planning. . . necessitate[s] a significant amount of costly enforcement and compliance activities by the IRS" (President's Economic Recovery and Advisory Board 2010, 88). Given all this, "[m]ost experts agree that the current hybrid U.S. system. . . embodies the worst features of both a pure worldwide system and a pure territorial system from the perspective of simplicity, enforcement, and compliance" (88).

Imposing excessive tax planning and compliance costs relative to the revenue raised is bad enough. However, the problems with the existing compromise system for taxing U.S. companies' FSI do not end here. Supporters of worldwide residence-based U.S. corporate taxation complain that the current system encourages rampant tax avoidance by U.S. multinationals, undermining broader tax equity and causing the companies to be unduly tax-favored relative to their purely domestic competitors. Supporters of exempting FSI complain, not only about the potential disadvantages of being a U.S. rather than a foreign multinational when one invests abroad, but also about the problem of "trapped" foreign earnings under our current rules, which may stay abroad for U.S. tax reasons even if they otherwise would come straight home to fund U.S. investments or be distributed to U.S. shareholders. Despite the seeming tension between these two accounts, both are largely correct.

Unfortunately, near-universal consensus that the existing U.S. international tax system is horrendously bad has failed to induce change, given the continuing dissensus about what to replace it with. An obvious solution might involve moving decisively to one of the two poles, by more fully adopting some version of either worldwide taxation or territoriality. This, however, has been impeded by the fact that, in politics no less than trench warfare, it is easier to defend one's own position than to advance through the enemy's.

Of late, there have been some signs of a possible shift toward territoriality. Long a Republican goal, there were occasional hints during the first Obama administration that Democrats might embrace it as well.[1] Factors encouraging the shift, beyond a generally pro-business and anti-tax political environment, include the rising pressures of global tax competition, and the fact that peer countries, such as the United Kingdom and Japan, have recently made their international tax systems more territorial. As a political matter, it is plausible that the United States would already have shifted to a territorial system if not for budgetary concerns. A recent Treasury estimate found that enacting a simplified territorial system without safeguards might reduce U.S. revenues by $130 billion over ten years (President's Economic Recovery Advisory Board 2010, 90). Moreover, while a package of international tax law changes that included exemption could, on the whole, pay for itself or even raise revenue, depending on the other items in the package, this might kill all the fun, so far as exemption's main political supporters are concerned.

Among the factors that have boosted exemption's political prospects is a shift in the intellectual climate of debate among U.S. international tax policy experts. Worldwide residence-based taxation used to be considered clearly superior by most experts—better for the world, and better for the United States. However, recent theoretical and empirical work has destroyed this consensus, and for a while seemingly raised the prospect of an emerging opposite consensus, in which a purely territorial tax was seen as better both for the world and for us. The main concern that continues to get in the way has less to do with taxing FSI as an end in itself, than with the view that worldwide taxation is indispensable to combating profit shifting by U.S. companies, which have become ever more adept at treating large shares of their U.S. (and other) profits as having arisen in tax havens for official reporting purposes (see, e.g., Kleinbard 2011a).

B. The Need for a New Framework

No matter how the short-term politics plays out—continued stalemate that might perhaps include tougher limits on multinationals' tax planning opportunities, or shift toward exemption—ongoing disputes concerning how the United States ought to tax domestic and foreign multinationals are unlikely to recede any time soon. Consider the episodes of media excitement in recent years over aggressive tax planning by such iconic U.S. companies as Apple, GE, and Google. The continuing rise of both global economic integration and tax planning technology, along with ongoing anxieties about U.S. job levels that both sides in the U.S. international tax debate invoke as favoring their preferred approaches, will keep these issues prominent indefinitely. Thus, it would be desirable to have a clear intellectual framework on hand. Best of all, of course, would be to find consensus "right answers" to all of the hard issues in the field. Even short of that, however, there is a need for better guidance regarding how to think about the main tradeoffs.

Making this more difficult is the fact that the international tax policy literature, despite a more than fifty-year history of frequently intensive academic study by exceptionally talented and knowledgeable economists and lawyers, at some point went badly off the rails. For many decades, its main terms of debate have too often reflected crucial misunderstandings of key issues and distinctions, along with a misguided focus on concepts that verge on being completely unhelpful.[2] We need therefore, to start again from first principles—albeit, principles that are routinely used elsewhere in public economics. To begin demonstrating the need for a new approach, consider the following five conceptual problems in the existing international tax policy literature:

C. First Problem: What *Is* the Problem? Is It Double (and Non) Taxation?

Popular and academic writers on international taxation—albeit lawyers more than economists—are largely at one in defining the basic problem that the rules in the field must try to address. It supposedly is "double taxation," which may arise when cross-border investment faces both a residence-based tax in the home country and a source-based tax in the country where the investment is made. Preventing double taxation from occurring—along with double nontaxation, which occurs when cross-border income is taxed nowhere—is thus identified as the supreme task of international tax rules.

To illustrate what "double taxation" is taken to mean, suppose that Acme Products, a U.S. company, earns $100 in Germany, and that the U.S. rate is 35 percent, while the German rate is 20 percent. Taking it as given that Germany will in fact charge Acme $20 of tax, the U.S. is thought to have only two legitimate alternatives. The first is to apply exemption, so that Acme's German income is only taxed in Germany. The second is to charge U.S. tax—it always is assumed, at the same 35 percent statutory rate that applies domestically—but to provide foreign tax credits, or a dollar-for-dollar reduction of the U.S. tax due by reason of the German taxes paid.

Under this second approach, the $35 of U.S. tax liability that Acme would otherwise have owed on its (pre-German tax) German income is reduced to $15 by reason of the allowable credits. Thus, while Acme is literally paying tax to two countries, it is not viewed as being "double-taxed," because the U.S. credits entirely wash out the burden on Acme of having to pay the German tax. Thus, it is just as if Acme had only been taxed by the United States, but with a side payment from the U.S. Treasury to the German Treasury, wholly compensating the latter for its forbearance.

Accordingly, the U.S. tax on Acme's German income ostensibly must be either zero or $15, as opposed to anything in between. This alone should excite suspicion. One would normally expect policy assessments to exhibit greater continuity. Given, for example, that raising the tax from zero to $1, or lowering it from $15 to $14, seems unlikely to change dramatically its practical effects (such as on the central tax policy concerns of efficiency and distribution), it is surprising to witness the evident assumption that everything in the middle must be ruled out.

Why is aversion to double taxation—leading to the assumption that the home country must either exempt foreign source income or offer foreign tax credits—so prevalent? The reasons appear to be several. First, there evidently is some sort of inchoate moral intuition lying behind it—although, as we will see, the intuition proves upon closer examination to be incoherent and formalistic.

Second, bilateral tax treaties, such as the existing one between the United States and Germany, invariably use the concept of avoiding double (and non) taxation as a coordinating device between overlapping tax systems. In the bilateral setting of a treaty, this concept may indeed be convenient and useful. But the United States is not operating in the treaty setting when it more generally determines how it should tax outbound investment.

The third ground for treating aversion to double taxation as a fundamental principle should help make its misdirectedness—as well as its relationship to what actually are serious concerns—somewhat clearer. Suppose, in the prior example, that the United States taxed Acme's $100 of German income at the full 35 percent rate, with the German taxes of $20 merely being deductible. Then Acme would end with only $52 after paying both German and U.S. taxes. Its overall global tax rate, on this income, of 48 percent would compare quite unfavorably with the global rates (i.e., just the domestic rates) that U.S. and German companies would face when investing at home. And German companies, of course, would face the same 48 percent global tax rate when they invested in the United States, if Germany taxed its residents' foreign source income at the full domestic rate, with U.S. taxes merely being deductible. The result would likely be significant discouragement of cross-border investment by U.S. and German firms.

The prospect of such discouragement is indeed relevant to U.S. policy making, whether we are setting our international tax policy rules unilaterally or engaged in strategic interaction with other countries. However, the use of such examples to support an anti-double tax principle confuses two distinct questions. The first is "How much?" The second is "How many times?"

To illustrate the distinction between these two questions, suppose the United States treated German taxes as merely deductible, but lowered its tax rate for FSI to 15 percent. Acme would now be getting double taxed, since the U.S. rules would no longer be entirely negating the separate impact of the German tax. But Acme's U.S. tax bill on its FSI would have declined from $15 under the full rate/foreign tax credit system, to just $12 (i.e., 15 percent of $80). So Acme's outbound investment would actually be *less* tax discouraged than previously, and the "crime" of double taxation would evidently be victimless.

Even Germany, while it could point to a clear treaty violation, would face no adverse consequence apart from one that actually is unrelated to double taxation as such. The change in U.S. policy might indeed make Germany worse off, since U.S. firms that were effectively subject to the U.S. worldwide tax would no longer be able to credit their German taxes against those levied at home. Thus, U.S. multinationals might be more eager than previously to minimize their German tax liabilities, whether through tax planning or actual shifts in where they operate. But they would likewise have this incentive if the United States, consistently with its tax treaty obligations, simply exempted those companies' FSI from the prospect of facing any residual U.S. tax. Indeed, under exemption they would care *more* about avoiding German taxes than under a worldwide/foreign tax deductibility approach with, say, a 15 percent U.S. tax rate on FSI, since the latter would reduce their after-U.S. tax cost of paying a dollar of German taxes from one full dollar to 85 cents.

This example helps to show that exemption is what I call an implicit deductibility system. That is, it has the same effect on U.S. companies' incentives, in trading off foreign tax liabilities against other foreign expenses (or forgone income), as would the adoption of explicit foreign tax deductibility with a positive U.S. tax rate (whether, say, 0.00001 percent or 35 percent) for foreign source income.

In sum, while there may be good reason to care about high versus low taxes on cross-border activity, or about even versus uneven taxes at a given margin, this does not imply that there is any direct normative reason to care about the *number* of taxes that are being levied on a given taxpayer or transaction. After all, most of us would rather be taxed twenty times at a 1 percent rate each time than once at 35 percent.

If double taxation is not objectionable as such, what about double non-taxation? Consider in particular the "stateless income" (Kleinbard 2011a) that multinationals are increasingly adept at locating for tax reporting purposes in tax havens where little productive activity occurs. As it happens, the point that zero is not a magic number is already widely accepted. Anti-tax haven rules (both actual and proposed) for resident companies' FSI, in the United States and elsewhere, generally do not provide any escape hatch for charging a very low tax rate that is not quite zero. However, a further issue about global tax minimization through the use of tax havens remains inadequately recognized.

Suppose we observe that Acme Products, in addition to having operations, affiliates, and taxable income in the United States and Germany, also has an affiliate in the Cayman Islands that purports to earn a significant percentage of Acme's global profits. We may reasonably suspect that little of Acme's global economic activity is actually taking place in the Caymans, and thus that this is "stateless income," relocated from either the United States or Germany by means of tax planning games. Suppose further that, despite having a nominally worldwide system, the United States does not get to tax Acme's Caymans income. (We will soon see why, under existing U.S. rules, this may be a realistic assumption.) What should U.S. policy makers think about this phenomenon?

A principle holding that everything should be taxed somewhere once would suggest unconditionally objecting to Acme's profit shifting to the Caymans. But in evaluating what has happened, there are two distinct possibilities to keep in mind. The first is that profits were shifted out of the United States, and that Acme has therefore used tax planning to avoid the source-based U.S. tax. The second possibility, however, is that Acme shifted profits out of Germany, thus avoiding the German rather than the U.S. tax. In practice, these two scenarios may be extremely difficult, and perhaps indeed impossible, to tell apart—and one might expect Acme's reported Caymans profits to include some of each.

But should U.S. policy makers regard the two scenarios as equivalent? To answer this question, we must turn to the second big problem with the existing international tax policy literature, which is its general failure to distinguish between domestic and foreign taxes even though they are very different from the standpoint of a given country.

D. Second Problem: How Should We Think about Foreign Taxes?

One of the most bizarre aspects of international tax policy analysis is its frequent indifference to the question of whether tax revenues go to the home country that is deciding what international tax rules to apply, or to some other country. As an analytical matter, such indifference is a necessary precondition to focusing exclusively on global rather than domestic tax rates as the key variable. It is at least implicit in the practice of offering foreign tax credits to resident multinational firms. And it is verging on explicit if we do not treat reciprocity as a precondition for offering foreign tax credits. That is, if we allow domestic taxpayers to credit, against their U.S. liability, the taxes levied by countries that do not similarly reimburse their taxpayers for paying U.S. taxes—such as by reason of offering exemption, which (again) is an implicit deductibility system—then we are effectively making a gift of the revenue to foreign Treasuries.

From a unilateral national welfare perspective—that is, one in which we care only about the welfare of domestic individuals rather than everyone in the world, and ignore or assume away other countries' strategic and other responses to our rules—it is clearly erroneous to treat foreign and domestic taxes as interchangeable. After all, the reason we typically regard taxpayers' incentive to reduce or avoid domestic taxes as socially suboptimal is that *we get the money* from those taxes.

Thus, in the purely domestic context, suppose I would decide whether to work for an extra hour based on how much of the earnings I would get to keep after-tax, and that I viewed the tax on these earnings as no less a cost to me than, say, the extra commuting expenses that I would incur if I accepted the assignment. From the social standpoint, this is an externality problem. I am ignoring the benefit to the domestic individuals who would reap the gain if this extra money went into the public fisc. Analytically, it is the same problem as if I were to ignore the pollution costs that my factory would impose on other individuals by releasing noxious fluids into an adjoining river. With respect to foreign taxes, however, *we don't get the money*—instead, it goes to foreign individuals, whose welfare we commonly disregard in making domestic policy choices (for example, in deciding whether to fund schools at home or abroad).

As noted above, this analysis is incomplete unless we assume, not just that we are exclusively concerned with domestic individuals' welfare, but also that there are no relevant strategic and other interactions between what we do and what other countries do. If, for example, all other countries were resolved to credit our taxes when paid by their own residents if and only if we credited their taxes in the reciprocal setting, then it is possible (depending on further information) that treating domestic and foreign tax payments as effectively equivalent would offer, at least, a plausible rough rule of thumb.

But the fact that there may be important interactions between our foreign tax rules and those in other countries does not establish that we generally should treat domestic and foreign taxes as if they were equivalent after all, from a domestic national welfare standpoint. All it means is that we need to think about those interactions. Viewing our treatment of foreign taxes as potentially relevant to how other countries treat our taxes is *not* the same thing as concluding that they are all effectively the same. Consider, for example, that our peer countries have generally shifted toward exemption, and thus toward an implicit deductibility system for the U.S. taxes that their resident companies pay. One can hardly argue that they would abandon foreign tax creditability if we did, when they have already done so without waiting for us to go first.

As we will see, from a purely unilateral national welfare standpoint, mere foreign tax deductibility—including that which results implicitly from having an exemption system for foreign source income—is clearly the right answer, unless and until some further consideration emerges to complicate the analysis. After all, when U.S. people pay foreign taxes, it truly is just an expense from our standpoint, no less than when they pay foreign fuel bills or labor costs, given that we don't get the money.[3]

There is, however, one last complication that we need to keep in mind. Recall the earlier example where Acme Products, a U.S. firm with domestic and German operations, reported significant profits as having arisen in the Cayman Islands, most likely due to tax planning games that shifted them, for official reporting purposes, out of the U.S. and/or Germany. Despite the ambiguity of from where the profits were shifted, there may be greater reason to suspect that true U.S. income is showing up in the Caymans than that it is showing up in Germany. After all, if U.S. profits are being shifted for official reporting purposes, the taxpayer has more to gain by placing them where the tax rate is actually zero. In addition, as we will see, shifting U.S. profits to a relatively high-tax country such as Germany may simply be the first step, for planning purposes, toward re-shifting them to a tax haven, which often is harder to do directly from home.

The bottom line that this suggests is a bit complicated, and thus needs to be stated carefully. On the one hand, if we regard foreign taxes, unlike domestic taxes, as purely a cost from the social as well as the taxpayer's individual standpoint, then presumably we should be glad when U.S. companies, owned by U.S. individuals, avoid German taxes by shifting their German profits to the Caymans for German reporting purposes. But on the other hand, when we observe U.S. companies reporting Caymans income, we may have reason to regard this, relative to their reporting German income, as effectively a statistical "tag" that is likely to be correlated with profit shifting out of the United States.

There indeed appear to be big numbers attached to this problem. Kimberly Clausing (2011, 1580) estimates that, in 2008, "the income shifting of multinational firms reduced U.S. government corporate tax revenue by about $90 billion." This estimate includes a 35 percent gross-up of the overall dollar amount to account for income shifting by non-U.S. firms that were outside the data set. Such firms are beyond the reach of the U.S. rules for taxing resident firms' FSI. However, even if one eliminates foreign firms from the revenue estimate, it suggests that profit shifting by U.S. firms reduced their 2008 U.S. tax liability by about $67 billion.

Against this background, if we want U.S. companies to treat foreign taxes as equivalent to any other cost that is incurred abroad, but also want to reduce the incentives for profit shifting out of the United States, we face a tradeoff. The former consideration calls for mere foreign tax deductibility, whether the statutory U.S. tax rate for FSI is 0 percent, 35 percent, or anything in between. But the latter consideration may call for treating low-taxed FSI less favorably than that which is higher taxed abroad, even though lowering foreign taxes on a fixed amount of FSI is exactly what we should want U.S. companies, if owned by U.S. individuals, to do.

It is in the nature of the tradeoff that we cannot advance the latter objective without undermining the former objective. After all, we reduce the reward that U.S. companies reap from overseas profit shifting if we treat it (in some cases, mistakenly) as evidence of domestic-to-foreign profit shifting. Nonetheless, given that this is a tradeoff between competing considerations, it would be a considerable surprise if the unilaterally optimal solution involved having, at any given margin, a company's U.S. taxes increase by a dollar when it reduced its foreign taxes by a full dollar (i.e., the creditability result, whether or not it formally reflects offering foreign tax credits). Instead, the optimal solution might involve companies reaping a worse-than-deductibility, albeit better-than-creditability, marginal result from reporting profits in tax havens.

E. Third Problem: The Issue of Multiple Margins

In thinking about international tax policy, issues of efficiency are widely agreed to belong at center stage, although distributional issues pertaining to individuals matter as well. But if there is one fundamental rule of clear thinking that one must follow, in order to analyze efficiency in an intellectually coherent fashion, it is that one must proceed, at least initially, by analyzing just *one margin at a time*.

Traditional international tax policy analysis has failed to satisfy this elementary maxim. Instead, a practice of obliviously conflating distinct and separable margins has, at least until recently, reigned as unchallenged orthodoxy in the field. Almost everyone seems to agree that the fundamental choice lies between worldwide/foreign tax credit systems, and those that are territorial. This, however, is a compound choice that sloshes together differences at two distinct margins. The first margin concerns *tax rates on foreign source income*. The second concerns *reimbursement rates for foreign taxes paid*.

Tax rates (both average and marginal) on foreign source income—The first, and more obvious, difference between worldwide and territorial systems lies in the tax rates that they impose on FSI. Under a worldwide approach as commonly conceived, the official statutory tax rate for FSI is the same as that for domestic source income. By contrast, under a territorial system, the tax rate for FSI is zero. Intermediate statutory rates are not so much consciously rejected as ruled out from the start, almost as if they were (for some unknown reason) logically impossible.

As it happens, the scope of the disjuncture may be less than it initially seems, if the worldwide system allows foreign tax credits. Thus, recall the earlier example in which Acme Products' operations and reported income were confined to the United States and Germany, with the U.S. rules taxing FSI at 35 percent but allowing foreign tax credits, while the German rate was 20 percent. If Acme earns $100 of German income (as determined by both systems) then, after paying $20 of German tax, it will owe only an additional $15 of U.S. tax. Thus, its actual average or effective U.S. tax rate on German source income is only 15 percent, as measured on a pre-German tax basis, or 18.75 percent (i.e., 15/80) as measured after deducting the German taxes.

Both marginal and average U.S. tax rates on FSI may matter for particular purposes. For example, suppose a U.S. company is considering opening a factory either at home or abroad. The average U.S. tax rate on the factory's expected income may matter more to this decision than the question of how its U.S. taxes would change, in either case, if it earned one additional dollar with all else remaining the same. But once the factory is in place, either here or abroad, the marginal U.S. tax rate may determine how much the company would pay to shift a dollar of profits, for official tax reporting purposes, from home to abroad.

Marginal reimbursement rates for foreign taxes—I turn now to the second, analytically distinct difference between the worldwide and territorial systems that traditional analysis fails to consider separately. This is what I call the marginal reimbursement rate (MRR) that they apply to foreign taxes.

In a worldwide system with foreign tax credits, the MRR is in principle 100 percent. After all, each dollar of creditable foreign taxes that you pay is fully reimbursed by the domestic government via a matching one-dollar reduction in domestic income tax liability. This is what it means to have a 100 percent tax credit.

In practice, two features of real-world foreign tax credit systems may lower the MRR that taxpayers actually enjoy. First, all foreign tax credit systems apply what are called foreign tax credit limits. That is, they provide that, while foreign tax credits can offset the domestic tax liability that would otherwise be due on FSI, they cannot go beyond this point.

To illustrate, suppose Acme Products earns $10 million in Germany, while having no other FSI. Once again, suppose that the statutory U.S. tax rate for FSI is 35 percent. Absent foreign tax credits, the U.S. tax on Acme's German income would be $3.5 million. Accordingly, Acme's potentially allowable U.S. foreign tax credits with respect to its FSI are limited to this maximum amount. If Acme paid, say, $4 million of German tax—as might conceivably happen, even if Germany's statutory rate is lower than ours, if Germany measures German-source income differently than we do—then Acme would end up not being able to claim U.S. foreign tax credits for its last $500,000 of German taxes. These would instead give rise to a foreign tax credit carryover, potentially allowable in some other year when Acme would otherwise face residual U.S. tax liability on its FSI. (Since Acme is assumed to have no other FSI, it cannot "cross-credit," i.e., use the extra German taxes to offset the residual U.S. tax on FSI from a low-tax jurisdiction.)

Permanent disallowance of the extra German foreign tax credits would mean that the U.S. MRR for German taxes switched abruptly from 100 percent to 0 percent when the foreign tax credit limit was reached. However, even if the excess credits became allowable in a future year, the MRR is effectively reduced to something below 100 percent, since Acme suffers a time value loss from the delay of the U.S. reimbursement.

Second, the effective MRR in a worldwide system with foreign tax credits may be lowered by the other really important domestic tax benefit for FSI. This tax benefit is called deferral, as it involves U.S. companies' getting to defer inclusion of their foreign subsidiaries' FSI for U.S. tax purposes until it is repatriated, such as through the payment of a dividend to the U.S. parent. This tax benefit is a legacy of realization doctrine, which holds that a change in the value of one's assets generally has no tax consequences until the gain or loss is "realized," such as through a sale or other exchange of the asset. Even in the case of a wholly owned foreign subsidiary, which in practice may be little different than a foreign "branch" whose operations the U.S. company conducts directly, realization doctrine causes the profits to be treated as tax irrelevant to the U.S. parent (which is a separate legal entity) until shareholder-level realization occurs.

In common perception, deferral and the foreign tax credit are respectively what one might call the "Goofus and Gallant" of U.S. international tax policy, referring to a hoary old cartoon series that contrasts bad and good versions of a white middle class suburban, perhaps eight-year-old, boy. Almost everyone recognizes that deferral, the "Goofus" of our system, is a terrible rule. In particular, it induces wasteful tax planning behavior by U.S. companies that must jump through hoops to make optimal use of their foreign earnings while avoiding a taxable U.S. repatriation. The reason for retaining it is that, from a pro-territorial perspective, replacing it with immediate U.S. taxation of resident multinationals' foreign earnings would be even worse. Deferral arose by accident—or, more precisely, through the mindless application of formalistic legal conventions, rather than as a deliberate policy choice—but it has become part of the forced ceasefire-in-place between worldwide taxation and territoriality. I will argue that the foreign tax credit, while it unjustifiably plays Gallant's noble part in common perceptions of our international tax rules, is in fact just as horribly Goofus-like as deferral, leaving aside the analytically distinct fact that each of them happens to lower the effective U.S. tax rate on FSI.

For now, the question of interest is simply how deferral affects the MRR from foreign tax credits. One generally does not get to claim a credit for a given foreign tax liability until the associated FSI is repatriated, and thus becomes subject to U.S. tax. In the interim, however, one's ultimately allowable foreign tax credits may grow at something like a market interest rate, as additional foreign taxes are paid on the accumulating earnings that remain abroad. This complicates the analysis, relative to the scenario for foreign tax credit limits, which involved straightforward loss of present value for the reimbursement when the claiming of a credit is delayed.

Exactly how deferral thus ends up affecting the MRR for foreign taxes paid is too complicated to discuss in full here, and will be addressed in chapter 3. For now, however, the main bottom line is as follows. One can describe hypothetical conditions under which the MRR would effectively still be 100 percent, despite the delay in claiming a given credit until the associated income is repatriated. Under realistic conditions, however, the actual expected MRR, and/or that which multinationals' managers will have in mind when they are making decisions, is potentially much lower, and even 0 percent in some common circumstances.

In short, deferral can in practice negate the incentive effect that the foreign tax credit would otherwise have (i.e., inducing indifference to foreign tax liabilities). We will see that the reverse holds as well: foreign tax credits can negate the incentive effects that might otherwise result from deferral – since, with enough credits, one can repatriate foreign earnings tax-free. But a crucial question in thinking about the future of the U.S. international tax rules is how to evaluate the efficiency of the system as a whole, given the two rules' interactions.

Despite these interactions, however, it is worth keeping in mind the point that, in principle, and except as modified in practice by interactions with other rules, foreign tax credits create a 100 percent MRR for foreign taxes paid by U.S. multinationals. Standing alone, this would induce zero cost consciousness with respect to foreign taxes. There would be no reason to care whether they were low or high, since they would be subject to full reimbursement by the home government.

A territorial system, by contrast, offers an MRR of 0 percent, since it ignores foreign taxes paid. However, of greater note than the fact that the MRR is 0 percent is its matching the marginal tax rate (MTR) that such a system applies to FSI. This is why territoriality functions as an implicit deductibility system for foreign taxes. That is, foreign taxes are in effect deductible from pre-foreign tax FSI, and it just so happens that the remaining amount of such net income is taxed at a 0 percent rate, rather than at any positive rate.

Calling territoriality an implicit deductibility system for foreign taxes may initially sound like a cute semantic point. In fact, however, it is an important substantive point. In a deductibility system for foreign taxes (whether implicit or explicit), the taxpayer has an incentive to maximize its after-foreign-tax income, and to treat $1 of foreign tax liability as equivalent to any other deductible $1 outlay or forgone $1 gross receipt. This condition holds whether the tax rate is 0 percent (as under exemption) or any positive number short of 100 percent. Deductibility therefore gives domestic taxpayers exactly the right marginal incentive with respect to foreign tax liabilities, given that the revenues go to people in other countries, rather than to us.

Why the distinction between the two margins matters—Understanding that the choice of domestic tax rate for FSI is analytically distinct from the choice of MRR for foreign taxes really is a key—and perhaps, *the* key—to unlocking the long-frozen terms of international tax policy debate, and deriving fresh insights. A relatively obvious point is that this analytical move encourages considering a much broader range of alternatives in taxing resident companies' FSI. For example, suppose one believes that deductibility offers the correct marginal approach to reimbursing resident companies' foreign tax costs, but that one does not want to raise (or even, perhaps, in the aggregate to change) the domestic tax burden on FSI. One now can see that these two aims are, at least in theory, simultaneously achievable, as one could make foreign taxes merely deductible but simultaneously lower the statutory tax rate on FSI so that the overall burden on outbound investment, or alternatively overall domestic tax revenues, remained constant (see Clausing and Shaviro 2011).

However, the analytical gain is no less fundamental if one rules out this particular policy response. Even if the worldwide/foreign tax credit and territorial approaches retain an exclusive hammerlock in practice, understanding the two distinct margins that they conflate is intellectually transformative. "Which of these two systems is better?" is simply not a well-posed question, if one fails to grasp its compound character. The questions that one is left with instead, after separating out the two distinct margins—"What should be the domestic tax burden on foreign source income?" and "How should we treat foreign taxes?"—while still not perfect, for example because "foreign source income" is an ill-defined term—are better-suited for coherent analysis.

F. Fourth Problem: Drowning in "Alphabet Soup"

Another big problem with the existing intellectual debate concerning U.S. (and other countries') international taxation is that, rather than starting from first principles, such as the welfare economics framework that typically is used in tax policy analysis by economists and their fellow travelers (such as myself), it all too often relies on what I call "alphabet soup" or the "battle of the acronyms." Under this approach, one starts by describing a single decisional margin at which (all else equal) it would be nice if international taxation were neutral in its effects on taxpayers' incentives. Each of these competing one-dimensional efficiency norms has its own acronym. During the era of the mainly pro-worldwide consensus, the debate focused on CEN (capital export neutrality), CIN (capital import neutrality), and NN (national neutrality). The recent shift toward a more frequently pro-territorial perspective has featured the addition of CON (capital ownership neutrality), NON (national ownership neutrality), and GPN (global portfolio neutrality).

Ostensibly, all one needs to do, in order to choose the right international tax policy, is not to consider tradeoffs (as one might have expected from the style of analysis typically deployed elsewhere) but rather to plunge into the alphabet soup, pick a single winner, and determine whether it supports worldwide taxation or exemption. Thus, if one had to say in a single sentence why support for exemption has gained ground recently in academic debate, it would be that, while CEN used to trump CIN, CON has now entered the fray. As we will see, however, a battle-of-the-acronyms approach to international tax policy issues is wholly inadequate.

This single-bullet, alphabet soup approach—if I may be forgiven for mixing my metaphors—would be ill chosen, and contrary to accepted public economics methodologies outside the field of international taxation, even under the best of circumstances. But the fact that it is used specifically in the international area, which one might have thought somehow related to justifying it, in fact makes using it even worse. Two considerations help to make a battle-of-the-acronyms approach even less suitable in the international realm than it would be as applied to a single country's internal policy choices. I call them the global welfare fallacy and the global convention fallacy.

The global welfare fallacy—A number of the global welfare norms—such as CEN, CIN, and CON—treat global, rather than national, economic welfare as the thing to be maximized. Thus, as we will see, CEN posits that it is a matter of utter indifference whether a dollar of taxes is paid at home or to some other country—even though, from a U.S. standpoint, we don't get the money unless it's our own tax. CON posits that, even if foreign investors would pay good money to the U.S. government for the privilege of getting to invest in U.S. corporations, we should let them do so for free—even though that likewise means throwing away money for no evident reason.

Now, there is nothing fallacious about actually favoring global welfare, rather than purely national welfare—just as there is no fallacy involved if a given individual decides to be a perfect altruist who values everyone else's welfare equally with her own. Indeed, from a purely ethical standpoint the selfless altruist stands on stronger ground than the rest of us, who fall short of sainthood by caring more about ourselves than about other people, who surely feel pleasure and pain just as strongly, and who matter just as much ethically, as we ourselves do.

But that is not what actually is going on here. Proponents of basing international tax policy on global welfare norms do not in general actually believe that the United States should, say, donate three-quarters of its GDP to poorer countries, or afford no preference to its own people in deciding where to build new schools. Instead, when they propound global rather than national welfare arguments, they are confusedly relying on a distinct and much more limited claim, which is that everyone (ourselves included) might end up better off if enough countries cooperated in pursuing global, rather than merely national, welfare.

The underlying point about the possible mutual gains from reciprocity and cooperation, as compared to acting unilaterally and aggressively playing "beggar your neighbor," is indeed important to international tax policy analysis. However, it calls for more concretely and critically examining how reciprocity and cooperation actually work—which the alphabet soup literature fails to do. Pervasive confusion becomes inevitable when ostensible global welfare proponents fail to express accurately, and therefore to analyze properly, what they actually care about. For example, one may end up failing to distinguish between areas where mutually beneficial cooperation is more feasible, and those where it is considerably less so.[4]

The global convention fallacy—Suppose we accepted, however, that U.S. international tax policy should be based on maximizing global, rather than U.S., economic welfare. The proponents of alphabet soup often act as if only one further analytical stage is needed: deciding which global welfare norm would be best if everyone adopted it, and then unilaterally implementing it in one's own country.

The problem with this reasoning is that global welfare does not necessarily improve, even if the analysis is otherwise correct, unless other countries generally adopt the same global welfare norm. Thus, as we will see, the United States might not actually succeed in advancing the objectives of CEN by pursuing it unilaterally while other countries focused, say, on CIN or CON (even if we were generously to assume that they were thinking in global welfare terms to begin with).

In earlier work (see Shaviro 2007), I posited that the global versus national welfare choice might resemble a prisoner's dilemma in which one is deciding whether to "cooperate" with the other players (by pursuing global rather than national welfare) or to "defect" (via a beggar-your-neighbor version of national welfare), but with the difference that one's choice was partly observable and thus might, to a degree, prompt reciprocal cooperation or defection. From this standpoint, it is perhaps conceivable that the United States' choice along the cooperate-to-defect spectrum would be emulated elsewhere (although this was more plausible when U.S. economic dominance was greater—as it was, say, in the 1960s). But when there are different ways of cooperating, based on distinct global welfare norms, one would need a further assumption, for which there is no contemporary supporting evidence, that other countries will follow the U.S. lead regarding, not just *whether*, but also exactly *how* to cooperate.

Once one recognizes the United States' evident inability to prescribe international tax rules that the rest of the world will follow, alphabet soup analysis rests on implicitly assuming that the question of interest to a given country's policy makers is the following: Suppose all countries were holding a convention to adopt universally binding rules regarding the taxation of FSI. What rule should this convention adopt, from the standpoint of global welfare? No need, apparently, to explain why we should think of the issues this way when no such convention is even remotely imminent.

National welfare norms—But this is entirely enough—or perhaps too much—time spent for now on explaining why we should not bark up the wrong tree by basing international tax policy analysis, intended for a given country, on global welfare norms. Do the national welfare norms that the literature has developed fare any better? As we will see, the answer is no, because they fail to offer any help in addressing the real question of interest, which is how to analyze the tradeoffs between competing efficiency margins, while also including distributional considerations in the analysis.

G. Fifth Problem: Lack of Conceptual Integration Between Entity-Level Corporate Taxation and the Taxation of Individuals

A final fundamental problem in the field relates to the fact that corporations are the main taxpayers in cross-border enterprise. All significant income tax systems around the world treat corporations as separate taxpayers from their actual owners, who ultimately are individuals. This is done predominantly for convenience, albeit verging on necessity. Corporations, multinational or otherwise, are not themselves flesh and blood people. They cannot themselves actually bear the burden of paying a tax, nor can they actually live anywhere. However, contemporaneous flow-through taxation of corporate income to underlying individuals, such as the shareholders, is widely considered impractical (see Shaviro 2009a, 154).

For this reason, worldwide residence-based corporate taxation unavoidably depends on corporations', rather than individuals', deemed residences. This proves to be of central importance in thinking about international taxation. So does the fact that legally separate corporate entities—say, a U.S. parent and its wholly owned foreign subsidiaries—are treated in many respects as separate persons, even though they are not in truth distinct like two human beings.

Yet corporations were long the key missing player in international tax policy analysis, which largely proceeded as if it made no difference that, for example, the "Americans" potentially being subjected to U.S. worldwide taxation were companies that had filed incorporation papers here, not people who were citizens or residents. More recently, as we will see with regard to the more recently coined acronyms CON and NON (which focus on the importance of which company owns a particular asset), this has begun to change, and corporations that are taxed as separate entities have at last taken their indispensable central place on the analytical stage.

While corporations are the principal direct actors and taxpayers in the international realm, they still are not (and cannot be) the true ultimate parties of interest. Thus, important and laudable though it is that the international tax policy field has begun in recent years to focus on the significance of their being the main taxpayers in the international realm, there has not as yet been much progress on the next step, which involves relating entity-level taxation back to the individual level. Here an important question is how international taxation relates to the distribution issues in tax policy.

Thus, suppose the United States is deciding how to tax U.S. multinationals. In so doing, it indirectly taxes the owners, all of whom ultimately (once one looks through all of the intermediate legal entities that own financial interests in the firms) must be either U.S. or foreign individuals. Accordingly, in evaluating how we tax U.S. multinationals, one must consider the possible effects on both of these two groups. This stage has generally been missing in analysis to date, and I plan to show its relevance in this book.

H. Toward a Better Analysis of International Tax Policy Issues

Having spent so much time summarizing what I believe is wrong with the existing international tax policy literature, it is only fair that I acknowledge the old schoolyard dare, "put up or shut up." In other words, how do I propose to improve the analysis? In general, I believe that this mainly involves addressing the following five—to a degree overlapping—questions.

1. *What companies should we define as U.S. residents?*—When we say an individual is a U.S. resident, we are defining her as a member of our community, a status that may be associated with our conveying both benefits and burdens. By contrast, when we define a corporation as a domestic resident for purposes of our international tax rules, the main thing it means is that we can, if we like, tax what we call its FSI.

As we will see, we would have good reason to tax the entire worldwide income of every company in the world—wholly without regard to whether it had connections of any sort to the United States—if this were legally, politically, and administratively feasible, as of course it is not. In particular, this approach would have the appealing feature, from an efficiency standpoint, of making the source-based domestic tax wholly unavoidable through locational choices (such as by investing abroad rather than here).

The question presented, then, is what subset of all the companies in the world, as among those that we *can* indeed define, if we choose, as U.S. residents, we should decide to make potentially subject to U.S. worldwide taxation. To what extent are the benefits of taxing all companies on all of their worldwide income merely scaled down, rather than lost, when we can only tax some of them? In choosing which attributes to use in identifying resident companies, a key question is tax elasticity. Thus, for clearly feasible attributes, such as one's place of incorporation or headquarters location, how flexible are taxpayers prospectively, and how easily can they alter what they have already done? Moreover, what attributes might we be reluctant to discourage through our tax rules, such as on the ground that their selection by corporate actors might have positive externalities for U.S. citizens and residents?

2. *How should we define foreign (and domestic) source income?*—In a world where governments claim exclusive authority within geographically limited realms, a source concept for income taxation verges on being inevitable. A country can be expected to at least consider taxing foreigners' "inbound" income, given that it has the power to do so. And for one's own residents, even if one imposes worldwide taxation, the question of whether a given dollar was earned at home or abroad is potentially of interest, given that one's control (and that of other governments) differs as between the two realms.

Unfortunately, the source of income is not a well-defined economic idea (Ault and Bradford 1990). Perhaps its meaning is clearest when a given individual, who is in a particular place, creates economic value by doing things exclusively there. Even if she has foreign sales, the work of production took place entirely at home. But even this simple case rapidly runs into several conundrums. For example, suppose people who are living abroad helped her to generate the foreign sales. Or suppose that the overseas "market" countries want to claim some of her income from selling items to their residents. What is more, even just for individuals, the inquiry into the source of income rapidly gets harder once we start thinking, for example, about where the income from financial instruments was earned, or about how to treat expenses that arguably relate to gross income earned in multiple locations. When we shift from the world of individuals to that of multinational corporate entities, the source inquiry gets exponentially harder still, and less resolvable even in theory.

So far, I have been treating source determinations as purely a factual inquiry into some underlying actual or partial truth. To the extent that there are correct answers about source, implementing them through one's international tax rules serves economic efficiency, from a national welfare perspective, at one particular margin. It avoids either encouraging or discouraging domestic taxpayers from integrating domestic operations with those conducted abroad. By contrast, if one mismeasures the domestic income component of cross-border operations, one may inefficiently encourage or discourage cross-border operations just for tax reasons.

Unfortunately, however, accuracy-based source determinations face the problem that there often is no "there" there. In addition, accuracy may not be the only value that matters from the standpoint of a given country's self-interest in setting international tax rules. Two further potentially important considerations are (a) deliberately discriminating between types of income, and (b) affecting what I call taxpayers' sourcing electivity (their ability to engage in cheap or even cost-free income shifting for tax purposes).

Discriminating between types of income—As we will see, countries may have good reason to use their source (and related) rules as a device for treating relatively mobile income more favorably than that which is more geographically fixed. The greater an item's geographical mobility, the worse the tradeoff between revenue-raising potential and the efficiency cost to the taxing jurisdiction of attempting to reach it. In principle, one could respond to this consideration by expressly applying lower tax rates to mobile than immobile income (albeit, taking account as well of the efficiency cost when taxpayers shift between the two types). However, permitting a degree of profit-shifting for mobile income may accomplish the same end with greater political and administrative convenience.

The principle that one may benefit from discriminating between types of income also applies to that which one classifies as FSI. Under existing U.S. law, income that is reported as arising in a tax haven, or that is highly mobile for reporting purposes and thus appears likely to be shifted to tax havens, often faces current taxation, in the hands of resident multinationals, even if one does not directly challenge their classifying it as FSI. This reflects that, from a practical standpoint, the source determination that one accepts for such income may matter less than how one actually taxes it.

Cheaper versus costlier sourcing electivity—Now suppose we are focusing on one particular type of income, rather than on how its level of taxation compares to that for other income. A country's international tax rules can make it easier or harder—cheaper or costlier—for taxpayers to succeed in treating it as foreign source rather than as domestic source. An important criticism of the existing U.S. source rules, such as in Edward Kleinbard's (2011a) discussion of the "stateless income" phenomenon, is that they create too much electivity, by making legally successful profit shifting too cheap, rather than too costly. This amounts to arguing as well that there is currently too much discrimination (even if the optimal amount is not zero) in favor of income that is earned by multinational companies.

In this book, while not attempting to provide definite suggestions for U.S. rule design, I will show that the cost-of-electivity framework can play an important role. Two particular issues stand out. The first is how to deal with debt (and thus the interest deductions) incurred by members of an affiliated worldwide group of companies. Economically speaking, the details both of intra-group debt and of who within an affiliated group is the borrower with respect to third-party debt, may matter very little, yet the tax implications may be great. The existing rules thus create very substantial sourcing electivity that probably ought to be reduced.

The second big electivity issue concerns the tax treatment of intra-group transactions, such as sales. Suppose, for example, that a U.S. member of a multinational group either sells productive inputs to a foreign affiliate in connection with an export, or buys such inputs with respect to an input. The deemed intra-group sale price (known as the transfer price) plays a key role in determining U.S. tax liability, despite the fact that it may not matter economically at all (since the group members are commonly owned).

Transfer pricing rules typically rely on the notion of a "comparable arm's length price" between unrelated affiliates. As has been widely discussed, however (see, e.g., Durst 2007), this concept is bad enough in theory, and even worse in current practice. Many have therefore proposed replacing transfer pricing with the use of an approach called formulary apportionment, under which the affiliated group's worldwide income would be apportioned through the use of a mechanical formula, typically based on the relative proportions of its sales, payroll, and/or tangible property in each country. This approach, however, is widely criticized as well, based both on the continued distortions and inaccuracy that it would entail and on the political difficulty of devising a common formula that all nations might agree to apply. Once again, however, a focus on the issue of cheaper versus costlier electivity can at least help to clarify the tradeoffs.

3. *Why should we want to tax (or not tax) resident companies' foreign source income?*— Suppose that we have now defined both domestic source and foreign source income, along with substantively related questions such as that of which member of an affiliated group earned a given dollar of income. Taking all this as given—although in fact, our preferred definitions of domestic source income and FSI might partly depend on how each is treated[5]—what motivations would one have for imposing a positive tax rate on resident companies' FSI?

The core reason should be obvious. If we also take as given the imposition of a source-based tax on domestic income (for reasons that I discuss in chapter 5), one faces a fundamental incentive problem. Absent a tax on FSI, all taxpayers can avoid the source-based tax by investing or reporting income abroad, rather than at home. But for anyone whose FSI is also taxed, and indeed under the same terms, the source-based tax becomes unavoidable through locational choices.

This is why, as noted above, at this margin it would clearly benefit the United States (or any other country) to tax all companies in the world on all of the income that they earned anywhere in the world. But this of course is impossible and would likely provoke adverse responses from other countries. So the potential benefit reduces to that available from taxing just resident companies on all of their worldwide income.

Further motivation for taxing FSI relates to the shareholder level. The United States imposes a worldwide income tax on individuals. The worldwide character of this tax clearly is necessary if we are using income as a metric for some underlying distributional concept such as "ability to pay." For example, one cannot really tell how well off Bill Gates or Mark Zuckerberg is, compared to people who are less materially fortunate, unless one counts all of their income, whether earned at home or abroad.

But with corporate income being taxed only at the entity level until there is a shareholder-level realization (such as from receiving dividends or selling stock), the tax on FSI becomes too easy to avoid unless we also tax the corporations in which U.S. individuals own stock on a current and worldwide basis. To be sure, here we face the same problem as that arising under the efficiency heading of making the source-based tax unavoidable. That is, the logic calls for taxing *all* companies' worldwide income (insofar as they have U.S. shareholders), but we can only impose it on companies that we define as U.S. residents.

A further potential motivation for taxing FSI relates to foreign shareholders. Again, suppose that we could tax them on their worldwide income no matter where earned, and no matter how (such as through a foreign company) they invested. This would potentially lead to wealth transfers from them to us. Even if we can only do this when they invest through U.S. resident companies, the possibility of such a wealth transfer remains. The key question, as we will see in chapter 5, is whether foreign investors can be induced to pay (such as through imposition of the U.S. worldwide tax) for the privilege of investing through a U.S. company.

If these are the motivations for taxing U.S. companies' FSI, what are the motivations for not doing so? To explain, suppose initially that U.S. corporate residence status, no matter how we defined it, would be entirely elective for all taxpayers. That is, it would have no practical effect on them of any kind, except for its causing their non-U.S. income to face a U.S. tax. Under these circumstances, the tax on resident companies' worldwide income would be expected to raise zero revenue. It would be pointless—albeit not affirmatively harmful, since no one would either elect it or be adversely affected by opting out.

Now suppose instead that U.S. corporate resident status is not entirely elective. That is, some people would be willing to pay for it in the form of expected higher U.S. taxes. Now the revenue estimate is no longer zero, but there are also potential efficiency costs to think about. In particular, U.S. individuals may incur deadweight loss to avoid it. And if U.S. people enjoy any positive externalities when investors choose the attributes that cause a company to be classified as a U.S. corporate resident, these may be reduced by the tax disincentive to choose them. All this, however, merely leads us to the next question, which is what tax rate we should apply to U.S. companies' FSI.

4. *How should we determine what average/effective tax rate to apply to resident companies' foreign source income?*—As noted above, the existing international tax policy literature generally contemplates just two possible domestic statutory tax rates for FSI: 0 percent or the full domestic rate. However, even strongly committed proponents of worldwide U.S. taxation, without deferral but with the allowance of foreign tax credits, evidently agree that the average or effective U.S. tax rate on FSI should be somewhere between those two endpoints.

How should we think about the criteria for determining optimal U.S. tax rates for U.S. companies' FSI? Fortunately, the existing tax policy literature—although not its expressly international component—can help in addressing this question. A starting point is the optimal commodity tax literature, founded by Frank Ramsey (1927). This literature addresses efficient rate setting if there are excise taxes on various consumer goods. It finds that varying, rather than uniform, rates are generally optimal when the potentially taxable items differ in their tax elasticity. More particularly, the "inverse elasticity" rule holds that, the more tax elastic a given item, the lower the tax rate on it should be, all else equal. Further and related insights can be gleaned from the existing tax policy literature concerning the marginal efficiency cost of funds (Slemrod and Yitzhaki 1996). Here a key idea is equalizing the ratio of deadweight loss to revenue raised as between alternative instruments (such as the tax on domestic source income as compared to FSI), in light of a common tendency for this ratio to grow worse, for any given instrument, as one uses it more (such as by raising the rate).[6]

To illustrate optimal commodity tax analysis (and how it relates to the marginal efficiency cost of funds), suppose a country needs to raise a fixed amount of revenue, with as little economic distortion as possible, solely through commodity taxes on two items—say, milk and orange juice. Suppose that these are the only available drinks apart from tap water, which let's assume cannot be taxed.

A narrowly focused neutrality-based approach might call for taxing both milk and orange juice at the same rate, so that people do not switch between milk and orange juice for tax reasons. However, while this consideration is indeed relevant to the choice of tax rates for the two items, it may be trumped by other considerations. In particular, suppose that orange juice consumption is much more tax elastic than milk consumption, perhaps because people are more willing to switch from orange juice to tap water. Then it turns out, as the optimal commodity tax literature shows, that the tax rate on milk should be higher than that on orange juice. And what should be equalized, rather than the two items' tax rates, is the marginal efficiency cost, in terms of deadweight loss, of the last dollar of revenue raised from each of the two levies.

In chapter 5, we will see that this mode of analysis is indeed relevant to international tax policy, with domestic source income taking the place of milk while resident companies' FSI takes the place of orange juice. (Investing abroad through foreign companies takes the place of drinking tap water.) This is why overall optimization—even if defined in terms of efficiency concerns *plus* those of distribution—depends on something very different from picking a particular neutrality (such as that either between orange juice and milk, or orange juice and tap water) and basing one's whole policy on it. Rather, it requires rejecting any analysis that is based on neutrality just at one particular margin.

Unfortunately, the optimal commodity tax and related literatures are unlikely in practice to yield definitive answers concerning the optimal U.S. tax rate on FSI. Yet they not only help clarify the terms of inquiry, but also may support general answers within broad ranges. For example, they help to show why exemption's zero tax rate is unlikely to be optimal. If one started with tax rates of zero for FSI and some positive rate for domestic source business income, it is highly likely that gradually raising the former rate and lowering the latter rate, in a manner that was revenue neutral overall, would have at least initial efficiency benefits, even if these disappeared well before the point at which the two rates had been equalized.

5. *How, or in what manner, should we tax resident companies' foreign source income?*—A standard maxim in tax policy outside the international arena holds that it generally is optimal to broaden the base and lower the rates. Taking a particular revenue target as given, this approach typically yields two distinct efficiency benefits. First, base broadening reduces the distortions that would result from treating some items more favorably than other items (assuming inadequate justification for the disparate treatment, such as from externalities or elasticity differences). Second, lowering the marginal rate, even if one does not lower the average rate over a broader range, can reduce tax distortions with respect to decisions that are made dollar-by-dollar (such as with respect to profit-shifting).

Applying this maxim to the taxation of FSI would suggest the likelihood of efficiency gain from a shift in policy that involved (1) eliminating deferral and repealing the foreign tax credit; plus (2) lowering the tax rate on FSI so that some underlying target, such as revenue raised or the average tax rate for FSI, remained the same. This point never seems to get mentioned, however (other than in my prior work), probably for three main reasons. First, the straitjacket of conventional thinking seems to rule out any statutory tax rates for FSI in between zero (or something close to it) and the full domestic rate. Second, pervasive confusion regarding how to think about foreign taxes impedes thinking about the foreign tax credit as an inefficient tax preference—as it clearly is, from a unilateral domestic standpoint. Third, the shift would violate dozens of bilateral tax treaties that the United States has signed, and might also raise additional administrative and political economy concerns.

Even if this last objection is dispositive, however, it is worth knowing whether the general base-broadening principle would otherwise apply here. For example, it might affect how we think about the range of choices that are indeed realistically available. (Territoriality is a treaty-compatible approach to repealing deferral and the foreign tax credit that merely happens to feature a lower tax rate for FSI than that which would otherwise be optimal.) But rather than simply assuming the applicability here of the general base-broadening principle, one should more particularly examine how deferral and the foreign tax credit affect taxpayers' incentives and behavior in practice.

With regard to foreign tax credits, we have already seen that a 100 percent MRR would cause U.S. taxpayers to be wholly non-cost conscious with respect to foreign taxes paid, likely to the detriment U.S. national welfare given the lack of general credit-granting reciprocity by other countries. And while often the MRR may be significantly lower than 100 percent in practice, mainly due to deferral, inefficiency still results from treating foreign taxes more favorably than other foreign outlays (although the "tagging" point about low foreign taxes must be kept in mind as well). Accordingly, the foreign tax credit is an inefficient tax preference that ought to be eliminated, holding to one side the question of what should be the overall tax burden on FSI.

What about deferral? As we will see in chapter 3, there are hypothetical conditions in which it would not actually have any distorting effect on U.S. multinationals' decisions regarding when and whether to repatriate funds that (tax considerations aside) could better be used at home. Unfortunately, however, these conditions do not generally apply in practice, and thus deferral causes large distortions that appear to be getting worse over time. The maxim that one should broaden the base and lower the rate therefore applies here as well.

Finally, what about a system that has both deferral and foreign tax credits? As noted above, each tends to blunt the other's worst incentive effects. However, a system featuring both of them is guaranteed to impose onerous tax planning and compliance costs relative to the revenue raised. An awful result would not, however, be similarly inevitable if the system instead applied an expressly lower tax rate to FSI. Even the fact that source determinations would now explicitly be necessary in all cases, rather than just when foreign tax credit limits potentially apply, would matter very little in practical terms. After all, under present law, U.S. companies pervasively must make determinations that have substantively similar effects, in the course of determining whether a given dollar of income belongs to the U.S. parent or to a foreign subsidiary.

So long as U.S. international taxation makes use of foreign tax credits and/or deferral, efforts to design or analyze reform proposals are confounded by what I call the "iron box." Cut back on foreign tax credits and you make deferral worse; cut back on deferral and you make foreign tax credits worse. A step forward as to either of these inefficient rules triggers a step back as to the other of them, even if the latter's technical terms have not been changed. Plus, one raises the separate question of whether the overall tax burden on FSI is being moved closer to, or further from, its optimal level. So long as U.S. international tax policy remains trapped in the iron box, significant overall progress is hard to achieve, and even marginal improvement is hard to judge.

In illustration, suppose we repealed deferral and went to a pure worldwide system with foreign tax credits. Even apart from the question of whether (absent other changes) this would unduly increase the effective U.S. tax rate on resident companies' FSI, it would result in worsening the incentive effects of the foreign tax credit rules. On the face of things, it might look as if those rules were unchanged. But in fact, U.S. companies would now have an effective MRR of 100 percent in *all* cases other than those where the foreign tax credit limit might apply. They would thus have a greatly reduced incentive, relative to today's law, to seek to reduce their foreign tax liabilities.

Now suppose instead that we changed the foreign tax credit in such a way as to make it much harder for U.S. companies to engage in cross-crediting (i.e., the elimination of any U.S. tax on repatriations of low-taxed FSI by pairing them with the repatriation of high-taxed FSI).[7] While this might effectively reduce U.S. companies' MRR with respect to foreign taxes, the resulting U.S. national welfare benefit would come at the cost of increasing the distortions associated with deferral, by making tax-free repatriations harder to arrange (Sullivan 2009).

Only by eliminating *both* foreign tax credits and deferral can we break out of the iron box that currently constrains U.S. international tax policy. And again, this need not imply increasing the effective U.S. tax rate on resident companies' FSI—the desirability of which depends on wholly separate considerations.

I. If We Now Know the Right Questions, What Is the Answer?

So much for the windup—what, then, is the pitch? Under the analysis that I am suggesting, what should the United States actually do in the international tax policy arena?

The answer to this question is complicated by the fact that it depends on how we interpret the choice set. How constrained are we in picking the best available solution? Consider, for example, the two core reasons why our international tax rules are so horrendously bad at present. The first is that we practice entity-level corporate income taxation, while the second is that existing worldwide systems use deferral and foreign tax credits. One cannot make a proper recommendation without knowing to what extent either or both constraints are binding.

As we will see in chapter 6, it is conceivable that the core dilemmas in current U.S. international tax policy could actually be eliminated. For example, replacing the income tax with a progressive consumption tax, depending on its form, could make both corporate residence determinations and transfer pricing wholly unnecessary. And even if the income tax remains in place for individuals, Alan Auerbach's (2010) recent proposal to replace the corporate income tax with a particular type of consumption tax could have the same effect. Even this, however, arguably is a more decisive Gordian knot solution to the existing dilemmas than we should realistically expect.

Now suppose that we are indefinitely stuck with entity-level corporate income taxation. What should we do then? Here, while we are deep in the realm of unappetizing and uncertain tradeoffs, I will end up (in chapter 6) suggesting the adoption of a modified territorial system, even though a zero tax rate for U.S. companies' FSI is likely to be too low. The main reason would be to eliminate foreign tax credits and deferral in a politically feasible and treaty-compatible manner, perhaps without requiring the effective tax rate on FSI to drop quite as low as one might initially have assumed was necessary under a system that is called "exemption."

It appears to be widely recognized that treaty compatibility does not actually require a zero rate on resident companies' FSI. Suppose—although the point is legitimately debatable—that 5 percent, or perhaps even 8 or 10 percent, is acceptable under an "exemption" system, if rationalized as an indirect way of taxing domestic source income that has been mislabeled. Then the horns of the dilemma become considerably less sharp, because one need neither violate treaties nor pre-commit to under-taxing FSI in the course of breaking out of the iron box.

In addition, as is common in putatively territorial systems, resident companies' foreign profits that they treat as arising in tax havens can be taxed at a higher rate than other FSI, albeit subject to the offsetting concern about undermining the companies' foreign tax cost consciousness. Quasi-exemption's repeal of deferral might also be accompanied by imposing a transition tax on U.S. companies' pre-enactment unrepatriated foreign earnings, which they accumulated under the expectation that they would face a U.S. tax at some future point.

Further associated changes that my analysis will support (or at least show to be highly plausible) include expanding the U.S. corporate residence rules, and toughening the source rules. In this regard, one important step, pertaining especially to debt, would be to reduce as much as possible the legal significance of formal entity lines within an affiliated corporate group. I will also argue that there may also be decent grounds to move part way toward a recent proposal (Avi-Yonah, Clausing, and Durst 2008) to replace transfer pricing with a version of formulary apportionment that gives the sales factor greater weight than property and payroll.

The rest of the book will more fully explore and develop the ideas set forth in this chapter, but with a very different organizational scheme. Whereas here I proceeded straight from the core dilemmas in international tax policy, to the defects in prevailing modes of analysis, to my own proposed analysis and its main policy implications, in the rest of the book I begin by taking a step back. In-depth discussion requires a thorough grounding in the general details of the current U.S. international tax system. Thus, Part 1, consisting of chapters 2 and 3, first reviews the basic U.S. international tax rules, and then addresses in greater detail the design challenges that they raise, along with their main incentive effects and planning implications. Part 1 could be skimmed or even skipped by readers who either are already well versed in the operational details, or else do not wish to delve too deeply into the U.S. international tax system's plumbing.

However, it does (chapter 3 in particular) develop some points that are important to the subsequent analysis.

Part 2 then shifts to a broader policy focus. To this end, chapter 4 addresses the global welfare perspective on U.S. international tax policy. Chapter 5 addresses the unilateral national welfare perspective. Finally, chapter 6 addresses the question of what practical steps might be taken to improve U.S. international tax policy.

Endnotes

1. During the 2011 debt ceiling fight between the Obama administration and congressional Republicans, Treasury Secretary Geithner reportedly stated that "[t]he goal is territorial" and that the Obama administration was "prepared to move off decades of Democratic orthodoxies" by agreeing to go "95 or 96 percent" of the way there (Woodward 2012, 242). During the 2012 presidential campaign, however, the Obama administration endorsed research suggesting that shifting to a territorial system, as proposed by Governor Romney, would cost 800,000 U.S. jobs (see Clausing 2012).

2. I first laid out pieces of this critique in articles such as Shaviro (2010) and Shaviro (2011b). While my critique of the existing literature may sound harsh, I am not alone in making it. Thus, consider the title of Graetz (2000), an article that stands as an important precursor to my work here: "Taxing International Income: Inadequate Principles, Outdated Concepts, and Unsatisfactory Policies." Or consider the statement in Auerbach (2010) that, while worldwide and territorial systems "are generally presented as the two reform options available... the United States could benefit by moving beyond these two heavily discussed choices."

3. It is true that the U.S. generally benefits if peer countries are able to maintain healthy and well-functioning tax systems. Accordingly, rampant tax avoidance that undermined their fiscal capacity might also harm us. However, this is a collective action problem—since all peer countries may benefit from each others' general fiscal health—that calls more for considering multilateral cooperation than for our unilaterally subsidizing tax payments to peer countries by resident U.S. companies. We may also benefit if peer countries maintain healthy economies with close to full employment and good wages. Yet it seems unlikely that we would want to respond by making U.S. companies' foreign wage payments better than deductible.

4. For example, I will argue in chapter 4 that multilateral cooperation is considerably more feasible with regard to information sharing and perhaps the "stateless income" or tax haven problem than with regard to reimbursing source-based taxes through the allowance of foreign tax credits.

5. For example, the greater the tax benefit from relabeling domestic source income as FSI, the tougher the source rules might need to be.

6. As I discuss in chapter 5, the optimal tariff literature also provides important and related insights. This literature shows that a country can benefit from levying tariffs on imports when it has significant market power—in particular, the ability to affect the world price for a particular commodity. Chapter 5 will show that issues of market power, like that which the optimal tariff literature emphasizes, are more generally central to the question of how heavily (if at all) both domestic source income and resident companies' FSI should be taxed.

7. As we will see in chapter 3, the Obama administration in 2009 proposed a so-called pooling rule for foreign tax credits that likely would have this effect.

I   The Rules and Their Main Effects

WHAT DOES U.S. international taxation have in common with the death penalty?

This may sound like a lame attempt at a riddle, leading either to a groan-worthy punch line or an overheated putdown of the U.S. international tax rules. In fact, however, the question aims to point out a genuine parallel between the ways in which politics has shaped legal structure in the two areas. In each, sharp political dissensus between closely matched forces has led to an outcome somewhere in the middle, partly satisfying but partly frustrating each side's preferences. But not just anywhere in the middle. Rather, in each case, the opposing political forces have battled to a stalemate characterized by such arcane legal complexity, yielding such contortions in actual practice, that arguably the outcome is in some respects worse for each side than outright defeat would have been.

Consider first the death penalty. In principle, a compromise—such as limiting it to a reduced roster of defendants whose crimes were the very worst by some agreed metric—might offer half a loaf to each side, while also potentially appealing to the unsure or ambivalent as superior to either pole. Even absolutist foes of the death penalty would gain something from taking it off the table for all the other defendants.

In practice, however, things have not worked out so neatly. With opponents of the death penalty having persuaded American courts to scrutinize it closely but not to abolish it altogether, capital punishment in the United States now features a "lengthy and elaborate legal process" that often takes decades to unfold

(Garland 2010, 45). Death penalty verdicts are subject to such extensive review litigation that the average lag between imposing and carrying out a sentence is twelve years, and it can exceed thirty years. For death penalty supporters, this eliminates any prospect of achieving swift retribution for terrible crimes, or a prompt sense of closure for crime victims' families. For opponents, it means that the eventually executed must first face years of excruciating uncertainty on death row. In addition, it creates the dismaying spectacle of an electoral death penalty cycle, as state governors work assiduously to time executions to coincide with their reelection campaigns. So it is hard to believe that anyone, even those who would favor a more straightforward compromise solution if one were feasible, regards the current U.S. death penalty status quo with anything far short of dismay.

In U.S. international taxation, the compromise emerging from decades of political struggle is similarly ill executed. Here, rather than simply and directly imposing on U.S. companies' outbound investment something in between a zero U.S. rate and the full U.S. rate, the rules are so convoluted and needlessly costly in practice that the overused term "Rube Goldberg machine" verges on being irresistible. At least in some respects, the compromise clearly is worse than going all the way to either pole. To help demonstrate this, chapter 2 reviews the basic rules, while chapter 3 examines the main planning and policy issues that they raise.

2 The Main Building Blocks of U.S. International Taxation

THE U.S. INCOME tax rules for cross-border activity are complicated enough to require vast forests of print for those not yet entirely wedded to reading on computer screens. Suppose you wanted to review all of the income tax statutes that particularly address international tax issues. Internal Revenue Code sections 861 through 999, where for the most part they are found, takes up no fewer than 282 pages in a prominent recent edition.[1] The Treasury regulations pertaining to those Code sections unfold luxuriantly across another 1,288 pages.[2] The leading international tax treatise (Kuntz and Peroni 2013), while inhospitable to a page count because its many (and nonconsecutively page-numbered) chapters have continually updated inserts and replacement pages, sprawls sideways in its loose-leaf binders over nearly a foot of shelf space.

Over the years, these primary and secondary source materials keep growing like kudzu as ever more authorities emerge, addressing ever more permutations in applying the U.S. international tax rules. Intellectually gifted attorneys at leading U.S. law and accounting firms can and do devote large portions of their careers just to studying how all these rules apply to and are best utilized by their clients, without feeling at any point that they have now seen and know it all.

Nonetheless, this welter of complexity has a surprisingly simple core. To grasp the basic elements of how we tax the income of multinational firms, taking as given the rules that would be needed to tax income in a purely domestic setting, just four or five basic concepts—depending on how one counts—go far indeed. First, there are the rules for determining corporate residence. Second are the rules for determining what I will call the source of income (defining this term somewhat more broadly than is customary in legal doctrine). Third are the rules concerning foreign tax credits. Fourth is deferral, or the lack of current inclusion for foreign source income that U.S. companies earn through foreign subsidiaries ("CFCs," for controlled foreign corporations, in the lingo of the Internal Revenue Code). Deferral generally ends when the U.S. parent repatriates or otherwise realizes the underlying CFC income, such as by receiving a dividend or selling CFC stock. Fifth, if we choose to list it separately from deferral rather than as part of the same broader concept, is subpart F of the Code. This is the rubric for a set of rules that potentially limit the scope of deferral by providing deemed dividend treatment for certain types of CFC income, thus making such items currently taxable to the U.S. parent.

A. Corporate Residence

Just as all social groups have at least an incipient sense of "us" versus "them," so all countries distinguish for multiple legal purposes between their citizens or residents on the one hand, and everyone else on the other. Typically only "we" qualify for specified benefits (such as the right to vote) and are subject to specified burdens or obligations (such as compulsory military service). Thus, it comes as no surprise to observe that income tax systems around the world, including in the United States, distinguish between those who are classified as domestic residents (or citizens) and those who are not.

The main reason this income tax classification matters is that generally only citizens and/or residents are potentially subject to domestic tax obligations with respect to income arising abroad. The United States cannot, after all, tax a foreigner on what it admits is FSI—by requiring, say, a German to pay U.S. tax on income earned in Germany or France. In addition, as we will see, in some respects the application of the source rules depends on whether or not a given person (either the taxpayer or the issuer of a financial instrument) is classified as a U.S. resident.

As applied to individuals, the residence concept requires relatively little elaboration. Most people unmistakably live within a single country's borders, and thus are its residents and no one else's. True, there are problems relating to temporary cross-border jobs, permanent expatriation, and the like, but these for the most part are fairly easily handled, such as by bright-line rules concerning the number of days one spends in a year in a given country.

A central fact about cross-border business activity, however, is that it is predominantly conducted by legal entities, such as corporations, that are themselves—largely for reasons of administrative convenience (Shaviro 2009a)—commonly treated as taxpayers distinct from their owners. This simple fact turns out to have far greater implications for the enterprise of international taxation than one might initially have expected, and one of the key reasons relates to residence. The idea of distinguishing between "us" and "them," so easy and natural most of the time when one is applying income tax rules to individuals, must also apply to corporations once they are being classified as taxpayers. But here it causes far greater problems, reflecting its lack of a meaningful core. How can an abstraction, such as a legal entity defined by pieces of paper, have a true "residence" in the same sense as a flesh and blood individual?

Suppose that there were no cross-border shareholding—that is, that Americans only owned stock in U.S.-incorporated companies, Canadians in Canadian companies, and so forth. Then not only would it be easy to assign each company a country of residence, but the fact that residence is determined at the entity level would make little difference. To be sure, taxation at the entity level rather than the owner level might affect such matters as the tax rate for a given quantum of income, as well as the deductibility of losses from one investment against income from another. However, if all individuals owned only home-country stock, entity-level taxation would not affect the question of what foreign source income is subject to domestic tax.

With cross-border shareholding, however, the issue of corporate residence gets both harder to resolve and more consequential. To begin with, the existence of cross-border shareholding weighs against basing corporate residence on the ultimate owners' nationality, even when those from one country predominate. Residence for tax purposes tends to be an all-or-nothing proposition, creating line-drawing problems if companies have owners all around the world. Moreover, ownership can change rapidly, especially for publicly traded companies. And even in the absence of ongoing trading, the underlying reality at the ultimate owner level can be hard to discern within a complex corporate structure in which particular owners may either hold distinctive combinations of rights, or place multiple tiers of intervening legal entities between themselves and the company whose residence must be determined.

Accordingly, with the ultimate owners' residence being hard to utilize as a decisive (or even a contributing) factor, corporate residence rules generally apply either of two approaches (Kane and Rock 2008, 1235). The first, followed in the United States, is to ask where the entity is formally incorporated. The second is to ask, with varying degrees of rigor, where the company's "real seat" appears to be located—that is, the main place where it is managed, or has most of its assets, employees, and business operations. This standard can range from simply asking where board of directors meetings generally are held—creating a "mild stimulus to the economies of Canada, Bermuda, or our Caribbean neighbors" (Tillinghast 1984, 263) if they build nice resorts for the meetings—to looking more rigorously at the "location of the administrative headquarters or. . . the firm's center of gravity as determined by the location of the employees and assets" (Kane and Rock 2008, 1235).

With corporate residence depending on an entity-level attribute, a fundamental legal divide emerges between entity-level and owner-level taxpayer residence. Thus, suppose Ann and Brian, who are American individuals, operate a multinational business through Cayco, a Caymans entity, while Carlos and Dolores, who are Spanish, do so through Cardol, Inc., a Delaware corporation. For purposes of the U.S. corporate tax, Cayco is a foreigner despite being American owned, while Cardol is a U.S. taxpayer despite being foreign owned. This ends up having important effects on the functioning of worldwide residence-based corporate taxation.

Even just conceptually, the entity-level focus on corporate residence can sow confusion. For example, if Ann and Brian put money in Cayco, which uses it to fund their U.S. business, this would appear to be "inbound" investment, coming to the United States from abroad. Likewise, if Carlos and Dolores use Cardol as a vehicle for investing their Spanish savings in Spain, this would appear to be "outbound" investment by a U.S. firm. If we try to rely on legally determined corporate residence in order to ascertain what actually is happening in the world economy (for example, what cross-border capital flows are taking place), we risk being misled.

More importantly, however, placing entity-level attributes at center stage has powerful effects on the practical reach of the U.S. international tax rules. In particular, it means that Americans' foreign business income generally will fall outside the reach of the residence-based U.S. corporate income tax when they invest through foreign corporations, whereas foreign individuals may face the U.S. worldwide corporate tax, through its impact at the entity level, when they invest abroad through U.S. corporations. What is more, if individuals are reluctant to expatriate physically, but are willing to invest through foreign rather than domestic entities, then focusing on entity-level attributes ends up increasing residence electivity, or investors' ability to select the corporate residence regime that they prefer, independently of what they are actually doing economically.

One of the most obvious ways electivity issues can arise is via an attempted midstream change in a given company's place of residence, or at least that applying to the underlying corporate businesses. In countries using headquarters rules, changing the parent's residence is relatively straightforward. At worst, if the country engages in a meaningful "real seat" inquiry rather than just looking at where annual meetings are held, it may require that enough of the company's high-level managers be willing to relocate abroad. The threat of such headquarters expatriations appears to have significantly influenced the U.K. government's recent decision to shift to a more territorial international tax regime for its resident companies.

In the United States, however, since we are a place of incorporation rather than a headquarters jurisdiction, the equivalent transaction would involve transferring the foreign businesses and their assets to a new foreign corporation that, assuming one does not want anything else to change, presumably would have the same owners as the old U.S. parent company. (There is no similar need to transfer the enterprise's U.S. assets and businesses, given that they would be taxed here on a source basis anyway.)

When done in a purely domestic setting, such asset (or stock) transfers from one corporation to another with identical ownership may result in a technical realization of any built-in gain from asset appreciation, creating the potential for taxation at both the entity and shareholder levels. For many decades, however, tax-free reorganization rules have generally permitted qualification for tax-free treatment at both levels, so long as (and to the extent that) assets remain in corporate solution and there are requisite showings of business purpose and lack of forbidden shareholder-level tax avoidance purposes, such as a plan to "bail out" corporate earnings at favorable capital gains rates.

In the international setting, however, concern about appreciated assets permanently leaving the reach of the U.S. tax system without ever being taxed is addressed by Internal Revenue Code section 367 and the regulations thereunder. This set of rules, though of "numbing complexity," contain a "basic idea. . . [that] is nearly fathomable. It aims to preserve for U.S. taxation all gains that originally arose within the reach of U.S. taxation" (Isenbergh 2006, 216), such as by imposing a "toll charge" via immediate gain recognition (or the denial of valuable tax attributes such as the allowance of net operating losses against subsequent taxable income) in certain situations where appreciated foreign assets are reshuffled out of ultimate U.S. ownership.

Starting in the 1990s, the expatriation game changed sufficiently to render Code section 367 far less responsive than it had previously been to tax-planning motivations and potential U.S. revenue concerns. U.S. multinationals with foreign subsidiaries increasingly began arranging what were called corporate inversions. In a typical such transaction, the U.S. parent would be replaced at the top of the corporate group by a foreign company, located in a tax haven such as Bermuda or the Cayman Islands. Once the dust had settled, the new parent would own both the U.S. company that continued to conduct U.S. operations and, through a separate chain of ownership, all of the foreign operations. The latter would thereby cease to be owned by a U.S. company, and therefore would no longer be subject in any way, via the former U.S. parent, to the U.S. worldwide corporate tax regime (Desai and Hines 2002).

The point of these transactions was not to remove appreciated assets from the U.S. company, which is the main concern addressed by Code section 367, but rather to avoid having the foreign subsidiaries' income ultimately subject to U.S. worldwide taxation via the former U.S. parent. A related goal was to facilitate tax planning to reduce the group's U.S. source income from its U.S. operations. Such corporate inversions became a huge U.S. domestic political issue, however, when Stanley Works, a leading toolmaker that had been a U.S. company since 1843, announced in 2002 its intention to expatriate to Bermuda. Although this transaction ultimately fell through, Congress responded in 2004 by enacting the so-called anti-inversion rules of new Code section 7874.

Under these rules, along with applicable Treasury regulations that ultimately tightened their application,[3] existing U.S. multinationals are now to a considerable degree stuck with their status as U.S. residents. Transactions in which at least 60 percent of the company's stock remains in the same hands as previously, and in which its new legal home is not a country in which it afterwards is conducting "substantial business activities," effectively are caught by the statute. However, even if these rules pervasively defeat fake expatriations that are merely tax planning arrangements, the expatriation of a given U.S. multinational is almost certain to be feasible if it is genuinely purchased by new owners, be they private equity funds or distinct foreign companies with their own share-holders and managers.

B. Source

1. Underlying Conceptual Problems

All countries with income tax systems distinguish between income that is deemed to arise at home and that which is deemed to arise abroad. I will call this the issue of "source," whether the question at issue is (1) classifying an item of gross income as either domestic source or foreign source; (2) determining whether a deduction reduces domestic source income or foreign source income; or (3) for a multinational group of corporate affiliates, determining how its global income is divided for tax purposes as between domestic and foreign members of the group.

As a matter of formal U.S. income tax terminology, only the first of these questions involves "source." However, the other two questions sufficiently overlap with it, as a matter of practical consequences, to make my broader usage of the term "source" conceptually clearer, and therefore more convenient. One can easily see how the treatment of deductions, which the U.S. rules may describe as being apportioned or allocated between domestic source and foreign source income, rather than as themselves having a "source," occupies the same substantive territory. However, the same is largely also true for issues in category (3). As we will see below, rules that determine the income split between, say, a U.S. parent and its foreign subsidiaries often effectively determine the amount of the group's U.S. source income—or, failing that, the amount of group income that the U.S. will currently tax.[4]

In a world of multiple sovereigns, each supreme within a geographically defined realm, source-based income taxation comes as no surprise. Partly, this reflects legal convenience. In any case where one cannot, or at least does not, tax income on a residence basis, source is the only jurisdictional hook that one has left. But source-based taxation is not just legally convenient. The concept also has great intuitive power. Its ruling metaphor is that of people who are physically located in a jurisdiction and who are doing things (i.e., earning income) there.

Once we accept this ruling metaphor, the inevitability of source-based taxation, in a world where governments have physically defined realms of sovereignty, seems almost beyond question. Why wouldn't a government impose taxes (including income taxes, if otherwise levied) on economic activity within its borders? After all, regulating or even banning particular activities within one's borders is par for the course, and merely taxing them would seem to be a more modest endeavor. What is more, if residents are being taxed on their local economic activity, it may seem unfathomable that foreigners, once they have chosen to enter the jurisdiction, would be specially exempted.

As we will see, however, the ruling metaphor of people physically located in a jurisdiction who are doing things there has a surprisingly weak connection to what source-based taxation actually means (or could mean) in practice. What is more, it will turn out that, even if source-based taxation could be made more workable than it actually is, the conclusion that it is a good idea would not necessarily follow. Indeed, if corporate income could be taxed directly to the individual owners, rather than initially just at the entity level, we'll see that there would a compelling argument, not just that source-based taxation ought to disappear (at least in most cases), but even that perhaps it would largely disappear.

However, under actual real-world circumstances, including entity-level corporate taxation that makes residence-based taxation a shaky enterprise, even those who are normatively skeptical about source-based taxation tend to agree that it is politically inevitable (Shay, Fleming, and Peroni 2002, 89). Thus, in practice one has no choice but to set about devising rules for determining the source of income. It therefore is unfortunate that this task proves so challenging in practice. Given the point that the source of income simply is not a well-defined economic idea (Ault and Bradford 1990), any attempted implementation faces grave conceptual problems.

These problems are especially great once we start considering multinational firms, which are the main economic actors in international taxation. But even just in simple cases involving individuals, at least two core conceptual problems rear their heads.

Origin basis versus destination basis—Suppose we have a cross-border transaction in which neither party leaves his or her home. For example, I might be an architect in New York who uses the Internet plus Skype calls to design someone's luxury apartment in Rome. For this design work, which might even include visual oversight of people's labor at the job site, suppose that I am paid $100,000. Which country ought to be deemed the source of this income: the United States or Italy?

Part of the apparent perplexity in this example may relate to the manner in which modern technology permits me, so far as Italy is concerned, to be there and yet not quite there. But even in a more old-fashioned example—say, if I construct furniture that I ship to my Roman customers—both the U.S. and Italian governments might feel that they had a compelling source-based claim. After all, the income from the transaction ineluctably depends on conditions in both jurisdictions, and could not have been realized absent both.

For any export of goods or services from one jurisdiction to another, it is basically just a matter of convention how we define source. Under what is called an *origin basis tax*, the producer or exporting country—the United States, in the above examples—gets to levy the tax. Under what is called a *destination basis tax*, the consumer or importing country—Italy, given the apartment in Rome—instead gets to do so.

In principle, over the long run, these should yield the same global division of the tax base. A country that could not engage in trade would get to consume just what it produced, no more and no less. With trade, it can swap some of its production for that in other countries. However, since trade is reciprocal, this should not alter the long-term equivalence between what its people produce and what they get to consume. Thus, at least roughly speaking, taxing domestic production and domestic consumption should eventually lead to about the same place.[5]

As it happens, consumption taxes, such as value-added taxes (VATs), typically use the destination basis, although some proposals to adopt a VAT-like U.S. tax would instead use the origin basis (see Shaviro 2004, 107). Income taxes generally use the origin basis, reflecting that (as we will see in chapter 6) use of the destination basis would create timing issues with respect to capital outlays, or those that are not supposed to be currently deductible. But, as we will see later in this chapter, many U.S. states, for purposes of their income taxes, use something that loosely resembles the destination basis to determine their share of multistate businesses' U.S. income, and a prominent recent proposal (Auerbach 2010) would switch to the destination basis after substantially modifying the existing U.S. corporate income tax.

Services versus property—Adopting the origin-basis convention leads to a clear answer as to source when an individual, working in a given location, provides services to consumers anywhere in the world. But things can rapidly grow muddy if one is able to steer one's efforts into the weeds of the long-standing income tax classification problem that lies at the boundary between selling (1) labor services and (2) property that one has created through one's labor.

For sales of property, the U.S. tax rules used to rely simply on where title passes, but now apply a complex web of provisions in which a whole range of different factors may determine the outcome, depending on the type of property involved and other relevant circumstances.[6] In some cases, the seller's residence determines the source, meaning that a U.S. seller will inevitably have U.S. source income, at least on the initial sale (such as to an exporter). But there are various complicated exceptions—pertaining, for example, to inventory, depreciable personal property, and intangibles.

Even just for individuals, accordingly, the source rules can founder on conceptual problems that create planning opportunities. But the problems grow exponentially harder once we shift to the setting of multinational firms that conduct integrated operations around the globe. The reasons these problems are so hard include the following:

- Multinationals' profits often depend more on the value of the intangibles that they own than on the currently observable production activities that they conduct in particular locations. While the intangibles presumably reflect someone's past labor or creativity, the time and place when their value arose (or became foreseeable) may be hard to identify.
- As Ronald Coase (1937) famously observed, firms (including multinationals) arise in settings where transaction costs make command-and-control a more efficient operating mechanism than ongoing market transactions with respect to integrated economic production by multiple parties. Firms therefore generally

do not have observable internal market transactions based on arm's-length prices. This makes it difficult to tell how profits or losses should be apportioned when a multinational firm engages in both U.S. and foreign operations. For example, there are no reliable market prices when one affiliate transfers goods and services to another. Likewise, internal financing choices, whether with respect to intra-group capital flows or borrowing from third parties, may not reliably indicate anything about where value and profits are actually being generated.

– The lack of true and observable arm's-length transactions extends not only to dealings between corporate affiliates, but also to those between employee-owners, such as founders, and the firm itself. Thus, consider Apple and Steve Jobs, during his many years at the helm, or Facebook and Mark Zuckerberg. Each was grossly "underpaid" by his firm for helping to create billions of dollars in expected profits, other than through the effect on the value of his shares. This, however, left the firm as the main taxpayer, giving it the opportunity to locate abroad, for tax purposes, profits that arguably reflected the work these individuals did while living in the United States.

2. The U.S. Rules' Approach to Sourcing Multinationals' Income

In describing how the U.S. rules address (and, many would agree, badly botch) the inevitably difficult task of determining the U.S. source and foreign source components of multinationals' income, two main topics merit particular attention. The first is transfer pricing, or how one determines the intra-firm prices that U.S. and foreign affiliates are deemed to have charged each other. The second is how deductions incurred by the various members of a multinational group are treated.

Transfer pricing—To give a general sense of the intra-group pricing problem, suppose that Acme Products' U.S. and French business operations, if conducted by separate owners, would earn $10 million each, for a total of $20 million. Given, however, the synergies that the two affiliates happen to realize by reason of their being jointly owned—pertaining, for example, to shared management, financing, and access to valuable intangibles—suppose that the unified firm earns $25 million. One really has no principled basis for determining the source of this synergy income (Shaviro 2009a, 108). What is more, this example, rather than being unusual or contrived, is fundamental to the existence of multinationals, which arise precisely to exploit synergies from common ownership where this works better than market-based arm's-length interactions (Avi-Yonah, Clausing, and Durst 2008, 5).

The U.S. tax rules, in common with those of most other countries, address these issues through transfer pricing, which involves attempting to require that companies' affiliates in different jurisdictions report the prices they would have charged each other if acting at arm's length. The starting point in transfer pricing is treating even wholly owned corporate subsidiaries as separate from their corporate parents—reflecting legal form, but not practical economic reality. The question then becomes one of asking what prices they "really," even if unobservably, must have charged each other when contributing goods or services to each other. Thus, suppose Acme United States spends $10 producing a widget, which Acme-France then sells locally for $40. The income split for the $30 of group-wide profit depends on the arm's-length transfer price that Acme United States is deemed to have charged Acme-France. Thus, if the correct transfer price is $18, the income split would be $8 United States and $12 France, whereas if it is $23, the split is $13/$7.

If one can determine what price the U.S. seller would have charged an unrelated French buyer in an otherwise identical transaction, that supposedly comparable price must be used for tax purposes in the related-company setting. But if the non-arm's-length relationship creates extra profit by reason of intra-group synergies, then by definition there cannot be market price evidence of how arm's-length parties would have agreed to split it. Even if unrelated parties were magically handed the unavailable extra profit, subject only to their agreeing about how to split it, they would face a bilateral monopoly bargaining problem, the outcome of which might be highly unpredictable. Thus, if Acme United States and Acme-France could make $10 million each operating separately but $25 million total if operating in tandem, all we could really say about the hypothetical income split that they would reach at arm's length is that each side would surely end up with somewhere between $10 million and $15 million of the total, with the exact breakdown depending on how the negotiations shook out.

In practice, therefore, transfer pricing is at once a puzzle without a correct solution and a sinkhole for substantial tax planning, compliance, and administrative expense (albeit providing gainful employment for numerous lawyers, economists, and accountants). Nonetheless, things would not be quite so dire if tax planning games were limited to keeping theoretically indeterminate synergy income disproportionately out of the United States. Instead, as we'll see further in chapter 3, in practice the observed problems are considerably worse than this. For example, U.S. companies' tax haven affiliates, which in practice often are little more than incorporated post office drops with their own bank accounts, often end up claiming large profit shares. Yet their true contribution to the firms' pre-tax profits may actually be negative, since, while operating them has a positive cost, they may actually contribute nothing to the firms' operations, other than the opportunity to reduce U.S. (and foreign) taxes.

Part of the blame for transfer pricing's working so poorly in practice lies with its central "comparable price" idea. For decades, the core practice in transfer pricing has been to look for real-world transactions that were similar to those occurring within the firm for which one needs to determine the transfer price, except that they involved unrelated third parties. At one time, this approach may have worked reasonably well. Michael Durst (2007, 1048) notes that, back in the 1920s, "available transportation and communications technology did not permit close centralized management of geographically diverse groups. Therefore, members of multinational groups functioned largely as independent entities, and benchmarking their income or transactions based on uncontrolled comparables probably made good sense." With improved communications technology, however, not only did central headquarters acquire the ability closely to control worldwide operations in real time, but a kind of market segmentation occurred that was directly adverse to the tax law's reliance on comparable arm's-length transactions:

> [I]n those industries and markets where common control poses advantages, it typically is economically infeasible to remain in the market using a noncommonly controlled structure (for example, by maintaining distributors that are economically independent of manufacturers). In those markets in which multinational groups operate (that is, in those markets in which transfer pricing issues arise), it is unlikely that reasonably close uncontrolled comparables can be found. For example, today... there are no independently owned distributors of mass-market automobiles in the U.S.; all of the distributors are owned by their manufacturers. (1049)

Companies were quick to react to the rise in tax planning opportunities. By the early 1960s it had become "standard practice" (Hellerstein 1963, 165) to establish tax haven subsidiaries that would attract substantial shares of multinational businesses' worldwide income. Moreover, it was already clear by this time that intangible assets, such as " 'know-how,' secret processes, the use of patents, providing personnel and a whole variety of technical and advisory services" offered especially rich opportunities for income shifting to low-tax jurisdictions, as "the reasonableness of the prices paid for these services and property... are customarily shrouded in a good deal of mystery" (165).

While these problems have not changed in kind since the 1960s, they have grown vastly more acute, reflecting ongoing advances in worldwide economic integration, along with the ever-rising importance of intangibles in global economic activity. Intellectual property, not bricks and mortar equipment, is increasingly the dominant factor in global economic production. And the transfer pricing rules cannot entirely impede shifting such property to low-tax jurisdictions long before it has demonstrably exhibited the economic value that its developers expect it to have.

In this brave new world of unique high-tech products, there frequently are no plausible arm's length comparables. Making things worse, many industries in which production has been globalized are wholly populated by multinational firms, such that even generally similar goods and services that arise within the stages of the production process are never sold at arm's length. Then the search for comparable prices often amounts to little more than a creative and flexible game of "find the strained analogy."

By reason of this problem, the comparable price method has largely been abandoned with respect to intangibles—unfortunately, however, without yielding great improvement. For a number of years, companies such as Apple and Google achieved astoundingly favorable results, with respect to new technologies developed in the United States, by exploiting transfer pricing regulations that pertained to "cost-sharing." For example, with respect to the iPhone, Apple appears to have done the following (see Sullivan 2011b).

First, it gave money to its subsidiaries that were located in tax havens such as Bermuda. Next, it had the subsidiaries give this money back to the U.S. parent, in a supposedly arm's-length deal in which they helped pay for developing the iPhone (through the work of engineers living almost entirely in the United States), in exchange for the parent company's giving them the right to market the iPhone overseas. Such methods have permitted Apple to treat about 70 percent of its global income as foreign source (Duhigg and Kocieniewski 2012), even though nearly all of its key value-creating work appears to have been done by people living in the United States (Sullivan 2011b). While the cost-sharing regulations were revised in 2009, apparently with an eye to addressing such techniques, U.S. companies may still retain "almost frictionless flexibility" to achieve comparably favorable results, with respect to intangibles that are actually developed at home, through alternative permitted valuation methods (Brauner 2008, 157).

Dismay about transfer pricing has led many commentators to suggest its replacement by a method called formulary apportionment, under which observed or hypothetical intra-firm transactions would drop out of the picture altogether. Instead, the proportion of a multinational firm's global income that was treated as U.S. source would depend purely on a mechanical computation that was based on the firm's U.S.-to-foreign proportion of one or more of the following objectively determined factors: (1) its property (typically limited to tangible items that have a determinate location); (2) its payroll, that is, wage payments to employees in different countries; and/or (3) its sales.

In illustration, suppose that Acme Products had $12 billion of global income, and that exactly two-thirds of each of the above three factors was located at home. Under a formulary approach that was based on any one or more of the three factors, Acme would be treated as having U.S. source income of $8 billion, and FSI of $4 billion. Or suppose Acme was a multinational corporate group, structured so that each affiliate was active only in its home country. Then the technical result of using formulary apportionment might be that the U.S. parent had $8 billion of income, all of it U.S. source, while the foreign subsidiaries had $4 billion of income that was not directly taxable by the United States (albeit effectively taxable as FSI of the U.S. parent upon actual or deemed repatriation).

For many decades, U.S. states with corporate income taxes have generally used formulary apportionment, rather than transfer pricing, to identify the in-state component of U.S. firms' national taxable income. Historically, it was most common for states to give equal weighting to the property, payroll, and sales factors. More recently, however, there has been a trend toward relying more (or even exclusively) on the sales factor, so as to avoid discouraging in-state investment and employment (see Avi-Yonah, Clausing, and Durst 2008). The European Union has also been moving toward the use of formulary apportionment by European firms, at least as a permissible method (see Weiner 2007).

As we will see in chapter 3, formulary apportionment, whether better or worse on balance than transfer pricing, is itself no panacea. For example, it can yield clearly incorrect or inappropriate results as to the source of income, and it is exploitable through tax planning (see, e.g., Altshuler and Grubert 2010). Moreover, even those who view it as clearly superior to transfer pricing often assert that its adoption should await broad international agreements to employ a common formula—a scenario that currently appears remote at best.

Treatment of Deductions—Further difficulties in sourcing multinationals' income, or otherwise affecting their domestic tax liability, pertain to deductions for outlays that may help produce gross income in multiple locations. Examples include (1) the central headquarters expenses of managing a worldwide group; (2) research and development (R&D) expenditures aimed at developing intangible assets that will be deployed in multiple countries; and (3) interest expense paid for the use of funds, either to third-party lenders or to affiliated companies that have made intra-group loans. The question presented is whether a given deduction should be taken against domestic or foreign source gross income, when it may have contributed to generating either or both.

Most countries base their treatment of deductions purely on where (and by which group member) the items were incurred, and do not attempt to match them against the particular source of the income that they helped to generate. Thus, all otherwise allowable expenses that are incurred locally, but only such expenses, are deducted against domestic income. The United States, however, departs in a key way from this practice. While likewise treating foreign affiliates as separate taxpayers, with the consequence that only the U.S. affiliates' outlays are potentially deductible, the U.S. rules in some respects take account of foreign subsidiaries for purposes of determining whether the U.S. companies' deductions will reduce their domestic source or their foreign source income.

In general, for a U.S. company's deductions that may have benefited foreign operations but that have no specific causal link to a specific item of income, several distinct sets of complicated rules require allocation and apportionment on some pro rata basis as between reducing U.S. source and foreign source gross income. For most expenses of a U.S. company that relate equally to all of its gross income, there is very broad discretion regarding the "pro rata to what" question.

Suppose, for example, that a U.S. multinational's headquarters provided support to all of its global operations. In allocating the headquarters expenses between U.S. source and foreign source income, the company could use the domestic to foreign ratio of, among other possibilities, its gross income, sales, assets, or expenses incurred that had a clear relationship to particular income items.[7] If assets are used, the foreign to domestic ratio can depend on their basis for tax purposes or their fair market value, again at the taxpayer's discretion.[8]

If income is being used to allocate deductions, the U.S. company's CFCs enter into the picture insofar as they may yield foreign source income, such as by paying dividends. If asset ratios are being used, shares of the CFCs' stock count as foreign assets of the U.S. company. Thus, suppose that Acme International is a U.S. multinational that incurs $10 million of headquarters expenses and elects to allocate them pro rata to asset basis. If the basis of its stock in its CFCs is 40 percent of its overall asset basis, then $4 million of its headquarters expenses will be treated as reducing foreign source, rather than U.S. source, income.

The same approach partly applies to U.S. companies' R&D expenditures, but with an extra wrinkle. Rather than use the above approach for all of the R&D expenditures, a fixed percentage (25 or 50 percent, depending on the taxpayer's choice of apportionment method) is sourced based on where they were predominantly incurred, with only the remainder being subject to the pro rata method. This part-fish, part-fowl R&D rule appears to be intended as a compromise between the usual pro rata rule and the U.S. agenda of encouraging domestic R&D, by permitting it to reduce domestic rather than foreign source income.

For interest expense—raising the most important deduction source issues given the ubiquity of both intra-group and third-party borrowing—the rules are generally similar, but in a key respect more complicated. Specifically, they look inside a U.S. company's foreign subsidiaries, as the headquarters and R&D rules do not, for purposes of gauging the proportionality of domestic to foreign interest expense. This in turn must be done relative to assets, rather than involving taxpayer discretion to use, say, income or sales instead.

To illustrate how the interest allocation rules work, suppose that parent company Acme United States has exclusively domestic assets, with an adjusted basis of $1,000, except that it also owns the stock of a foreign subsidiary, Acme China, which the rules treat as a foreign asset. If Acme U.S.'s adjusted basis in its Chinese subsidiary's stock is $500, then its overall assets are two-thirds domestic for purposes of the interest (or any other) allocation rules.

If the interest allocation rules worked like those for headquarters expenses, then two-thirds of Acme U.S.'s interest expense would be treated as reducing its foreign source, rather than its domestic, income. The interest rules depart from this approach, however, by considering Acme China's interest expense for purposes of determining domestic to foreign proportionality.

Suppose Acme United States has interest expense of $80, while Acme China has interest expense of $25. The total is therefore $105, of which only two-thirds, or $70, can be treated as reducing domestic source income. Accordingly, while Acme United States' deductible interest expense remains $80, the rules require treating $10 of that amount as reducing its foreign source taxable income.

Now suppose instead that Acme China's interest expense totaled $55. Accordingly, the global Acme total is $135, and seemingly $90 of interest expense should be treated as reducing U.S. source income. This does not happen, however. Acme China is not a U.S. taxpayer, and thus its expenses have no direct effect on Acme United States' taxable income under the U.S. rules. Instead, all that happens is that Acme United States need not treat any of its $80 of interest expense as reducing foreign source, rather than domestic, income.

By thus considering foreign subsidiaries' interest expense for the limited purpose of assessing the group-wide domestic to foreign proportionality of U.S. companies' interest expense, the interest allocation rules take a step away from separate company accounting and in the direction of what might be called full global consolidation. The rules still fall short of the latter, however, not just because only the U.S. group members' items are directly includable or deductible for U.S. tax purposes, but also by virtue of their only considering foreign subsidiaries of U.S. companies, as distinct from all foreign affiliates.

Thus, in the above example, suppose Acme China were the corporate parent and Acme United States the subsidiary. Or suppose Acme United States and Acme China were merely sibling affiliates in a group with a Bermudan parent. In either of these scenarios, since Acme United States would not own any of its foreign affiliates' stock, its assets would be 100 percent domestic, and the affiliates' interest expense would be entirely disregarded for U.S. income tax purposes. Thus, all of Acme United States' $80 in interest expense would reduce its domestic source taxable income, even if its foreign affiliates had no debt or interest expense whatsoever.

To call the interest (and other) allocation rules exceptionally complex, both on their face and in how they apply to inevitably intricate facts, would be if anything an extreme understatement. While no other country attempts anything similar, many countries evidently share the U.S. concern about multinationals' use of domestic interest deductions to fund operations that produce foreign source income, thus effectively stripping out income from the domestic tax base. To protect themselves, they commonly apply "thin capitalization" or "earnings-stripping" rules, under which interest deductions may be disallowed if excessive relative to equity or domestic gross income—and in particular when paid to non-residents (Ault and Arnold 2004, 411).[9] While such rules do not directly pertain to source, and may apply to companies with purely domestic operations that are funded by a high ratio of debt to equity financing, they can reasonably be viewed as a functional substitute for the U.S. response to concern about excessive domestic as compared to foreign leverage.

3. The Tax Advantages of Being a Multinational

As both the transfer pricing and the interest allocation sagas make clear, the source rules permit a great deal of profit shifting by U.S. companies. Reported profits can readily migrate, not just to lower-tax countries in which significant productive activity may be occurring, but to tax havens that often lack sufficient resources, such as land and population, to support more than a trivial amount of such activity.

Suppose that all one needed to do, in order for profit shifting from home to foreign tax havens to be effective, was to establish a shell subsidiary with a postal box and a bank account, in some convenient jurisdiction such as the Cayman Islands. This might make the source-based U.S. corporate tax wholly unfeasible, even as applied to purely domestic businesses that were owned and operated by U.S. individuals. Shifting profits abroad, in this scenario, might function almost as if it were an explicit election for all U.S.-incorporated businesses, permitting their owners to avoid any U.S. (or other) tax on their profits until they needed to withdraw the funds—and perhaps not even then, if they could simply borrow in consideration of the value of the stock.

In actuality, however, things are not quite so simple. Thus, Clausing (2011, 1580) finds that only about 30 percent of the domestic U.S. corporate tax base, rather than all of it, ends up escaping proper attribution under the source rules. This evident limitation on effective profit shifting both shows and reflects that the U.S. source rules are not entirely—even if they are often substantially—empty and manipulable. And it reflects in particular the fact that, to a considerable extent, successfully gaming the U.S. source rules requires that the taxpayer actually be a multinational company in practice, with discernible operations both in the United States and abroad, rather than just pretending to be a multinational on paper (as in the case where all that one owns overseas is a shell corporation in the Caymans).

Once a U.S. company has significant foreign operations, giving at least surface plausibility to the claim that a sizeable share of its profits may actually have been earned abroad, overstating the true foreign operating component may only be the first step. As Kleinbard (2011b, 754–755) notes, once profits have been labeled as FSI rather than as domestic source income, shifting them to a tax haven tends to become far easier. For example, a foreign subsidiary that is more than just a mail drop with a bank account can more easily claim a high transfer price on inter-company transactions with the U.S. parent. And once one has shifted the profits to an actually operating foreign affiliate, "straightforward earnings stripping technologies that are unavailable for domestic income can be used to move that income to a low-tax affiliate" (755).[10]

For this reason, actual foreign economic activity, even if it must be located in non-haven countries, serves for U.S. companies the role of tax-planning complement to activity in the United States. Or, as Kleinbard (2011b, 755) more colorfully puts it, U.S. multinationals have an "odd incentive. . . to invest in high-tax foreign countries, to provide the raw feedstock for the stateless income generation machine to process into low-taxed. . . [foreign] earnings" that may end up never being taxed anywhere.

Kleinbard (755–757) argues that U.S. (and perhaps other) multinationals are able, by reason of this practice, to derive "tax rents," or above-normal after-tax returns that are not competed away by global capital flows. Ordinarily, if Country A has a lower tax rate than Country B, one would expect A to attract global capital at B's expense until the marginal pre-tax returns that it was offering were sufficiently below those in B for the two countries' after-tax returns to be equalized. After all, investors would have something to gain by shifting funds from B to A until this condition prevailed. However, if multinational firms, unlike purely domestic businesses, can uniquely escape this process without becoming the marginal investors that determine prevailing relative pre-tax returns in different countries, then they can get B's higher pre-tax return without actually paying B's tax rate.

Alternatively, multinationals might collectively dissipate these tax rents by competing with each other sufficiently to become the true marginal investors that determine prevailing relative pre-tax returns. However, this would not relieve purely domestic businesses from facing a significant tax disadvantage in comparison to the multinationals. Either way, the Coase story, in which multinationals arise where they can lower the transaction costs associated with cross-border economic activity, ends up being supplemented, and perhaps even in some cases replaced, by a "tax synergy" story in which the tax advantages that can be derived from operating in multiple countries end up fueling the use of multinationals.

4. Determining the Source of Portfolio Income Earned by Investors

A corporation's tax residence may matter for purposes of the source rules even when it is not itself the taxpayer. Consider its portfolio investors, or those owning non-controlling financial interests in it such as stock and debt, respectively yielding dividends and interest income. For those investors' portfolio or passive income, the source question is even harder to resolve satisfyingly than it is with respect to the company's active business income, which at least may have some discernible connection to where economic activity actually takes place.

Suppose the rules simply flowed through entity-level source determinations, making them applicable at the portfolio investor level as well. Thus, if I were a shareholder in Acme Products and received a $100 dividend, the source of this income would depend either on the company's overall ratio between U.S. source and foreign source income over a given period, or else on how my funds (or those from the original issuance of my stock) were deemed to have been used.

Attempting to base the source of portfolio income on such entity-level determinations would be administratively challenging, to say the least, but in any case it generally is not attempted. Perhaps the logic of treating corporations as separate taxpayers from their owners encourages not looking too intently within the entity when its own tax treatment is not the thing at issue. Rather, the question of apparent interest might be thought of as where the investor notionally "went" in order to earn the portfolio income. However, given the difficulty of devising any substantively meaningful answer to this question, the U.S. rules, and those of numerous other countries, respond with arbitrary formalism.

In general, for U.S. federal income tax purposes, the source of interest or dividend income depends on the residence of the issuer. Thus, debt and equity issued by a U.S. corporation yields U.S. source interest and dividends, while that issued by a foreign corporation generally yields foreign source income (with an exception for dividends paid by foreign corporations that earn too high a percentage of their gross income in the United States).

There is a different rule, however, for income from notional principal contracts (NPCs), in which parties agree to offsetting payment obligations based on the returns that each would have earned on an underlying notional amount if invested in a particular way. Parties A and B might agree, for example, that A will owe B the amount that

$10 million would have yielded during a given year if invested in a fixed rate debt instrument, while B will owe A whatever the same amount would have earned if invested, say, in a given company's stock (taking account both of dividend payments and changes in the market price of the stock). At the end of the period, they settle by netting the obligations against each other, leading to a single payment by the party that owed more. The source of any such payment is the residence of the recipient, rather than that of the payer.

There also are financial instruments that defy clear characterization as fitting any such present law category as equity, debt, or NPC. For income from such instruments, source questions may be impossible to resolve with any confidence, using existing precedent (Walker 2009).

There are two different senses in which these rules could potentially cause the legally determined source of income from portfolio investments to verge on being elective with the taxpayer, rather than depending, say, on where she is taking particular local economic risks. First, by choosing between issuers, one may be able to pick the preferred source outcome without much changing the actual set of economic risks that one is bearing. Second, one can choose between financial instruments that are governed by different source rules, again without much changing the actual economics. For example, as I further discuss in chapter 3, NPCs can be used in lieu of stockholding to bet that a particular company's stock will do well, with the consequence of changing the applicable source rule so that it depends on one's own place of residence, rather than that of the company.

A further important feature of the U.S. tax rules for U.S. source passive income responds to potential collection difficulties. In order to sidestep the constraint of lacking direct income tax jurisdiction over foreigners whose only U.S. connection lies in their owning the stock or debt of U.S. companies, the United States imposes a 30 percent withholding tax, collected from the payer, on their U.S. source dividend income (and certain interest). However, various bilateral tax treaties between the United States and foreign countries reciprocally reduce or eliminate the withholding tax for each other's residents.

Tax planners often respond to the presence of these treaties through treaty shopping, or attempting to qualify under an especially favorable treaty even if the true beneficiaries have little or no connection with the treaty's non-U.S. signatory. This in turn is combated by anti-treaty shopping provisions, both in the treaties and in U.S. tax law. These provisions typically attempt to ensure that the foreign country residence claim has some underlying economic substance, as opposed to simply reflecting one's having, say, incorporated a conduit entity there that passes through all of its perfectly matched income and deductions.

C. Foreign Tax Credits

1. Mechanics and Incentive Effects of the Credit

Suppose a U.S. company conducts branch operations abroad. The income from these operations is currently taxable at home because it was earned by the company directly, rather than by a legally distinct foreign subsidiary. In computing U.S. taxable income, the allowable business expenses of these foreign operations, such as for labor, fuel, and rent, are merely deductible. However, the foreign income taxes paid where the operations take place generally give rise to U.S. foreign tax credits, rather than merely to deductions. The company therefore effectively gets a 100 percent, dollar-for-dollar, refund from the U.S. government of its foreign taxes paid, assuming that no foreign tax credit limits apply.

To illustrate the importance of the distinction between credits and mere deductions, we can start with an example where foreign taxes are zero. Suppose that Acme Products' foreign operations have gross receipts of $140 and deductible expenses of $40, yielding net income of $100. If Acme pays no foreign taxes, it would owe the U.S. $35 of tax at the currently prevailing U.S. corporate rate, and end up with $65 after paying that tax. Had Acme incurred one more dollar of deductible expenses, reducing its net income to $99, the U.S. tax would have been only $34.65, and Acme would have ended up with $64.65. Thus, given the effect on its U.S. tax liability of earning a dollar less, Acme's extra one-dollar outlay ended up costing it only 65 cents. One could say, therefore, that it has a marginal reimbursement rate (MRR) for business expenses of 35 percent—equal, of course, to its marginal tax rate (MTR).

Now let's change the example so that Acme also pays foreign taxes that are creditable in the United States. Suppose initially that the foreign tax rate is 20 percent. Acme therefore pays foreign taxes of $20 on its $100 of pre-foreign tax net income. Because the foreign taxes are creditable, they reduce Acme's U.S. tax liability from $35 to $15, leaving it with the same $65 after paying all taxes as if the foreign rate were zero. Or suppose the foreign tax rate had been 30 percent, increasing Acme's foreign tax liability to $30. Acme would pay only $5 after claiming foreign tax credits, and therefore still would end up with $65. In short, so long as U.S. foreign tax credits are allowable immediately and in full, Acme has a foreign tax MRR of 100 percent.

Where effectively applicable, a 100 percent MRR for foreign taxes eliminates all cost consciousness, or incentive by a U.S. taxpayer to care how much it pays. Indeed, with a 100 percent MRR, a U.S. taxpayer would lose out, after U.S. tax, from paying one dollar out of its pocket in order to avoid $1 billion in foreign taxes. Similarly, suppose that a third party asked a U.S. taxpayer to pay that party's billion-dollar foreign tax bill, in exchange for just a dollar, and that the U.S. taxpayer would indeed be allowed to treat this tax payment as creditable, immediately and in full. Even if the dollar it received was taxable at home, the U.S. company, while losing $999,999,999 before U.S. taxes were considered, would end up 65 cents better off after U.S. tax. As we will see in chapter 3, there actually have been real-world transactions based on something resembling this idea, although the U.S. foreign tax credit rules use multiple mechanisms to impede them.

The story is more complicated where a U.S. company operates abroad through a foreign subsidiary, creating the possibility that deferral of the subsidiary's FSI will apply. This affects both the mechanics for claiming foreign tax credits and, at least potentially, the true MRR. Let's start with the mechanics. Given that a foreign company (even if wholly U.S. owned) is not itself a U.S. resident, the foreign income that it earns is never literally or directly taxable in the United States. Rather, the U.S. parent is taxable when it realizes income, in its capacity as a shareholder, from the subsidiary. This could involve, for example, its receiving a dividend—or, as we will see, a deemed dividend under the so-called subpart F rules that limit the U.S. tax benefit of deferral.

Given this formally indirect approach to imposing U.S. tax on a foreign subsidiary's foreign source income, the subsidiary's business expenses are not literally or directly deductible by the U.S. parent. Rather, they are implicitly deductible, in the sense that they reduce the amount of taxable income that can be repatriated to the U.S. parent. This implicit deductibility, in turn, has two elements. First, every dollar of business expense that the subsidiary has to pay (such as for wages or rent) thereby becomes unavailable to be paid to the U.S. parent. Second, under U.S. tax law generally, amounts paid by companies to their shareholders are taxable as dividends only insofar as they do not exceed the company's earnings and profits (E&P). For this reason, U.S. parents are supposed to keep track of their foreign subsidiaries' E&P, and a distribution in excess of E&P merely reduces the parent's basis in the payer's stock.[11]

This brings us to the foreign subsidiary's foreign tax payments. If they, too, received no direct consideration in U.S. tax law other than reducing available cash along with E&P, the result would be effective denial of foreign tax credits to U.S. companies that operate abroad through foreign subsidiaries rather than mere branch operations. To prevent this result, the rules allow U.S. parents to claim a deemed-paid or indirect foreign tax credit when they include actual or deemed dividends from their foreign subsidiaries.

To illustrate, suppose in the prior example that the $100 of pre-foreign tax income had been earned by Acme's foreign subsidiary, rather than through branch operations, and that the subsidiary had paid $20 of income tax in the source country, leaving it with $80. If the subsidiary then paid $80 to Acme as a dividend, the deemed-paid foreign tax credit would be used to create the equivalent of direct creditability. Specifically, Acme would treat the foreign tax attributable to the dividend amount both as grossing up its U.S. taxable income and as generating an allowable credit. Thus, upon receiving the $80 of cash, Acme would have U.S. taxable income of $100, generating pre-credit U.S. liability of $35. However, the $20 foreign tax credit would reduce its U.S. tax bill to $15, leaving it with the same $65 of free cash as in the branch example.

Considered by itself, the deemed-paid or indirect foreign tax credit preserves tax equivalence between branch and subsidiary operations abroad, including with respect to the multinational group's 100 percent MRR for foreign taxes paid. Deferral, however, makes the story more complicated. While deferral is a tax benefit that subsidiaries enjoy but branches do not, it potentially reduces the value of foreign tax credit claims, for reasons that I discuss in chapter 3. Indeed, if one *never* repatriates particular foreign source income, then the associated foreign tax credit will itself presumably never be claimed, thus reducing the MRR (as well as the U.S. MTR for the income) to zero.

Despite deferral's potential mitigating effect on foreign tax MRRs, foreign tax credit-ability remains so potentially generous that the existence of a plethora of provisions limiting its availability comes as no surprise. These provisions are of two main types: foreign tax credit limits, which prevent the credits from offsetting more than the U.S. tax otherwise due on particular foreign source income; and a host of what I call gatekeeper rules providing that particular taxes (or claimed taxes) are not creditable.

2. Foreign Tax Credit Limits

Under a long-standing though frequently changing set of rules, allowable foreign tax credits are limited to the amount of U.S. tax otherwise due with respect to one's foreign source income. Excess credits are neither refundable (in the sense of generating a net cash payment from the U.S. Treasury) nor allowable to offset the U.S. tax due on U.S. source income. They can, however, be carried over to the previous taxable year or any of the next ten taxable years.

To illustrate the operation of the foreign tax credit limit, suppose that, in the earlier example, the foreign tax due on Acme's $100 of foreign source income was $40, and that Acme had no other FSI. While it still would get to use $35 of U.S. foreign tax credits to reduce its U.S. tax liability on this income to zero, the extra $5 of credits would be disallowed—even if Acme also had U.S. source income on which it owed U.S. tax. Only if Acme had other FSI, unsheltered by otherwise available foreign tax credits, at any time during the carryover period would these credits be usable against its U.S. tax liability.

Foreign tax credit limits provide the reason why the source of a U.S. company's taxable income can affect U.S. tax liability even if a given item (such as interest expense under the interest allocation rules) will appear on the company's U.S. tax return in any event. Thus, when interest deductions of a U.S. company are treated as foreign source under the interest allocation rules, the reason this matters is that it reduces the limit, potentially causing the disallowance of credits that otherwise could have been claimed. Where this happens, the rules' effect turns out to be arithmetically equivalent to directly disallowing the interest deductions that triggered such disallowance (Shaviro 2001). For U.S. companies that need not be concerned about credit disallowance, however, the interest allocation rules are effectively irrelevant.

Absent any ability to claim disallowed excess credits in another year, the credit limit, at the moment when it is reached, suddenly shifts the MRR for foreign taxes from 100 percent (ignoring deferral) to 0 percent. It thus (as in the interest allocation example) more generally has the effect of dividing U.S. taxpayers into two groups: (a) those that are "excess credit," and thus may have an MRR as low as zero; and (b) those that are "excess limit" (i.e., have foreign source income that is unsheltered by foreign tax credits), and thus may have an MRR as high as 100 percent. This divide can powerfully influence foreign investment patterns as between U.S. firms, such as by inducing excess-credit firms to invest in low-tax countries so that their excess credits will become usable, while excess-limit firms may prefer to invest in high-tax countries given their ability to make full use of the credits generated there.

As both sides of this divide suggest, one obvious taxpayer response to foreign tax credit limits is to seek "cross-crediting" opportunities. Suppose initially that the foreign tax credit limit applied solely with respect to the sum total of all one's foreign source income. Thus, if Germany had a higher tax rate than the United States, causing disallowance of foreign tax credits when a U.S. company invested there, all the company would need to do is invest as well in low-tax countries, thus lowering the average foreign tax rate paid to the U.S. rate or lower.

To illustrate, recall the earlier example where Acme paid $40 of tax on $100, and suppose this happened in Germany. If Luxembourg had a 10 percent rate, Acme might respond by shifting $20 of income that it otherwise would have earned in the United States to arise instead (at least for tax purposes) in Luxembourg, on which it would pay $2 of Luxembourg tax. Absent the German tax problem (and ignoring deferral), this would have failed to reduce Acme's worldwide tax bill, given the residual U.S levy on lightly taxed foreign source income. Now, however, Acme's overall foreign source income would be $120, on which it would have paid $42 of foreign taxes—exactly the amount creditable under the U.S. rules, given the 35 percent rate and the foreign tax credit limit. Thus, Acme would in effect have "liberated" its excess foreign tax credits by using the low-taxed Luxembourg income to soak them up.

The U.S. rules respond by seeking to limit cross-crediting. The method they use is creating separate "baskets" of foreign source income, the taxes on which can only be used against income from the same basket. Thus, suppose Acme pays $40 of foreign tax on $100 of foreign source active business income, and $2 of tax on $20 of foreign source passive income (just as in the Germany-Luxembourg example). Since the U.S. rules generally place active business income and passive income in separate baskets,[12] only $35 of the active business foreign tax credits would be allowed, and Acme would owe $5 of U.S. tax ($7 gross minus the $2 credit) on the income in the passive basket.

The motivation for dividing foreign source income into active and passive baskets is that income in the latter basket, since it can be earned almost anywhere given competitive global financial markets, is far easier to move for tax purposes to low-tax countries. For example, only so much active business income can plausibly be claimed to arise in the Cayman Islands, given its limited population and industrial capacity. But in theory, all one's passive income could be located there for tax purposes, if one feels comfortable with investing one's entire portfolio in Caymans banks and companies (that could in turn, as an economic matter, have investments around the world, thereby providing substantial diversification).

Thus, allowing taxpayers to pool low-tax passive income with potentially higher-tax active business income would make cross-crediting especially easy. Luckily for U.S. companies, however, there are various low-tax jurisdictions—for example, Ireland and Singapore—in which one may reasonably be able to place significant business assets, relying on transfer pricing and financing patterns to increase the amount of income treated as arising there.

The attempted rigor of the U.S. response to cross-crediting has fluctuated substantially over the years. From 1932 through 1976, the U.S. rules contained various versions of a per-country limitation—preventing, for example, the use of excess French tax credits to offset the U.S. tax on German income. The rules have separated passive income from active business income since 1962. There has also been ebb and flow in the creation of other separate baskets designed to isolate particular categories of income and thereby limit cross-crediting. For example, the Tax Reform Act of 1986 created no fewer than nine separate FSI "baskets," as between which cross-crediting was impermissible. At present, however, only the active versus passive distinction remains.

3. Gatekeeper Rules That Make Particular Items Non-Creditable

In addition to providing credit limits and at least modestly addressing cross-crediting, the U.S. rules respond to the potential for a 100 percent foreign tax MRR by providing that particular taxes, or claimed taxes, are not creditable. Examples of this approach include the following:

"Specific economic benefit" rule—The credit, by treating foreign taxes paid so much more favorably than other overseas business expenses, creates an incentive for U.S. taxpayers to seek to convert what would otherwise be merely deductible (or capital) outlays into creditable income tax payments. Suppose, for example, that building an overseas factory would cost Acme U.S. $100 million. Arranging instead to pay the local government a $120 million "tax" in exchange for its furnishing the building would potentially benefit both Acme and that government, at the expense of U.S. individuals. Treasury regulations respond by providing that payments to a foreign government, even when collected pursuant to its taxing power, are not creditable if received in exchange for a "specific economic benefit," or one that is "not made available on substantially the same terms to substantially all persons who are subject to the income tax that is generally imposed by the foreign country."[13]

Income taxes only—Another apparent policy response to the foreign tax credit's extreme generosity is its being expressly limited to foreign income taxes, or those whose "predominant character. . . is that of an income tax in the U.S. sense."[14] Relevant factors in making this determination include whether a given tax generally uses realization accounting, requires inclusion of gross receipts, and allows deductions so as to produce a measure of taxable net income. This rule may help in screening out disguised fees for particular benefits, and it also ensures that other countries' VATs will not be creditable against U.S. income tax liability. Otherwise, however, its rationale is not entirely clear.[15]

Other miscellaneous rules—Various other specific rules address particular gambits that respond to the foreign tax credit's 100 percent MRR. For example, only a "compulsory payment" of foreign taxes, rather than one that is effectively voluntary, can give rise to a foreign tax credit.[16] Likewise, foreign tax liabilities that could potentially be challenged are not creditable until the U.S. taxpayer "exhausts all effective and practical remedies" with the foreign government.[17] To address real-world cases in which U.S. taxpayers would buy foreign stocks just before a declared dividend was paid, and sell it immediately afterwards, in order to be able to claim foreign tax credits for the withholding tax that the host country was levying, there is now a 15-day minimum holding period for the foreign stock in such cases.[18] To address so-called splitter transactions, in which taxpayers devised creative new ways to bring home foreign tax credits without having to repatriate the associated FSI, there is now a statute that suspends the credits if there has been a "foreign tax credit splitting event."[19] All this is an ongoing cops-and-robbers process, as new transactions necessitate the enactment of new rules limiting the allowance of foreign tax credits.

Anti-abuse and economic substance rules—The IRS also periodically responds to new foreign tax credit planning gambits by attempting to apply anti-abuse rules, such as the common law (and now statutory) requirement that tax-effective transactions have requisite economic substance and business purpose. Indeed, on such grounds the IRS unsuccessfully challenged both withholding tax seeking and splitter transactions,[20] which legislative responses could address only prospectively. The need for anti-abuse rules is of course not unique to the foreign tax credit area, but the 100 percent MRR that credits can offer adds to the economic stakes.

D. Deferral

As noted above, U.S. multinationals operating abroad can use either a branch or a subsidiary structure. A branch is simply a set of operations in the source jurisdiction, conducted directly by the multinational firm through on-site employees and other agents (typically described as giving rise to a "permanent establishment" within the jurisdiction—a status that nonresident firms are often eager to avoid). A subsidiary, by contrast, is a separate legal entity, incorporated in the source jurisdiction but, in the pure case, wholly owned by the multinational firm.

For most practical business purposes, it makes no difference whether one operates through a branch or a subsidiary. Either way, the multinational firm has complete control over the local operations and ultimately owns all of the profits. However, using a subsidiary may permit the multinational to take advantage of limited liability with respect to the local operations. Its use may also have other (typically favorable) domestic legal consequences, insofar as the local government treats resident corporations differently from foreign ones and accepts that foreign multinational parents are not directly subject to its jurisdiction. For these among other (such as tax) reasons, multinationals typically use subsidiaries rather than branches in their overseas operations. The one big exception is banks, which regulators may require to use branches so that the entire global group will support local solvency.

However close the branch and subsidiary modes of operation may seem economically, they look very different doctrinally from the standpoint of a realization-based income tax. Foreign branch profits ineluctably are part of the domestic parent's current operating results. So far as realization is concerned, a U.S. company's office in Paris is no different than an office in Phoenix. In the case of a profitable foreign subsidiary, however, all that technically has happened to the domestic parent is that its stock in a legally distinct entity presumably has appreciated. Thus, the realization doctrine, unless expressly modified to ignore the parent-subsidiary line, suggests ignoring what happened at the subsidiary level until the parent either sells the stock or receives dividends.

For this reason, foreign subsidiaries' non-U.S. income has never directly been includable in the U.S. parents' income until something happens to trigger domestic realization. The very fact that this is called deferral, however, seems to imply a harsher critique than one might normally expect from the application of something so familiar and widespread as realization doctrine. This choice of term presumably reflects both the well-understood arbitrariness of the branch versus subsidiary distinction and the fact that, in the eyes of the U.S. tax system, the subsidiary would itself have taxable income, rather than merely unrealized appreciation, if it were being classified as a U.S. taxpayer by reason of its (at least entity-level) ultimate U.S. ownership.

While deferral arose for formal or doctrinal reasons, its retention to this day is a deliberate policy choice, reflecting Congress's reluctance to choose either pure worldwide taxation at one pole or exemption at the other pole. Deferral thus is effectively rationalized as a tax preference, given the otherwise worldwide character of U.S. residence-based taxation. Even proponents tend to view it as half a loaf toward achieving territoriality, rather than as making sense on its own terms.

Deferral's formalistic origin still matters, however, in that it causes the tax preference of choice to have a particular structure that surely no one would have deliberately chosen from a design standpoint. Its two main features are that one only gets to defer one's foreign earnings if one (a) earns them through a subsidiary and (b) avoids repatriating them. While (a) is immaterial to the extent that a given U.S. multinational would operate abroad through subsidiaries anyway, (b) has important practical implications that essentially no one in U.S. international tax policy debate considers desirable. After all, why would one want to discourage U.S. companies from bringing money home that they then might use domestically?

As it happens, the question of why and how deferral discourages the repatriation of foreign earnings is more complicated than it may initially seem. Thus, suppose that Acme Bermuda has $100 million of wholly untaxed profits, which would cause Acme U.S. to pay $35 million of current year tax liability if foreign subsidiaries were treated like foreign branches. Suppose that all of Acme's global funds earn a 10 percent return, and that Acme would be forced for business reasons to repatriate its funds in Bermuda next year. Is there any benefit from the one-year delay, resulting here from deferral, in collection of the economically accrued $35 million liability? At a first approximation, the answer is no.

After all, in a year Acme Bermuda will presumably have $110 million (given the assumed 10 percent return), thus triggering a repatriation tax of $38.5 million. The present value of this tax at a 10 percent discount rate—$35 million—is exactly the same as that of the tax that deferral permits Acme to avoid today.

We will see in chapter 3 why deferral nonetheless is a substantial tax benefit. The answer turns on varying tax rates between years, and the fact that Acme might never have to repatriate its Bermuda funds, at least during the lifetime of the repatriation tax that is currently part of U.S. law. For now, however, suppose we simply assume that deferral highly benefits U.S. multinationals, and thus that they have "trapped earnings" abroad.

Under this assumption, almost the only plausible rationale for using such a zombie relic of formalistic realization doctrine, rather than a deliberately designed tax preference to achieve a compromise outcome somewhere in between pure worldwide taxation and territoriality, is political. The ongoing stalemate or ceasefire in place regarding U.S. international tax policy makes retaining deferral convenient, and suggests that any effort to replace it could lead to a political bloodbath (at least among competing lobbyists and their pet legislators) as the prospective winners and losers from rival replacement proposals jockeyed for position.

One peculiar political side effect of deferral's perverse structure is that *both* sides in the worldwide versus territorial debate can point to "trapped earnings" abroad as an important reason for adopting *their* preferred changes. There would be no possible problem of trapped earnings if foreign subsidiaries' income was taxable in the United States either immediately or never. In 2004, on the ground that trapped earnings were a problem, proponents of exemption won an important battle, though not (as it turned out) the war, through the enactment of a "tax holiday" providing that, for one year only, qualified foreign dividends would be taxed in the United States at only a 5.25 percent rate, rather than the usual 35 percent. The provision triggered a huge response, with the amount repatriated greatly exceeding official expectations. In the end, $312 billion worth of dividends came home for 2005, the holiday year (Redmiles 2008, 103), as compared to only $30 billion that would have been expected otherwise (Kleinbard and Driessen 2008).

Since U.S. tax law generally defines dividends as distributions made out of E&P, deferral requires U.S. shareholders to keep track of their foreign subsidiaries' E&P, as defined under U.S. tax law principles. The amount of such foreign E&P currently exceeds $2 trillion.[21] Its ongoing rapid growth reflects, not only the actual profitability of U.S. companies' foreign operations, but the companies' ability to label profits, wherever earned, as foreign source.

However significant the actual economic benefit of deferral may be, the managers of publicly traded companies often care more about accounting benefits, or the ability to state high reported earnings on their financial statements. In the words of a knowledgeable insider, "saving taxes is all very nice, but earnings per share make the world go round" (see Shaviro 2009d, 449). Thus, deferral might not affect U.S. multinationals' behavior as much as it actually does, if it did not permit them to state higher current earnings.

As it happens, generally accepted accounting principles (GAAP), which govern U.S. financial reporting, do not in fact permit companies to treat deferred taxes more favorably than current ones. For reasons that are difficult for non-accountants to understand, GAAP generally ignores time value considerations—even though any rational investor surely understands that a dollar today is worth more than a dollar in the future. Thus, in the Acme Bermuda example above, Acme would have to report a $35 million tax expense, for purpose of determining current year earnings, even if it anticipated benefiting from the deferral indefinitely. Only if it stipulated, to its auditors' satisfaction, that Acme Bermuda's funds were *permanently* reinvested abroad, would it get any accounting benefit as to current earnings. But with such a stipulation, it would be able to drop its reported U.S. tax liability, for financial accounting purposes, all the way from $35 million to zero.

Given the magnitude of this discontinuous benefit, it has become common practice for U.S. multinationals to report that the profits they have treated for tax purposes as arising in tax havens are permanently reinvested abroad. In practice, this may cause the companies to have "trapped earnings" abroad after all—trapped, that is, by the managers' reluctance to take the earnings hit that would result from contradicting their prior stipulation to the auditors that a U.S. repatriation tax would never be paid.

Despite the tax and accounting stakes, taxable repatriations of U.S. companies' foreign source earnings do in fact happen. In such cases, however, the key factor determining the magnitude of the U.S. federal income tax hit is how much in the way of foreign tax credits can be claimed. For example, if you bring home $100 million of foreign earnings but this frees up $35 million of foreign tax credits, the resulting U.S. tax liability is zero.

Needless to say, companies do not leave the U.S. tax hit purely (or even substantially) to chance. Instead, a "forced move" repatriation of earnings from either a high-tax or a low-tax country frequently prompts offsetting repatriations, designed to optimize the overall U.S. tax consequences. The common result from this interaction between deferral and the foreign tax credit rules is tax planning and compliance costs that are very high relative to the U.S. tax revenues that end up being generated.

E. Subpart F

The first clear proof that deferral has become a deliberate U.S. policy choice, not simply the logical consequence of a realization-based income tax, came in 1962, when the Kennedy administration proposed almost completely repealing it. In support of making the earnings of controlled foreign corporations (CFCs) immediately taxable to their U.S. parents, the administration argued that CFCs were effectively identical to foreign branches, and noted that deferral is simply a tax preference if one accepts worldwide taxation and branch equivalence. In denouncing deferral, the administration made classic anti-tax preference arguments, based on issues of fairness and tax neutrality, and also expressed concern that tax-favoring U.S. companies' outbound investment would reduce domestic U.S. investment and jobs.

The attack was in a sense two pronged. While the administration targeted deferral generally,[22] much of its rhetoric and argumentation focused more narrowly on U.S. companies' use or abuse of tax havens. These generally were small countries (such as Luxembourg or Bermuda) with two linked characteristics: extremely low (if any) income tax rates; and a lack of sufficient domestic resources, including population, to support significant levels of local economic production. In light of these characteristics, taxable income that U.S. companies attributed to havens might reasonably be suspected of reflecting economic activity that actually took place elsewhere. Under the source rules, however, such income shifting was hard to combat, given transfer pricing opportunities plus the ability to use intra-group debt to place interest deductions in high-tax countries (including the United States) and the offsetting interest income in tax haven subsidiaries.

Not surprisingly, this proposal prompted intense opposition from U.S. multinationals. In the main, however, rather than challenging the logic of branch equivalence or defending realization doctrine as applied to wholly owned foreign subsidiaries, the companies responded with their own competing policy claims—about worldwide taxation, as distinct from deferral as such. In particular, they argued that increasing the U.S. tax burden on outbound investment would gravely handicap their ability to compete abroad with non-U.S. companies that only faced local source-based taxes.

The companies were perhaps less eager than the Kennedy administration to discuss tax planning designed to shift income to tax havens. They could, however, note two defensive rationales in favor of these practices: (1) that foreign competitors were also shifting income to the havens, thus making it a part of remaining competitive; and (2) that thereby saving foreign, as distinct from U.S., taxes, was something that the U.S. Treasury should welcome, rather than condemn.

Congress responded to this closely fought cage match by splitting the difference. Rather than generally ending deferral, it enacted a set of rules commonly known as subpart F, under which specified types of CFC income are taxed currently to U.S. shareholders, through the mechanism of being treated as deemed dividends. These rules arguably focus on tax havens, but only indirectly. Rather than distinguishing between, say, countries like Germany and those that are more like Bermuda, the subpart F rules target income that is relatively mobile (and thus easy to locate in a tax haven), along with indicia of tax planning designed to shift income from one country to another.

For purposes of subpart F, CFCs are defined as foreign corporations that are more than 50 percent owned by U.S. shareholders, counting only such shareholders who own (including through attribution from related parties) at least 10 percent. Those owning less than 10 percent not only are disregarded in measuring U.S. control, but are not treated as receiving deemed dividends even if the ownership threshold is otherwise met for the foreign company.

In defining the circumstances that give rise to deemed dividends, subpart F is quite wide ranging. For example, it addresses paying illegal foreign bribes, as well as participating in international boycotts, such as by Arab countries of Israel.[23] Its principal effect, however, is to create the following three main categories of items that give rise to a deemed dividend:

(1) passive income, such as interest and dividends on portfolio financial assets held by the CFC. One important application of this category is to intercompany financial flows, such as interest income that one CFC earns on debt owed to it by the U.S. parent or another CFC. Such related-party passive income generally is taxable under subpart F—reflecting the concern about income shifting—even though, from the standpoint of the entire worldwide group, one might view it as a wash. The subpart F rules do, however, provide for disregarding intra-group interest payments if the borrower and lender are in the same country.[24]

(2) Overseas tax planning is even more clearly the focus of a second set of rules defining subpart F income. These rules address the "base company" scenario, in which a conduit entity, located in a tax haven, effectively diverts taxable income from higher-tax countries by serving as an ostensible middleman, using transfer pricing to claim a share of the overall worldwide group profit that exceeds its true value added.

To illustrate, suppose that Acme Products produces goods for the European market, most of which would be sold in high-population but high-tax countries such as France and Germany. Rather than shipping the goods directly to its French and German affiliates, Acme might insert a Luxembourg subsidiary in the middle that ostensibly provided, say, storage and marketing services, and arrange the reported transfer prices such that this affiliate ended up with a significant slice of the group's overall income from its export activities. This would increase Acme's benefit from using transfer pricing to shift taxable income abroad. But even if the United States did a good enough job of transfer pricing enforcement to squelch such shifting entirely, Acme could still benefit abroad from the arrangement, by transfer-pricing income out of France and Germany.

The subpart F rules address such arrangements as follows. When a CFC earns sales income with respect to property that is neither produced nor consumed within the country where the CFC operates (e.g., Luxembourg in the above example), such income is generally taxable as a deemed dividend to the U.S. parent.[25] A similar rule applies when a CFC receives income from the performance of services when it is neither in the country where the services were performed, nor that where they were consumed.[26] As a result, Acme will likely have no tax incentive to establish a Luxembourg affiliate, given that each dollar of taxable income shifted out of France and Germany would show up as current U.S. taxable income.

(3) A final major category of inclusion under subpart F pertains to investments by CFCs in U.S. property, such as real estate or stock in U.S. corporations. Such investments, when made by CFCs with unrepatriated profits, give rise to a deemed dividend even though they do not reflect direct receipt of the profits by the U.S. parent. One rationale for this rule might be that the case for perpetuating deferral, if based on permitting foreign operations to fund their growth through retained earnings, no longer applies when the earnings have come back to the United States. A second might be that treating U.S. investment as a taxable repatriation makes it harder for U.S. companies to avoid the residual U.S. tax indefinitely. For example, if they are concerned that keeping the funds abroad would expose them to foreign economic risk that they would prefer to avoid, U.S. real estate investment might be an attractive alternative, but for its giving rise to subpart F income. However, the rule's efficacy in this regard is greatly reduced by the fact that a U.S. company's foreign subsidiaries can hold U.S. dollars or U.S. government and private securities, thus effectively bearing U.S. in lieu of foreign economic risk no less than if they held U.S. real estate, without this being treated as a taxable repatriation (Linebaugh 2013, 1).

What should we make of subpart F as a whole? However murky and disparate its rules may be, it actually has a surprisingly coherent (whether or not persuasive) conceptual core. Again, the basic idea is that, when a U.S. multinational invests abroad, it should not face pre-repatriation U.S. tax so long as it not only keeps the money abroad but (a) is actually using retained earnings to expand its active business operations, rather than to hold an investment portfolio that can easily be placed in a tax haven; and (b) does not appear to be avoiding meaningful source-based taxes abroad by shifting its income from the "true" place where it was likely earned. The rules make no effort to answer the hard question of whether, for these purposes, it is U.S. or foreign taxes that either directly or ultimately are being saved. And, while seemingly aimed at tax haven income, they address this issue purely by reference to the type of income that is involved (or the structure used in earning it), rather than by focusing directly on where the taxpayer actually reports it.

However conceptually clear subpart F's main structure and purposes might be, it is considerably less pellucid in practice. Indeed, it is "widely regarded as one of the most complex and difficult pieces of legislation in existence" (Isenbergh 2004, 70:8). This complexity has multiple causes, even beyond the difficulty of identifying either passive income or arrangements that raise suspicion about income shifting abroad. One set of issues relates to the need to keep track of foreign subsidiaries' E&P, so that one can determine whether deemed distributions are dividends. Moreover, for deemed dividends no less than actual ones, one must determine the foreign taxes that are attributable to them, while continually coordinating to make sure that neither earnings nor foreign taxes paid are counted twice. Finally, because U.S. shareholders who own less than a 10 percent interest, as well as foreign shareholders, are not subject to the receipt of deemed dividends under subpart F, one must take care to "assign the right earnings to the right owners at the right time.... The upshot [of all this] is a very busy statute" (Isenbergh 2004, 70:8).

F. Bilateral Income Tax Treaties

One last feature of U.S. international tax law that is worth briefly mentioning is the existence of bilateral income tax treaties, which the United States presently has with more than sixty nations. Under U.S. law, treaties have no higher standing than statutory law, and thus give way if contradicted by a later-in-time enactment, but this is relatively rare, reflecting that the treaties and the Internal Revenue Code generally reflect a shared or at least consistent vision.

While the treaties are not entirely uniform, their terms, along with those of other bilateral income tax treaties around the world, tend to have various common features. In general, the treaties state as their principal goal the "avoidance of double taxation and the prevention of fiscal evasion with respect to taxes on income" (United States Department of the Treasury 2006). In other words, they generally seek to ensure that cross-border activity involving the treaty partners is taxed exactly once, rather than twice or not at all. A key tool for preventing evasion is information sharing.

To prevent double taxation, the treaties generally use two distinct approaches. For business activity in a source country that is conducted by a foreign entity through a permanent establishment, they require the residence country to offer either foreign tax credits (effectively rebating the source country tax) or else exemption. By contrast, for passive income earned from portfolio investments in the source country, they often lean toward exemption (or at least a reduced rate of withholding tax) by the source country.

Even with these rules in place, however, double taxation or double non-taxation may result if source and residence countries apply different source rules, or otherwise measure income differently. Thus, suppose that Acme Products earned $100 million worldwide, all of it in either the United States or France. If both countries claim that $60 million was earned within their own borders, $20 million of Acme's global income may effectively be taxed twice (if only in the sense that the U.S. foreign tax credit limit, if Acme is a U.S. company, will reflect FSI of only $40 million). Accordingly, fully avoiding double taxation and double non-taxation would require tax base coordination, not just foreign tax credits or exemption by one country or the other.

Tax treaties generally do not prevent tax base or source rule differences from arising. While they may offer mechanisms for abating it, such as by providing for consultation between the treaty partners' "competent authorities" to address issues such as transfer pricing, these mechanisms generally have limited scope. In particular, they can only address purely bilateral issues, such as the transfer price that is applied to a transaction between a given multinational's affiliates in the treaty countries. Source rule differences of broader geographical scope—for example, those pertaining to interest deductions, which generally are not country specific, as they merely distinguish domestic source from foreign source income—generally cannot be handled this way.

Given the limited scope of bilateral sourcing reconciliation efforts even if the competent authorities are eager to reach agreement, a logical next step—if countries placed a high enough priority on ensuring that income wax taxed exactly once—might be the creation of a multilateral tax authority, akin to the World Treaty Organization (WTO) in trade matters, with a mandate to assure that income is generally included somewhere exactly once. In fact, however, while various multilateral institutions—for example, the Organization for Economic Coordination and Development (OECD), the International Monetary Fund (IMF), and the United Nations' Committee of Experts on International Cooperation in Tax Matters—may offer advice and coordination in support of the one-tax end result, nothing like the WTO exists in international tax, nor does the creation of any such institution appear imminent (or likely to attract U.S. support). Even more limited initiatives, such as arranging common global approaches to formulary apportionment or the sourcing of interest deductions, have proven unachievable.

G. Summary

U.S. international taxation uses five core concepts: residence, source, foreign tax credits, deferral, and subpart F exceptions to deferral. Each, in different ways, rests on shaky foundations and leads to difficulties in practice. The residence concept works well, for the most part, with respect to individuals, but is poorly suited to the task of classifying legal entities such as corporations. The source of income lacks fundamental economic meaning, but is even worse in practice than one might expect from its theoretical limitations. The main tools used to exploit it are transfer pricing and the strategic use of borrowing to shift net income from high-tax to low-tax jurisdictions. Foreign tax credits can eliminate all cost consciousness by U.S. taxpayers with respect to foreign tax liabilities, and prompt a need for complex rules limiting their use or allowability. Deferral helps to ensure that tax planning costs are high relative to the revenue raised. The subpart F rules that limit deferral's reach, mainly in situations where one might suspect that income is being shifted to tax havens, create still more pyramiding complexity in practice.

Endnotes

1. I am referring to the winter 2013 edition of the Commerce Clearing House (CCH) compilation, where Code sections 861 through 999 go from pages 2551 through 2833. This admittedly includes not just the text of current statutes, but information about recent amendments thereto.

2. In the winter 2013 CCH compilation of income tax regulations, those pertaining to Code sections 861 through 999 appear at pages 45,940 through 46,359; 48,801 through 49,470; and 50,801 through 50,998, making for a total of 1,288 pages.

3. The issuance of IRS Notice 2009-78, 2009-2 C.B. 452, played an important role in tightening the anti-inversion rules' application, addressing gaps and defects in the initial proposed regulations.

4. Even if income that is assigned to the U.S. parent ends up being classified as FSI, it will be currently taxable under the U.S. rules, and the source determination will matter solely for purposes of applying the foreign tax credit limitation. Income of a foreign subsidiary that avoids any direct U.S. presence is not directly taxable under the U.S. rules—although, as we will see below, in some cases it may in effect be currently taxable to the U.S. parent, by reason of its giving rise to a deemed dividend under subpart F.

5. This assumes that one is taxing production or consumption by the same people—and not, for example, taxing consumption by foreign visitors or failing to tax that by one's own residents when they travel abroad.

6. See IRC section 865.

7. See Treas. Regs. sections 1.861-8(b) and 1.861-8T(c).

8. See Treas. Regs. section 1.861-8T(c)(2).

9. The United States also has a thin capitalization rule, but not an especially rigorous one. See Code section 163(j).

10. These earnings-stripping technologies rely on the existence and limited reach of subpart F, discussed later in this chapter and in chapter 3.

11. Once the basis of the subsidiary's stock has been reduced to zero, further distributions generally are treated as giving rise to capital gain.

12. See generally Code section 904(d).

13. Treas. Reg. §1.901-2(a)(2)(ii)(B). Absent a generally imposed income tax in the foreign country, the regulation instead defines a specific economic benefit as one that is "not made available on substantially the same terms to the population of the country in general." Id.

14. Treas. Reg. §1.901-2(a)(1)(ii).

15. The rule providing that only foreign income taxes are creditable was recently the subject of a U.S. Supreme Court decision. PPL Corp. v. Commissioner, decided on May 20, 2013. This decision directly affected only a few U.S. taxpayers, and its broader significance to U.S. international tax law appears to be limited.

16. Treas. Reg. §1.901-2(a)(1)(i).

17. Treas. Reg. §1.901-2(e)(4)(ii).

18. IRC section 901(k).

19. IRC section 909.

20. See Compaq Computer Corp. v. Commissioner, 277 F.3d 778 (5th Cir. 2001); IES

Industries, Inc. v. United States, 253 F.3d 350 (8th Cir. 2001); Guardian Industries Corp. v. United States, 477 F.3d 1368 (Fed. Cir. 2007).

21. Linebaugh 2013 notes a recent estimate of $1.7 trillion in U.S. public companies' foreign earnings, counting only that portion, which (as discussed below) the companies have classified as permanently reinvested abroad.

22. The Kennedy administration proposed retaining deferral for investment in developing countries, but as a deliberate tax preference to promote their economic advancement.

23. See IRC sections 952(a)(3) and (4).

24. See IRC section 954(c)(3)(A).

25. See IRC section 954(d).

26. See IRC section 954(e).

3 Planning and Policy Issues Under the Existing U.S. Rules

THERE IS AN old saying that, if you don't know where you are going, any road will do. Given this point, one cannot fully evaluate the U.S. international tax rules, or draw conclusions regarding how they ought to change, until one identifies the underlying policy aims, which I will start addressing in chapter 4.

However, roads do not just differ in where they go. In addition, some are bumpy while others are smooth, some are slow while others are fast, and some have steep hills and hairpin turns while others are flat and straight. So the ultimate destination is not the only evaluative criterion. Hence this chapter examines some of the main incentives and tax planning opportunities that the existing U.S. international tax rules create, and discusses how marginal changes to the rules might affect things. A further aim is to show why the current system has such a horrendous ratio of tax planning, compliance, and administrative costs to U.S. revenue raised.

A. Corporate Residence

As we saw in chapter 2, the main direct consequence of qualifying as a U.S. resident corporation is at least potential U.S. taxability of one's FSI. Often, a more important indirect consequence is making it harder for the taxpayer to reduce (or save taxes by reducing) U.S. source income (via subpart F and/or the interest allocation rules). Either way, however, being classified as a U.S. corporate resident frequently is tax disadvantageous. Peer countries generally are closer to the territorial pole in their treatment of resident firms. Better still, from a global tax planning standpoint, may be establishing corporate residence in a tax haven. Or, for that matter, one can reside nowhere, like Apple Operations International, an affiliate that Apple incorporated in Ireland and manages in the United States, hence avoiding both countries' corporate residence rules and making it, in the words of Senator Carl Levin, a "ghost compan[y] which for tax purposes, exist[s] no-where" (see Flynn and Doyle 2013).

A key question, therefore, is how easy taxpayers are likely to find it in practice to avoid U.S. corporate resident status, either under the existing rules or others that could plausibly be prescribed. If avoiding such status is sufficiently easy—even for existing companies—there presumably is no point to considering a worldwide regime with significant teeth, even if it would otherwise be desirable, given that the prospective targets could then simply respond by opting out. I call this the issue of corporate residence electivity.

1. The Parameters of Corporate Residence Electivity

By relying formalistically on where companies are incorporated, rather than on where their headquarters or main operations are located, the U.S. residence rules seem to invite ease of avoidance. After all, dozens of reasonably well-governed countries around the world have domestic incorporation statutes or the equivalent. Some, such as Bermuda and the Cayman Islands, are specifically in the business of attracting outside investors.

Nonetheless, over the sweep of decades, the place of incorporation rule has only recently become problematic. Historically, people's places of residence and where they choose to incorporate and invest have been closely linked, despite the seeming ease of severing the two. Home equity bias, or investors' substantial preference for largely avoiding foreign equity, has remained prevalent in recent decades (see Coval and Moskowitz 1999; Tesar and Warner 1995). To this day, U.S. individuals hold predominantly U.S. stock (Gravelle 2009, 481), and are U.S. companies' predominant shareholders.

While home equity bias remains significant, it has been declining with the rise of globalization (Obstfeld and Rogoff 2000, 43). Even as things stand, incorporating at home and holding domestic rather than foreign stock clearly are widely viewed as choices, rather than as inevitable. Thus, it is useful to think about U.S. corporate residence as to some extent a choice or election by taxpayers.

To be sure, companies cannot formally or explicitly elect whether they want to be classified as U.S. residents. If they incorporate in the United States, they unavoidably so qualify. Yet the presence or absence of formal electivity does not tell us whether a given tax classification is actually elective in substance.

Even in the case of formal electivity, taxpayers may face either an explicit or a substantive exercise price for making a particular election. Thus, suppose the IRS charged the U.S. founders of foreign-incorporated companies a $10 million fee. Or suppose that incorporating abroad would reduce a U.S.-owned business's appeal to consumer and investors, or one's ability to lobby Congress effectively. Then the election to incorporate abroad would have an implicit exercise price, equaling the disvalue or cost of these adverse consequences.

Likewise, taxpayers may enjoy substantive tax electivity even if each fact pattern is associated with a determinate legal outcome. All this requires is sufficient flexibility in establishing the requisite fact pattern. The question is simply whether and to what degree the choice of fact pattern, for purposes of determining the applicable rule, actually makes an important difference to the taxpayer.

In illustration, consider the general rule that unrealized gain or loss from an asset's change in value is not taken into account for tax purposes. If realization were formally elective, taxpayers generally would choose it with respect to loss assets, while avoiding it with respect to appreciated assets.[1] Given, however, that it is formally nonelective, and generally depends on whether there has been a sale or exchange of the particular asset, substantive electivity depends on the cost to the taxpayer of departing from its nontax preferences with regard to the occurrence or nonoccurrence of a sale or exchange.

Suppose you hold an appreciated asset, such as stock in a publicly traded company, which your tax advisor says you should retain until death (at which point it will get a tax-free basis step-up under Internal Revenue Code section 1014). Why might you nonetheless sell it, despite the adverse tax consequences, assuming for now that sell and hold are the only alternatives? There are many possibilities. For example, you might need the cash and find a sale more convenient than taking out a loan. Or you might feel the company's stock is overvalued and likely to decline in price. Or you might dislike your risk exposure to this company's stock price performance and want to rebalance your portfolio.

The more important and far from equipoise that these considerations tend to be, the more often you will end up, in practice, not doing the tax-preferred thing. Where tax considerations tell you to hold (or, in the case of a loss asset, to sell), you could think of yourself as having an effective election to attain the tax-preferred result, but at the cost of incurring an exercise price: the disvalue to you of doing the wrong thing, tax considerations aside. Thus, substantive electivity is potentially costly. And the higher the exercise cost, the less substantively elective the tax consequences actually are. At a prohibitive exercise price, electivity is effectively gone.

The effective exercise price of the sell-or-hold option does not, however, depend just on your particular preferences regarding whichever of the underlying factors potentially constrains tax optimization. It also depends on the other means available to you for achieving your nontax goals, and on how the tax law would treat them. For example, can you readily use the stock to secure a loan, and do so without triggering a tax realization? What about buying put options to sell the stock, thus cushioning the downside risk, and/ or selling call options that permit you to monetize and transfer the appreciation potential? Both the completeness of financial markets and the tax law's treatment of effective substitutes for an outright sale will help determine the degree of effective electivity of gain and/or loss realization in practice.

Returning to the issue of U.S. corporate residence, while the place of incorporation rule is formally nonelective, its degree of substantive electivity depends on what nontax consequences attach to having a U.S., as opposed to a foreign, place of incorporation. In countries that define corporate residence in terms of headquarters location, the degree of electivity depends on the malleability of the factors that will end up determining the legal outcome regarding this issue.

A useful rubric in evaluating corporate residence electivity, suggested by Kane and Rock (2008, 1239–1240), is to consider the "tax surplus" as opposed to the "corporate surplus" (i.e., the factors affecting value, taxes aside) that would result from alternative residence choices.[2] For a company whose principals would prefer U.S. incorporation as a business matter but want to avoid U.S. residence as a tax matter, the exercise price of electing to be a non-U.S. corporation is equal to the value of the corporate surplus that this would sacrifice. In my terminology, tax electivity would be complete if the corporate surplus from choosing or avoiding U.S. residence was always zero. By contrast, an always-prohibitive exercise price for departing from one's nontax preferences would lead in practice to complete nonelectivity.

There are four distinct settings in which the degree of electivity of U.S. corporate residence may matter. The first involves new U.S. incorporation of a start-up business. Here, obviously, in principle one can do whatever one likes, but actual electivity depends on the U.S. versus foreign alternatives' nontax consequences.

A second scenario involves existing foreign companies that have reason to consider becoming U.S. companies. This scenario is apparently a very real one, hallucinatory though it might seem to tax officers in U.S. companies who desperately wish they could expatriate. (Lewis Steinberg (2010) has dubbed this mutual desire to change places the "reverse endowment effect.") A well-known example involved Rupert Murdoch's News Corporation, an Australian company that reincorporated in Delaware in 2004.

A third setting for electivity involves existing U.S. companies that may want to expatriate. The anti-inversion rules, which attach adverse tax consequences (including continued U.S. resident status) to transactions that might otherwise have permitted low-cost effective expatriation by existing companies, play an important role in limiting effective electivity for such companies.

The fourth setting for electivity is the least obvious, yet arguably the most important. It involves tax law's impact on new investment by existing U.S. and foreign firms that themselves have fixed places of residence. To illustrate, suppose a new investment in a given capital-importing country could either be made by a U.S. firm or a non-U.S. firm. China, for example, was recently reported to be considering a $60 billion to $100 billion upgrade to its electricity infrastructure, prompting expected competition for the business between GE and Siemens, among other non-Chinese prospective entrants (McGuire 2010). Suppose that China picks the company that offers it the best bid, and that each company's bid reflects its own need to offer the requisite after-tax return to the investors who ultimately would supply the financing in integrated world capital markets. Then the winning bid presumably depends on the interaction between corporate surplus (i.e., relative expected pre-domestic tax returns)[3] and tax surplus (i.e., relative domestic tax burdens). One could fruitfully think of this as if the investors were electing between the use of GE and Siemens to make the investment, even if the only party consciously making a choice—the Chinese government—is looking exclusively at the bids, and thus does not itself care about the winning supplier's place of corporate residence.

2. *Assessing Electivity under Current U.S. Law*

The degree of corporate residence electivity is neither innate nor unalterable. It depends not only on various market actors' preferences, along with available tax planning technologies and the completeness of various markets, but also on the legal rules that determine corporate residence. Thus, its current level under U.S. law depends on the existing rules, which could in principle be changed. In analyzing the extent to which electivity affects the potential efficacy of U.S. worldwide residence-based corporate taxation, I will first assume retention of present law, and then ask how changing the definition of resident companies might affect this bottom line.

a. *New incorporations by U.S. individuals*—Again, the electivity of U.S. corporate residence depends on the value of the nontax surplus that relevant market actors would enjoy if they selected whatever attributes (such as domestic incorporation or headquarters) the U.S. tax law treats as establishing domestic residence. The greater this surplus, the more the United States can "charge," through expected effects on tax liability and on tax planning and compliance costs, by imposing worldwide taxation on the companies that possess the relevant attributes. One might expect the surplus generally to be greatest for U.S. individuals, for whom using local corporate law and lawyers is likely to be most convenient.

Unfortunately, electivity is hard to measure directly, especially given that only companies engaged in cross-border economic activity would find the degree of U.S. worldwide taxation potentially relevant. For those operating exclusively in the United States, the fact that we have more of a worldwide regime than most countries is irrelevant, and domestic incorporation may continue to make perfect sense.

As Mihir Desai and Dhammika Dharmapala (2010, 726) have noted, even just for new incorporations, a "full empirical assessment [of electivity] would require worldwide data on incorporations, and an empirical strategy that credibly identifies the relevant counterfactual—i.e., incorporations that would have occurred in the United States, but occurred in other countries for tax reasons." Both the data and the strategy are hard to come by. For example, even for public offerings, it is unclear what available data sources could be used to distinguish between prospective multinationals and other companies, or to identify the cases in which the organizers are American individuals. Data about incorporations around the world (including in tax haven countries) and concerning the universe of closely held companies, may also be hard if not impossible to assemble. Apparently for these reasons, to date there has been relatively little empirical work bearing on electivity, although numerous international tax economists understand the issue's importance.

This does not, however, mean that we know nothing. Thus, for each of the main settings where effective electivity may play out, I next discuss what is currently known or can reasonably be discerned. In doing so, I draw not only on existing empirical work where available, but also on my own knowledge about current tax practice, including that gained from discussions with leading New York practitioners.

New Start-Ups—The Microsofts and Facebooks of tomorrow, especially when founded by U.S. individuals, involve a key battleground in which electivity must be limited if worldwide residence-based taxation of U.S. corporations is to achieve its main purposes. In particular, if a central aim is to back up the individual income tax by ensuring that a future Bill Gates or Mark Zuckerberg can be effectively be taxed (at the entity level) on his worldwide rather than just his U.S. profits, it is important that his successors frequently continue to follow his lead by incorporating their main businesses in the United States. Should we expect this when global capital markets are increasingly integrated and when foreign incorporation may become ever more familiar, accepted, and cheap?

In support of the view that electivity is rising, Desai (2009a) notes that firms increasingly are separating their legal homes (i.e., where they are incorporated) from their homes for managerial talent and their financial homes (i.e., where they mainly raise capital). This clearly would tend to raise the electivity of where one incorporates, by reducing its dependence on where its managers live or it raises capital.

Yet empirical evidence of changing incorporation patterns remains elusive. For example, Desai and Dharmapala (2010, 728) examined a data set of initial public offerings (IPOs) listed on the New York Stock Exchange and NASDAQ during the period from 1988 through 2009, which included the new firms' place of incorporation. They found that, whereas no firms were being incorporated in tax haven jurisdictions early in the period, such incorporations had risen to 10 percent of the listed incorporations by the period from 2005 through 2009 (and peaked at 30 percent thereof in 2008). This appeared to suggest that U.S. individuals might increasingly be choosing to incorporate their new companies in tax havens. It subsequently turned out, however, that the rise in tax haven incorporations was driven by firms headquartered in China and Hong Kong—not by U.S.-headquartered firms (Allen and Morse 2011).

What about anecdotal evidence? In Shaviro 2011b, I reported on conversations with knowledgeable New York City tax practitioners who consult on start-ups and other corporate business deals. They described a complicated picture, featuring three distinct types of common situations.

First is the typical start-up, often based on a business idea that is not inherently global in intended scope. When U.S. individuals are behind such a start-up, their initial plan is simply to launch a U.S. business. Global aspirations would only come into focus later, if the firm hit enough of a "home run" to suggest expanding it abroad.

In such situations, U.S. incorporation has continued to predominate, for reasons that include the following:

– Not everyone is thinking that far ahead. While such lack of foresight, if it were the only explanation, might suggest the possibility of irrational failures to optimize, this would not be unprecedented. Joseph Bankman (1994) has written about start-ups during the 1990s Internet boom that arguably left money on the table by failing to use tax structures that could have permitted them to monetize the tax value of losses early in the business cycle. One need not posit this, however, given the remaining factors that encourage domestic incorporation.

– Start-ups often need to be highly cost-conscious in the early stages, when they may need to make large capital outlays, are not yet generating revenue, and cannot be certain that they ever will. Incorporating abroad, rather than in one's home state or a familiar domestic locale such as Delaware, may raise costs initially—for example, by making routine managerial and governance transactions costlier to execute (such as due to the need to recruit more remote and specialized outside legal advisors).

– For an initially domestic start-up that is indeed thinking ahead, the relevant U.S. income tax analysis is not limited to the admitted desirability of avoiding future U.S. taxation of foreign profits. Incorporating a foreign parent of the domestic operating company in a tax haven gives rise to concern about potential U.S. withholding tax liability if the need to access or extract cash requires the making of upstream dividend payments. Use of a U.S. tax treaty partner to avoid the withholding tax may raise problems under the limitation of benefits (LOB) rules that such treaties typically deploy in order to impede such "treaty-shopping." LOB rules typically require more of a real presence in the treaty partner than mere incorporation provides, and thus may make use of the treaty too costly or inconvenient.

– At present, the residence-based worldwide U.S. corporate tax is not actually all that onerous. After all, even firms that rely on exploiting deferral plus foreign tax credits so as to avoid indefinitely the U.S. worldwide tax have so many tools available that, as Kleinbard (2011a, 1027) puts it, "in practice and as used by sophisticated multinational firms, the U.S. tax system operates [for the most part] as an ersatz territorial tax regime." The incentive to exercise foresight, by incorporating abroad to pave the way for a hypothetical future expansion abroad if the start-up hits a "home run," would be greater if the U.S. worldwide tax were more onerous. Thus, the fact that new start-ups so frequently do not incorporate abroad given the current rules (and expectations about them in the future) does not tell us how much latitude the U.S. might have to toughen its international tax regime without significantly affecting current practice.

A second category involves niche start-ups in particular industries. For some types of business, the norm of choosing U.S. incorporation just because it is convenient does not apply. In a few areas—for example, defense contracting or operating an airline inside the United States—domestic corporate residence is legally or politically necessary, or at least highly advantageous. There also are areas in which foreign incorporation has become the norm. Companies engaged in reinsurance, for example, commonly incorporate in Bermuda. And funds that engage in strategic investment and trading, typically on behalf of high-net-worth individuals, frequently choose tax haven incorporation in one place or another. One important reason is that, under Internal Revenue Code section 864(b)(2), they can run active trading desks through a U.S. office, using U.S. individuals who are deemed crucial to the expected profitability of the enterprise, without thereby generating income of a U.S. trade or business. Accordingly, they can save U.S. taxes by incorporating abroad even in the absence of future expansion.

Finally, a third category involves prospective multinationals that are indeed thinking ahead strategically, and that therefore make incorporation decisions that reflect explicit assessment of the relevant tax and other considerations. During the planning process, U.S. tax lawyers, if consulted, commonly make the point that domestic incorporation is potentially tax-disadvantageous, given in particular that it will require either paying future U.S. taxes on foreign source income, or engaging in careful and potentially cumbersome planning to avoid this result. They do not always win this argument, however, as U.S. incorporation may also be perceived as having nontax advantages. For example, it may show one's willingness to face the U.S. corporate governance and securities law regimes, and it may ease trading on U.S. capital markets. Apparently, these concerns are not always fully addressed by the fact that foreign firms can enable U.S. trading of their shares, and signal their willingness to face U.S. securities laws, by using American depositary receipts (ADRs) or other cross-listing mechanisms.

While all this suggests that the United States retains (at least for now) some market power to impose worldwide taxation on start-ups of prospective multinationals that are explicitly evaluating the question of where best to incorporate, one should not exaggerate how great this power is. Again, the current U.S. worldwide regime is not all that onerous. What is more, start-ups in this category frequently engage in careful planning to make sure that valuable intellectual property (IP) is assigned to foreign affiliates at an early stage, thus limiting the U.S. source income that will result from profitably exploiting it. This tax planning might not work, of course, if the U.S. tax rules were sufficiently aggressive in currently reaching resident multinationals' foreign source income. But if the U.S. had such a regime, and thus greatly raised the tax price of domestic incorporation, U.S. tax lawyers might start winning more of the in-house arguments regarding where to incorporate.

b. *Foreign individuals who value U.S. incorporation*—The preceding paragraphs focused on start-ups by U.S. individuals, who generally are the most likely to value incorporating here, or at least to regard it as the default option. However, foreign individuals also may have reason to favor U.S. incorporation, even given that they can access U.S. capital markets simply through cross-listing. One reason is that using, say, Delaware corporate law may create corporate surplus because it is perceived as high quality (Kane and Rock 2008, 1267–1268), leading to the hope among a firm's organizers that "it brands them legally, reputationally, and otherwise as a real company with high standards" (Steinberg 2010, 79).

According to Lewis Steinberg (2010, 81), this is not the only reason why investment bankers "see lots of [existing] non-U.S. companies that today are small but would like to become multinationals," and that are eager to reincorporate in the United States as an important step in that direction. Such companies also may respond to data suggesting that U.S. companies' stock may trade at higher price-earnings ratios than that of their foreign peers, notwithstanding the powerful economic forces in global capital markets that push toward convergence. Steinberg attributes this asserted effect of U.S. incorporation on share value to the existence of "a variety of different investors for whom U.S. incorporation is every bit as important as U.S. listing." Often, these are U.S. investors with home equity bias that may reflect legal constraints, in the case of various institutional investors such as U.S. pension funds and certain insurance companies, along with the desire to avoid currency conversion issues, and the perceived value of being better able to join U.S.-focused indices such as the S&P 500. And even where U.S. incorporation would not boost share value, new companies' founders in countries such as Israel and India often view U.S. incorporation as a prestige factor (82).

While this conceivably could support charging foreigners a fee for U.S. incorporation (whether or not by means of taxing foreign source income), Steinberg cautions against assuming too readily that it will continue. He notes, for example, that legal restrictions against holdings of foreign stock by U.S. institutional investors have been easing, and that private equity sponsors and hedge funds are exerting pressure toward global price-value convergence (81–82). To similar effect, consider recent evidence that, when the Sarbanes-Oxley Act of 2002 raised the securities law compliance costs associated with U.S. incorporation, companies organized by foreign individuals responded by shifting what might otherwise have been U.S. IPOs to non-U.S. locales such as London (Ribstein and O'Hara 2008, 711).

c. *Expatriation by existing U.S. companies*—If existing U.S. companies want to escape their status as U.S. residents—or more precisely, to extract their foreign operations from the U.S. international tax umbrella, leaving only a subsidiary here that conducts purely domestic operations—the anti-inversion rules that Congress enacted in 2004 stand in the way. Again, transactions in which at least 60 percent of the company's stock remains in the same hands as previously, and in which its new legal home is not a country in which it afterwards is conducting "substantial business activities," effectively are caught by the statute.

It has been understood from the start that these rules would not prevent economically meaningful merger and acquisition (M&A) activity from being deliberately used to expatriate U.S. companies in response to the tax incentive for doing so. To date, the response appears to be detectable, although not huge. Desai and Dharmapala (2010, 730–731 and Figures 2–3) find it suggestive that, during the period from 1988 to 2009, the percentage (for all U.S. M&A deals) in which the acquirer was a foreign company located either in a tax haven or an exemption country more than doubled. Moreover, looking just at transactions with a foreign acquirer, the percentage in which that company resided in a tax haven country roughly tripled.

With respect to which company ends up on top in a genuine strategic merger between U.S. and foreign peers, practitioners report that "social" considerations, such as which company's managers have more clout, can matter along with the tax analysis. Nonetheless, there is statistical evidence supporting the unsurprising conclusion that taxes do indeed matter. Huizinga and Voget (2009, 1218–1219) estimate that, if the U.S. tax system had featured exemption in 2004, the proportion of cross-border deals in their sample that resulted in a U.S. parent would have been 57.6 percent, rather than 53.1 percent, "correspond[ing] to an 8.6 billion dollar increase in the difference between outward and inward takeovers for the United States."

In the tax planning world, practitioners initially reported that the anti-inversion rules were indeed extremely difficult to circumvent. Even "investment bankers like to say, because we're very upbeat... [that] it's 'very challenging'... [by which we mean] are you out of your mind, if we were so smart, we'd be taking every company offshore" (Steinberg 2010, 79). Some predicted, however, that the "severe chilling effect on inversions of publicly held companies" would prove temporary and that such inversions would "stage a comeback" (Vanderwolk 2010, 700).

To a degree, this appears to already be happening. For example, according to Brett Wells (2012), creative minds have increasingly been finding ways to play games with the change-of-ownership inquiry, or to claim "substantial business activities" in low-tax countries that are not actually major production sites. And while it apparently remains the case that "the current inversion planning strategies are largely event-driven exercises"—meaning that one must take advantage of economically significant changes in a company's ownership or operations that are not just tax driven—"the events that must concurrently occur with the inversion transaction are foreseeable events. Those events may not be routine, but they also are not uncommon" (Wells 2012, 430).

An example is the case where a U.S. multinational happens to want to (or at least is willing to) expand its operations into a country that also would be a tax-advantageous headquarters site. Once one is there, the "substantial business activities" exception to the anti-inversion rule's application can be met. Where this is done by acquiring a small foreign company with the aim of using it in substance, at least to a degree, but also to avoid section 7874, Wells calls this a "bootstrap of inversion benefits onto minnow acquisitions" (434).

Since this is not as yet happening en masse, however, the bottom line appears to be as follows. On the one hand, imposing worldwide taxation does lead some U.S. companies to exit, and this problem may grow worse over time, due both to tax planning advances and expanding global M&A. However, many existing U.S. companies are indeed to a significant degree trapped here, and the United States probably has more leeway to apply worldwide taxation to them than to tomorrow's start-ups.

d. *Effects on New Investment by Existing Companies*—Perhaps the most important, though least visible, mechanism by which electivity could undermine achievement of the aims of worldwide residence-based corporate taxation concerns the making of new investments by existing companies. Foreign direct investment (FDI) from around the world, much of it made by existing multinational corporations, typically exceeds $1 trillion annually. According to Bureau of Economic Analysis data, FDI outflows just from the United States averaged about $200 billion annually between 2000 and 2007. If U.S. international tax rules significantly reduce the extent to which FDI (whether ultimately funded by U.S. or foreign individuals) is made through U.S. companies, then electivity is playing a significant role—no less than when new companies decide to incorporate abroad, and potentially on a larger canvas.

Unfortunately, this issue has not, to my knowledge, been studied empirically as yet, presumably reflecting the difficulty of the task. As in the case of measuring how worldwide tax regimes affect new incorporations, one would need adequate data about new investment by companies from around the world, along with an empirical strategy credibly identifying the investments that would have been made by U.S. companies, but instead were made by foreign companies by reason of the differences in domestic tax regime.

Anecdotal evidence on this question is also harder to come by than it is with respect to new incorporations. U.S. tax lawyers who work for particular clients generally do not get to observe the determinants of whether a U.S. or foreign company will end up exploiting a given investment opportunity. They also tend not to work on foreign investments by foreign companies, which typically would pose no U.S. tax issues.

3. Possible Rule Changes to Reduce Electivity

The U.S. corporate residence rule appears to be more formalistic than the common foreign alternative of relying instead on the location of the headquarters or other "real seat" where the company's predominant assets, employees, or business operations are to be found. However, while formalism often correlates with high electivity, since people typically care more about matters of actual substance, this may not be entirely the case here. Indeed, there is evidence suggesting that headquarters location (at least as determined by the tax authorities) may tend to be more tax elective than place of incorporation.[4] This presumably reflects the fact that headquarters location can be changed at any time, whereas the place of incorporation is determined up front and then becomes irrevocable absent an acquisition that would satisfy the anti-inversion rules. It also reflects that often the people operating a given firm, especially if they are U.S. individuals, may have a strong preference at the start-up phase for U.S. incorporation.

However, even if we assume continued primary reliance by the U.S. tax system on a place of incorporation rule for domestic residence, electivity could still potentially be reduced through the adoption of a disjunctive test, or one treating companies as U.S. residents if they qualify based either on incorporation or some alternative test. The most obvious approach, given practice in other countries, would be defining U.S. companies as those that are *either* incorporated or headquartered here. Or perhaps one could extend resident status to any company that was listed on a major domestic stock exchange— although this would aggressively extend U.S. resident status to companies, such as Siemens, that unmistakably have stronger affiliations elsewhere.

The use of a headquarters-based alternative test for domestic residence has indeed recently been proposed. Under Senator Carl Levin's Stop Tax Haven Abuse Act,[5] a foreign-incorporated company with U.S. headquarters would be classified as a U.S. resident if it either had at least $50 million in gross assets or was publicly traded. A corporation would qualify as United States-headquartered if "substantially all of the executive officers and senior management. . . who exercise day-to-day responsibility for making decisions involving strategic, financial, and operational policies of the corporation are located primarily in the United States."

How should one analyze such proposals, assuming that they can succeed in significantly reducing corporate residence electivity in practice? As it happens, their merits are difficult to separate conceptually from those associated with imposing any worldwide residence-based taxation to begin with. After all, the question of whether the United States should tax the foreign source income of the companies that Senator Levin's proposal would add to the list of domestic companies obviously has a lot in common with the question of whether it should do the same to companies already so qualifying. However, two points worth noting are as follows:

1. A tax on companies' worldwide income that is conditioned on their having a particular attribute is in part a tax on that attribute itself (albeit depending as well on the U.S. rules for FSI). Thus, just as the existing residence test discourages U.S. incorporation, so the Stop Tax Haven Abuse Act would discourage foreign-incorporated companies from having U.S. headquarters. This could be a downside to thus expanding the residence definition if one believes, for example, that corporate headquarters create positive externalities for people living in the countries where they are located (see, e.g., Hufbauer and Assa 2007, 115–116). On the other hand, such expansion would reduce the U.S. tax system's discouragement of U.S. incorporation, the avoidance of which would no longer help unless one also could avoid having a domestic headquarters.

2. Suppose one is choosing between two alternative means of raising the U.S. tax burden on FSI, where the first would be raising the tax on companies that already qualify as U.S. residents, while the second would be broadening the residence definition, such as through the addition of a disjunctive headquarters test.

A good way to think about the choice is as follows. Companies that already are U.S. residents face, on average, some particular effective U.S. tax rate on their FSI. Those that the second alternative would newly classify as U.S. residents would see their U.S. tax rate on such income increase from zero to a similar rate. In general, as a given tax rate increases, the proportion of deadweight loss created to revenue raised goes up as well (Rosen and Gayer 2009, 340). This implies that, if the efficiency tradeoffs presented by taxing the two groups of companies on their FSI are otherwise similar, it may be better to broaden the residence definition than to make the system tougher on companies that already are U.S. residents.

B. Source

Given the possibility that declining home equity bias will make residence-based worldwide taxation ever less promising, it would be nice if one could report that source-based taxation, at least, is holding its own. Unfortunately, however, this is not the case. Residence-based and source-based taxation are jointly weakening, such that analysts view any choice between them as a "race between two very slow participants" in which there can be "few cheers for the winner" (Auerbach 2012, 20).

Their joint decline reflects overlapping causation. The ongoing globalization of business, investment, and finance, crucial to the dimming prospects of residence-based worldwide corporate taxation, also makes a source-based system harder to operate effectively. The rising importance of intangibles as a productive input, and financial innovation that expands tax planning opportunities, have also helped to undermine source-based taxation, by increasing the mobility of both actual and reported income.

Nonetheless, for source-based as well as residence-based taxation, the decline has been occurring in slow motion and remains incomplete. In theory, the death knell for source-based corporate taxation should be a race to the bottom in corporate rates, leaving very little, if anything, to be taxed at the entity level, at least with respect to large, publicly traded companies. To date, however, and confounding widespread predictions about the likely rate and pace of the race to the bottom, "source-based corporate income taxes—many of which were introduced over a century ago—have survived and continue to raise significant amounts of government revenue in many countries" (Mirrlees et al., 2010, 432). This is not to deny, however, that the orderly retreat—in that corporate rates around the world have indeed been declining—may at some point turn into a rout.

In this regard, a key battlefront is transfer pricing. In recent years, its difficulties have accelerated under the double whammy of explicit rate-cutting abroad and increased tax planning by U.S. multinationals (Sullivan 2008a, 2008b). This has recently enabled many firms to enjoy a dramatic increase in successful profit shifting, (Sullivan 2008c), evidenced by their commonly reporting mysteriously higher profit shares in countries with low tax rates (Grubert 2009b; United States Government Accountability Office 2008b).

These developments have been sufficiently dramatic to prompt comments by experts that "the IRS is losing its battle to rein in aggressive transfer pricing abuse" and indeed that "[t]ransfer pricing is dead" (Sullivan 2008c, 1078).

All this has been occurring despite efforts by the U.S. government to push back. The IRS does in fact extensively, and on a regular basis, review major U.S. multinationals' transfer pricing claims. In many cases, the parties negotiate broad agreements under the shadow of potential litigation. Moreover, applicable Treasury regulations have continued evolving, reflecting ongoing efforts to place them on a sounder economic basis and reduce their manipulability.

Why haven't these efforts been more successful? For one thing, case-by-case inquiries are very expensive for the government. And while in theory the government has vast resources, in practice it often has only limited staff and cannot realistically litigate more than a very few selected cases. Thus, it often lacks negotiating leverage. In addition, companies inevitably know their own facts best, even when the government gives its auditors long-term assignments to a given taxpayer (which raises its own issues of auditors "going native" or being subject to taxpayer "capture").

Making things worse, the search for ostensibly meaningful economic factors within the setting of an integrated firm has at times created new paper-shuffling opportunities, in which economically trivial intra-group arrangements end up driving legal outcomes worth millions of dollars. A recent example involves the view, taken by transfer pricing authorities in both the United States and Europe, that the affiliate "actually" earning the lion's share of the profits from a flourishing business line is the one that takes commensurate economic risks. This may sound logical if one is thinking about arm's-length financial markets, in which risk takers typically can demand higher expected returns, and then ex post may enjoy very high observed returns if they happen to win their bets. But for an integrated corporate group, only the overall risk position really matters, not which affiliates would be assigned particular gains and losses on paper.

Consider a famous U.S. transfer pricing case from many years ago, involving the contact lens company Bausch & Lomb. Here it mattered to the court—although surely irrelevant economically—that the group's Irish affiliate (assigned by its U.S. parent the opportunity to manufacture lenses for $1.50 each and then sell them back to the parent for $7.50) formally bore the intra-group risk that the underlying technology might not work well.[6] Yet while this was a risk the group bore as a whole, there was little reason to care, U.S. taxes aside, which affiliate bore it. Similarly, in Europe, companies have found that risk standards permit them, "at the stroke of a pen" (Vann 2010), to shift income to tax havens through the use of Caymans or Bermuda captive insurance companies (i.e., those that are self-owned and thus don't really change the group's overall risk exposure). While one might conclude from this simply that intra-group risk assignments are not a promising avenue for giving transfer pricing greater economic substance, the broader point is that the quest for any such substance is likely to be quite challenging when commonly owned entities are being compared.

A recent trend in transfer pricing has been to rely more on objective criteria, such as the relative profit rates of affiliates in a multinational group. This tends to increase the resemblance in practice between transfer pricing and formulary apportionment, making the choice between these two approaches more a matter of degree than an either/or fork in the road. Accordingly, whether or not formulary apportionment ever officially replaces transfer pricing, it is effectively gaining at least partial sway in practice. This suggests explicitly considering how one should think about the merits of relying on one or more of the three objective factors—property, payroll, and sales—that formulary apportionment typically emphasizes.

Few proponents of formulary apportionment would be so naïve as to argue that the approach can actually get sourcing determinations right—whereas, for transfer pricing, that is evidently the aim, however unsuccessful in practice. A company's property and payroll, although not its sales, are indeed factors used in economic production. However, there is no reason to think that they yield local profitability on a proportionate dollar-for-dollar basis. What is more, intangible property, often the key to a given multinational's economic prospects, generally is excluded from the calculus because it has no readily identifiable location.

The sales factor, meanwhile, is easier to reconcile with a destination-based than an origin-based approach to determining the source of income. After all, if Californians create goods and services that they sell to consumers in New York, then seemingly California should get to claim all of the income, given that (as noted in chapter 2), income taxes generally take an origin-based approach to the source of income from cross-border sales. Use of the sales factor therefore appears to reflect something other than an effort to solve the source conundrum consistently with standard income tax norms. Not that there's anything wrong with that (as the characters in *Seinfeld* might say).

Surely a key rationale for using formulary apportionment, instead of attempting to improve transfer pricing, is pessimism about the feasibility of achieving accurate source determinations. Further relevant considerations include the following:

(a) *Coordination*—In principle, formulary apportionment appears well-suited for multijurisdictional coordination regarding how to divvy up multinationals' global income. If all countries use the same formula, then in practice their source determinations should generally be consistent, even if in some cases they differ either in how they define the underlying factors or in their measures of taxable income.

On the view that such consistency is extremely important, many commentators conclude that no country should adopt formulary apportionment unilaterally. Instead, even the countries that want to proceed ostensibly should await global agreement regarding the use of a consistent formula. As I argued in chapter 1, however, the importance to either global or national efficiency of taxing each dollar of income exactly once—by different countries and at varying rates—is not as great as it may initially seem. Clearly no such qualms have prevented the United States from applying its own interest allocation rules in the international tax realm, or the U.S. states from using distinctive approaches to formulary apportionment.

(b) *Costliness of electivity*—Suppose one believes that transfer pricing, no matter how one tweaks its design and enforcement, can never adequately constrain multinationals' profit shifting. Formulary apportionment might then be viewed as a way of making profit-shifting costlier. Thus, consider the payroll factor. If high-value employees would demand greater compensation to relocate tax havens, or if the replacement workers whom one could find in low-tax countries were less productive than those whom the firm would otherwise hire, then using it effectively increases the exercise price of the election to play sourcing games. The same consideration may hold for using property that is located in low-tax rather than high-tax countries. To be sure, the resulting deterrence comes at a price, since it gives multinational firms an incentive to locate their payroll and property in low-tax rather than high-tax countries (and all the more so if only the high-tax countries are using formulary apportionment). But if profit shifting is itself socially costly from the high-tax country's perspective, then raising the exercise price may be desirable up to a point, depending on the tradeoff between the competing considerations.

From this perspective, use of the sales factor has potential advantages. As Avi-Yonah, Clausing, and Durst (2008, 15) have noted, "sales are far less responsive to tax differences across markets than investment in plant, and employment, as the customers themselves are far less mobile than firm assets or employment. Even in a high-tax country, firms have an incentive to sell as much as possible."

This may understate the effective manipulability of the sales factor. As Altshuler and Grubert (2010, 1172) have noted, companies could respond to use of the sales factor in a number of ways. For example, they could increase marginally profitable (or even unprofitable) sales in low-tax countries, while reducing routine sales in high-tax countries. Suppose, for example, that Apple or Google, in order to increase the extent to which the income from its highly profitable global operations were attributed for tax purposes to Ireland (a relatively low-tax country), acquired an Irish retail grocery chain that had high sales volume along with low profit margins. Unless the sales factor was applied separately to distinct lines of business, the apparent result would be to shift reported taxable income from the United States to Ireland. Another tax planning option would be to use independent resellers in low-tax countries, thereby diverting sales that would otherwise have been observed as occurring in high-tax countries. Altshuler and Grubert therefore question whether the sales factor is actually less manipulable than the other two. Again, however, there clearly would be costs associated with the income-shifting behavior, affecting the amount of it that one would expect to occur.

(c) *Effect on the character of the tax*—A further consideration in evaluating the use of formulary apportionment is how a reliance on each of the factors affects the economic character of the tax that is being levied. Ever since the pathbreaking work of Charles McLure (1981), economists have understood that, with regard to corporate income taxes levied by the U.S. states, the choice of factor may fundamentally transform how a corporate income tax operates. The same analysis presumably applies at the global level to international taxation.

Use of the payroll factor in formulary apportionment causes a state-level tax to resemble economically a tax levied directly on in-state employment. After all, increasing in-state labor costs increases one's tax liability, just as it would under an express payroll tax, although the resemblance is not quite perfect given the role played by national-level corporate income in determining one's liability. Likewise, use of the property factor causes the ostensible income tax to resemble a standard property tax, while use of the sales factor yields resemblance to a conventional sales tax.

What if the U.S. international tax rules instead continue to use transfer pricing? If this method actually succeeded in accurately determining the source of income, the U.S. corporate income tax would reach two main things: the returns to capital investment in the U.S. through corporate entities, and the labor income that owner-employees (such as the Facebook and Google founders), earn through such entities via stock appreciation. But if transfer pricing permits profit shifting at the corporate level, these two levies are reduced or avoided, and the character of the tax that remains is ambiguous, as it depends on what company or income attributes limit the ability to re-label U.S. income as FSI. Insofar as those attributes overlap with those that are expressly used under formulary apportionment, the economic consequences of the two approaches could be similar.

Source issues pertaining to passive income—A further set of ever-worsening problems in determining the source of income pertains to portfolio income earned by passive investors. As noted in chapter 2, the U.S. attempts to tax foreign investors (unless protected by a tax treaty) on the dividend income that they earn from U.S. companies. But over the last twenty years, financial innovation has made the withholding tax ever easier to avoid. In particular, as early as the mid-1990s (but increasingly in the 2000s), instruments called total return swaps began playing an increasingly prominent role in this regard.

Such swaps are notional principal contracts, the income from which is sourced based on the residence of the recipient (rather than that of the payer, as with dividends). To illustrate a typical transaction, suppose a foreign investor wants to buy $1 million worth of stock in Acme, a dividend-paying U.S. corporation. Rather than calling a broker to buy the stock, the investor agrees to a total return swap with a U.S. bank that is in the business of arranging them. Under the swap, on the first anniversary of the transaction date:

1. the investor will owe the bank an amount equal to (a) one year's interest on $1 million at the LIBOR[7] rate (adjusted upwards to provide the bank's fee); plus (b) the amount, if any, by which Acme stock worth $1 million on the transaction date (the "reference amount" of such stock) declined in value during the year; and

2. the bank will owe the investor an amount equal to (a) the dividends paid on the reference amount of Acme stock during the year; plus (b) the amount, if any, by which that amount of Acme stock increased in value during the year.

On the settlement date, the parties resolve their offsetting obligations via a net payment by whichever owes more. Counterparty default risk and the bank's fee aside, the outcome is economically equivalent to that if the investor had purchased $1 million of Acme stock, using the bank as its broker or agent, via debt financing that the bank supplied at the LIBOR rate.

For tax purposes, however, since the foreign investor is not a shareholder of record with respect to any stock, Acme (which has no way of knowing about the transaction) does not withhold when it makes dividend payments to the bank. Likewise, the bank does not withhold when it effectively forwards dividend payments (minus its return) to the investor, as would have been necessary were it acting explicitly as the investor's agent or broker. Emboldened by its fee to disregard the risk of legal liability for the forgone withholding tax, the bank relies on the transaction's form as a notional principal contract, rather than a debt-financed customer purchase of Acme stock.[8]

Under long-standing law, one could argue that withholding tax is indeed due from the bank. U.S. tax law includes broad (though vague) common law principles requiring transactions to be taxed in accordance with their economic substance, rather than their form (Shaviro 2000b). In addition, a specific regulation concerning "substitute dividend payments" arguably applied given the exact match between dividends paid and amounts added to the investor's gross return.[9] But with the IRS being slow to address the transactions in published guidance, total return swaps became enough common enough to create the sense, as then-Joint Committee on Taxation Chief of Staff Edward Kleinbard put it, that "only fools pay withholding taxes on dividends today."[10]

Congress finally responded in 2010 by enacting Code section 871(m), which provides that withholding tax is due on "dividend equivalent payments" such as the above. However, the scope of final implementing regulations remains unclear. The Treasury has suggested that fairly broadly written proposed regulations will be significantly "simplified," even, apparently, if this makes them more avoidable (see Sheppard 2013). Accordingly, the use of swaps in lieu of direct stock ownership remains feasible for taxpayers who do not insist on precise economic equivalence between the two.

C. Foreign Tax Credits and Deferral: Significance of the "New View"

1. Applying the Basic New View Assumptions

To evaluate the incentive effects and planning responses associated with the foreign tax credit and deferral rules, one must first understand the so-called new view of dividend taxation, as applied to the international setting (initially by Hartman 1985). The new view shows that, under specified assumptions, deferral's incentive effects, both on repatriation decisions for foreign subsidiaries' FSI and on paying the foreign taxes that become creditable upon such repatriation, differ from what one might have initially expected. What is more, even if these specified assumptions turn out to be false, the logic that underlies the new view may significantly reshape how one understands foreign tax credits and deferral.

We can start with a point that may seem obviously correct, but in fact is not. Deferral of a fixed liability always reduces its present value (assuming a positive interest rate). Thus, one might think that opting to defer the repatriation of one's foreign subsidiaries' FSI, and thus delaying the date on which a U.S. repatriation tax will apply to such FSI, inevitably reduces the present value of this tax. The assumed result would be, not just the enjoyment of a tax benefit by U.S. multinationals, but discouragement of taxable repatriations that would bring the deferral period to an end. Hence, it would seem, deferral must inevitably create "lock-out," by giving U.S. multinationals an incentive to avoid, or at least delay, repatriating their foreign subsidiaries' FSI.

Now consider foreign tax credits. As we saw earlier, a credit that is allowed immediately and in full creates a 100 percent MRR for the underlying foreign tax payment. But credits generally are not allowed until the associated FSI is repatriated. Once again, the principle that deferral of a fixed amount (here, the U.S. reimbursement of the foreign tax) generally reduces its present value would seem to indicate that deferral automatically reduces actual MRRs, causing them to be less than 100 percent. Here, however, just as with the repatriation tax, things turn out to be more complicated.

To illustrate, suppose we adopt two assumptions that are crucial to the analysis, plus a third assumption that is just for initial convenience. The crucial assumptions are that a taxable repatriation will occur at some point, and that the U.S. repatriation tax rate will never change from what it is today. (For simplicity, let's start out by ignoring foreign tax credits, and thus focusing purely on the "gross" or statutory U.S. tax rate for FSI.) The assumption just for initial convenience is that U.S. companies will earn the same rate of return on their accumulated foreign earnings, after considering all source-based taxes, no matter where they invest these funds (e.g., whether in the United States or abroad). This permits the analysis to focus purely on the incentives that are created by the U.S. repatriation tax.

Under these circumstances, suppose that Acme U.S.'s Belgian subsidiary has $100 of accumulated earnings that will bear a 35 percent U.S. tax whenever they are brought home, and that, in either case, these funds will earn 10 percent a year after considering all source-based taxes. To take foreign tax credits out of the example, suppose the Belgian tax rate is zero. If Acme brought its Belgian earnings home immediately, it would pay a repatriation tax of $35. This would leave Acme with $65, which after a year would have grown to $71.50.

By contrast, if Acme awaited a year to repatriate its Belgian funds, it would have $110 to bring home. This would trigger a repatriation tax of $38.50, leaving Acme with the same $71.50. Not surprisingly, the repatriation tax would also have the same present value either way: $35 today, as opposed to $38.50 in a year. Thus, in the example, deferring the repatriation for a year would *not* reduce (or otherwise affect) either Acme's overall position or the present value of the repatriation tax. Hence, there would be no lock-out, as Acme would have no tax incentive to defer repatriating its Belgian earnings.

How could a year's deferral have failed to reduce the present value of the repatriation tax? The answer is that there were two offsetting effects. On the one hand, the tax payment was deferred for a year, reducing (at a 10 percent discount rate) the present value of the taxes that were initially due. But the amount to be repatriated, and thus the amount of the repatriation tax that ultimately was due, grew at the same 10 percent rate, leading to no net effect on present value.

For readers who prefer a more general algebraic demonstration of this point, let x equal a U.S. company's foreign earnings that benefit from deferral. In addition, let r equal the after-tax return that is available no matter where the cash is being invested, and let t equal the U.S. repatriation tax rate. Immediate repatriation leaves the taxpayer with $x(1 - t)(1 + r)$. Repatriation at the end of the period leaves the taxpayer with $x(1 + r)(1 - t)$. These terms are mathematically identical.

Suppose we were to change the example such that there was a difference between the after-tax rates of return that were available in the United States and Belgium. For example, suppose that Acme's pre-tax rate of return, rather than that available after paying source-based taxes, was 10 percent everywhere. Given the 35 percent U.S. tax rate (reducing the after-tax rate return here to only 6.5 percent), Acme would have a strong incentive to invest in Belgium rather than here.

The broader point that this example makes—even if we might expect after-tax returns to be equalized by market forces once capital flows have responded to tax rate differences—is that Acme may have an overall tax incentive to invest in Belgium, rather than the United States even if the U.S. repatriation tax is constant (and certain to be incurred at some point). But this has nothing to do with the incentive effects of the U.S. repatriation tax as such. The overall tax incentive to invest in Belgium rather than the United States, under the assumed differences in source-based tax rates, would still be there if the U.S. tax system was purely territorial, and thus did not include a repatriation tax for FSI. Differences between source-based tax rates, while important, are conceptually unrelated to deferral as such, and do not create an incentive for companies in deferral countries to avoid repatriating accumulated foreign earnings in particular, as distinct from generally preferring to invest abroad so long as the rate of return differential persists.

The conclusion therefore is clear. If a repatriation tax at the current U.S. rate will paid at some point, then the most common critique of deferral, which is that it discourages U.S. companies from repatriating their foreign subsidiaries' earnings, is false. As we will see, however, the real import of this reasoning is not that there is no "trapped earnings" problem, but rather that we must look more closely at those two assumptions in order to see why there is a problem.

Now let's add foreign tax credits to the analysis. Suppose that Belgium has a tax rate of 20 percent, but that the after-tax rate of return in both the United States and Belgium is 10 percent. This would do nothing to change the above equivalences. After all, the above equation still applies to deferring the U.S. repatriation tax, even though its t has been reduced from 35 percent to 15 percent (computed as a percentage of the pre-Belgian tax earnings).

Thus, suppose Acme-Belgium's $100 of accumulated earnings had borne $20 of Belgian tax, leaving $80 in the subsidiary's coffers. An immediate repatriation of these funds to Acme-United States would be treated as a $100 repatriation on which $20 of foreign taxes had been paid, leaving a $15 residual U.S. tax and $65 in Acme-United States' coffers, which after a year would grow to $71.50.

If the repatriation instead occurred a year later, Acme-Belgium's $80 of after-Belgian tax earnings would have grown to $90 pre-Belgian tax, or $88 after paying an additional $2 of such tax. Repatriating Acme-Belgium's funds would now be treated as yielding $110 of U.S. dividend income, on which the pre-credit U.S. tax liability would be $38.50. However, the $22 of foreign tax credits would reduce the U.S. tax liability to $16.50. Subtracting this amount from the $88 that was actually brought home, Acme-United States would once again end up with $71.50.

Not surprisingly, the equivalence here extends to the present value of the foreign tax credits that end up claimed. Immediate repatriation would have resulted in Acme's claiming $20 of foreign tax credits. Waiting a year caused the credits to grow to $22, which has the same present value as $20 a year earlier, given the 10 percent rate of return. Algebraically, if foreign earnings grow at a fixed annual rate of return (r) that is subject to tax at a fixed foreign rate, then my available foreign tax credits likewise grow by r annually, causing their present value, as determined up front, to remain the same.

Real-world foreign tax credit examples may of course be more complicated. For example, suppose companies can shift funds between countries that have different tax rates while offering the same after-tax rate of return. Or suppose we have a cross-crediting story, in which the residual U.S. tax depends on the repatriation mix between earnings from high-tax and low-tax countries. Then the timing and other details of the eventual repatriation may end up mattering.[11] But the basic "new view" point still holds. That is, deferring repatriation does not reduce the present value of foreign tax credit claims, so long as (1) they will be claimed eventually, and (2) in the interim they will grow at the requisite after-tax rate of return.

This in turn suggests the following. In a simple new view scenario, deferral not only fails to reduce the present value of the repatriation tax, and thus does not induce lockout, but it also does not reduce the present value of foreign tax credit claims, even though they generally must be deferred alongside the associated income. So if the MRR for foreign taxes that the credits offer is 100 percent in the absence of foreign tax credit limits and deferral, in this scenario it remains 100 percent even with deferral.

2. What If the New View Assumptions Do Not Hold?

In practice, the new view's two crucial assumptions do not generally hold. First, repatriation may not be inevitable. In an affiliated corporate group, a taxable repatriation merely shifts funds from one pocket to another—an act that may not be highly meaningful economically. Even when a foreign affiliate reaches a "mature" size, such that it has no further use for retained earnings to finance expansion, there may be many ways of directing the funds to where they are needed without a taxable repatriation. For example, as noted by Altshuler and Grubert (2003), the U.S. parent may find itself able to borrow more by reason of the overseas asset accumulation. Or the parent may cause a mature affiliate in one country to invest equity in a growing affiliate in another country, thus eliminating the need for repatriation as an intermediate step. Or, exploiting the interaction between deferral and foreign tax credits (further discussed below), the parent may have created tiered CFC structures in which high-tax affiliates own low-tax affiliates, thus facilitating the use of cross-crediting to eliminate the repatriation tax on dividends back home.

The existence of a financial accounting category for "permanently reinvested earnings" (PRE), which ostensibly will never come home, adds to real-world divergence from behavior that reflects the new view. Once the accounting nirvana of PRE status has been attained, deferred U.S. repatriation taxes are booked at zero, and the foreign taxes paid therefore have a zero MRR for U.S. financial accounting purposes. In practice, this may often outweigh the opposite scenario, in which full current deductibility from accounting income of the future U.S. taxes, net of foreign tax credits that are booked as an asset, effectively creates an accounting MRR of 100 percent.

Managers of publicly traded companies often notoriously care more about reported than actual earnings (see Shaviro 2009d). The PRE rule can thus turn into a self-fulfilling prophecy, inducing managers not to repatriate for accounting rather than economic reasons. The stakes here may include not only the one-time negative adjustment to earnings when PRE is repatriated, but managerial concern that this will undermine the credibility of other PRE claims that they make to their accountants (Graham, Hanlon, and Shevlin 2011). Accordingly, accounting incentives, as much as or more as economic ones, may end up reducing the extent to which repatriation is inevitable in practice. The results include both lockout and a reduction in the expected MRR for foreign taxes paid to as little as zero (as it is in any case where the credits definitely will never be claimed).

Second, the U.S. repatriation tax rate may not remain the same. So long as there is any prospect that, at any time in the future, the rate will be lower than it is today, keeping the funds abroad has option value. Moreover, there are indeed several systematic reasons for anticipating that future repatriation tax rates may be lower than current ones. First, exemption may eventually be enacted, without a significant transition tax on past earnings. Second, Congress may lower the general U.S. corporate rate, as has recently been much discussed, causing the repatriation tax rate to decline with everything else. Third, Congress may at some point enact a repeat of 2004's temporary tax "holiday," providing a temporary reduction in repatriation tax rates. There is sporadic talk in Washington of enacting another holiday, encouraged by the fact that a handful of companies, by no means lacking in political influence, would benefit enormously. To date, the bad odor from last time has helped to discourage reenactment. In the interim, however, dividend repatriations have indeed declined, as U.S. companies apparently wait for it to happen again (Brennan 2010).

What, then, is left of the new view, given that its assumptions do not in fact hold? A common, but mistaken, conclusion holds that this means we can simply ignore it. But in fact it is a vital touchstone for thinking about how deferral and the foreign tax credit operate in practice. It shows the importance of thinking about the relationship between current and expected future repatriation tax rates, in order to understand deferral's significance in practice. And it teaches us that—accounting incentives aside—the reasons for lockout, and why foreign tax credit MRRs may in practice be as low as zero, are that (1) avoiding a taxable repatriation may be feasible indefinitely, and (2) future expected repatriation tax rates may be lower than current ones. These are variables that we can study—thus helping us to better understand the incentives that companies actually face under present law—and that we can also potentially change.

D. Foreign Tax Credits in Practice

1. Actual U.S. Taxpayer MRRs for Foreign Taxes

As noted above, despite the existence of foreign tax credits, U.S. companies actually are cost conscious regarding foreign taxes in many circumstances. Perhaps the expected MRR is never quite actually zero, given the possibility that even supposed PRE might come home someday. Yet managers of publicly traded companies who have short time horizons and who focus purely on reported earnings may act as if the MRR is zero for foreign taxes that are associated with PRE.

When the expected MRR is 100 percent, however, U.S. taxpayers should have zero cost consciousness with respect to the foreign taxes that they pay. This implies indifference, not just to the choice between investing in high-tax versus low-tax foreign countries if the pre-foreign tax return is the same, but also to tax planning opportunities in foreign countries. Even if the expected MRR is less than 100 percent, however, U.S. taxpayers' foreign tax planning incentives can be importantly affected. So long as the MRR exceeds the MTR, a given taxpayer rationally should not be willing to pay as much as $1 in order to reduce its foreign tax liability by $1.

In some situations, the effects on U.S. taxpayers' incentives are transparently perverse. For example, there are real-world cases in which a U.S. taxpayer effectively paid a fee (either directly to foreigners or by incurring wasteful transaction costs) just for the privilege of at least purporting to pay a given foreign tax liability. Thus, consider a transaction that an IRS Notice, issued in the late 1990s, identified as abusive and legally ineffective.[12] The hypothetical facts in this transaction (presumably based on actual transactions that had come to the attention of the IRS) were as follows. A foreign copyright is about to expire after generating one last payment of $100 that will be subject to a $30 foreign withholding tax. Shortly before this payment is made, a U.S. company buys the copyright for $75. It then receives $70 (net of the withholding tax) as the new copyright owner, plus $30 from the U.S. Treasury, via the value of foreign tax credits that reimburse it for the withholding tax. The U.S. company accordingly scores a $25 after-tax profit almost overnight. The United States, however, is $5 poorer, since we sent $75 abroad and got only $70 back. In effect, then, the U.S. purchaser pays the foreign copyright holder $5 (the excess of $75 over $70) for the privilege of being considered the party that paid the foreign withholding tax.

For an example involving the incurrence of pointless transaction costs in lieu of directly compensating foreigners, consider the notorious case of *Compaq v. Commissioner*,[13] in which the taxpayer ostensibly purchased almost a billion dollars' worth of Royal Dutch Petroleum stock moments before a pre-announced dividend was paid, and then sold the stock (by pre-arrangement) moments afterwards. This resembled a total return swap in reverse. Compaq claimed legal ownership of dividend-paying stock while avoiding any economic risk of gain or loss with respect to the stock, whereas in total return swaps the foreign taxpayer seeks out the economic risks while avoiding legal ownership. The government challenged the *Compaq* transaction—successfully in the Tax Court, but only to be reversed by the Eighth Circuit Court of Appeals—on the ground that the transaction lacked economic substance and business purpose.

When all the dust had settled on the contested transaction in *Compaq*, the taxpayer had roughly broken even economically, except for the fact that it owed a $1 million fee to the investment bank that arranged the transaction. It had thus, taxes aside, paid $1 million for nothing. However, it now could claim that a $3.4 million withholding tax on the dividend—levied by the Dutch government without regard to the identity of the shareholder—was actually its own tax liability, and therefore qualified for full reimbursement via foreign tax credits.

In effect, then, Compaq created more than a million dollars[14] of after-tax profit out of thin air by incurring the transaction fee, solely so that it could claim to be the party that had paid the withholding tax. Legislative concern about such transactions was high enough that, even before *Compaq* was decided, Congress enacted a statute prospectively denying foreign tax credit claims for withholding taxes on dividends unless the taxpayer truly owned the underlying stock for at least fifteen days.[15] This apparently succeeded in discouraging similar transactions, at least by publicly traded U.S. companies, because managers were leery of having to take the responsibility for the companies' bearing fifteen days of price risk with respect to other companies' stock (Shaviro 2000, 229).

Cases such as these, in which foreign tax credit-seeking behavior makes the United States poorer because our taxpayers ignore the cost to other Americans of reimbursing their foreign tax payments, may lead one to think that the problem is simply one of "abuse." As the legislative aftermath to the rise of *Compaq*-style transactions shows, anti-abuse and economic substance rules can indeed significantly discourage foreign tax credit deals in which essentially nothing is happening apart from U.S. taxpayers' creating foreign tax credit claims. In fact, however, the same incentive to ignore foreign taxes that will be reimbursed, and thus to accept lower after-foreign tax returns that leave the people in one's country on the whole poorer, operates more generally.

Thus, suppose a U.S. multinational, wholly owned by U.S. individuals, can choose between earning (a) $100 pre-foreign tax in a country that, like the United States, has a 35 percent corporate tax rate, or (b) $90 in a zero-tax jurisdiction. Ignoring deferral, U.S. individuals would reap only $65 from the former choice, as compared to $90 from the latter. Accordingly, the United States as a whole is $25 richer if the company chooses option (b). However, with credits that offer 100 percent reimbursement of foreign taxes, option (a) turns out to be preferable. It offers the company a $65 bottom line after using the foreign tax credit to avoid any U.S. liability. By contrast, under option (b), after paying a 35 percent U.S. tax on its $90 foreign return, it will end up with only $58.50.

Obviously, no plausible interpretation of the foreign tax credit anti-abuse rules could treat this transaction as within their scope. The effect is inherent to the design of the foreign tax credit, with its 100 percent MRR that can make domestic taxpayers wholly indifferent to how much in foreign taxes they pay.

2. Foreign Tax Credits and U.S. Companies' Tax Planning Costs

From a unilateral U.S. national welfare perspective, paying higher foreign taxes than necessary and thus reducing one's after-foreign-tax return, because the MRR for such taxes exceeds the MTR for foreign source income, is itself an example of deadweight loss. But even if you look just at tax planning, compliance, and administrative costs, the foreign tax credit and its associated rules contribute heavily to the U.S. international tax system's horrendous ratio of deadweight loss to revenue raised.

Conceptually, there are two main reasons for this. First, credits cause the marginal tax rate that potentially can apply to FSI to be much lower than the average tax rate that actually is being collected. Thus, the United States gets relatively little revenue from taxing FSI overall, yet taxpayers have to plan against potential instances of taxation at a 35 percent marginal rate.

Second, as I noted in chapter 2, the hazards associated with the extreme generosity of offering 100 percent reimbursement of foreign tax liabilities have triggered the creation of a plethora of rules that rein in available credits and thus defend the U.S. fisc. These rules give rise to significant tax planning and compliance costs for U.S. companies that have extensive overseas operations in multiple locations. Indeed, I have been told by people associated with such companies that foreign tax credit issues consume more in-house and outside staff attention and time, at least from personnel such as lawyers and accountants, than any other set of international tax issues—although this may understate transfer pricing's contribution to overall costs incurred, since there a different set of personnel (such as economists and valuation experts) play a comparatively large role.

Anti-abuse provisions—Provisions that respond to arguably "abusive" transactions like that in *Compaq*, whether by establishing broad economic substance and business purpose requirements or through black-letter rules such as the 15-day holding period, offer a nice illustrative example—albeit, far from the most important one in practice—of legal complexity in response to the generosity of foreign tax credits. However needed and justifiable such provisions may be on balance, they result not only in occasional legal uncertainty, but in what would otherwise be needless and counterproductive distortion of how taxpayers structure their transactions.

In this regard, consider *Compaq*-style transactions and the fifteen-day rule. If we were to assume that the taxpayer would have purchased the Royal Dutch Petroleum stock in any event, there would be absolutely no reason for the U.S. government to care whether the taxpayer bore any economic risks of ownership with respect to that stock. No one else would be substantially affected by whether Compaq decided to hold the stock for fifteen minutes, fifteen days, or fifteen years. Why, then, should the government require a minimum period of ownership as a prerequisite for claiming foreign tax credits, when this would inconvenience Compaq (if it did not want the associated risks) without benefiting anyone else?

The answer is that economic substance and business purpose requirements reduce effective electivity, by raising the cost of acquiring foreign tax credits when taxpayers prefer not to hold risky positions in foreign stock. Thus, while in some cases the requirements may result in extra deadweight loss, as taxpayers both get to use foreign tax credits *and* otherwise inconvenience themselves to no one's benefit, in other cases the result is to deter tax -motivated transactions altogether.

As I have argued elsewhere, "[f]rom this perspective, economic substance is just a tool for accomplishing aims that have little to do with how one might define it as a matter of internal logic. Leaving aside the institutional reasons why (for courts in particular) economic substance is a particularly suitable tool for deterring undesirable transactions, one might as well condition favorable tax consequences on whether the taxpayer's chief financial officer. . . can execute twenty back-somersaults in the IRS National Office on midnight of April Fool's Day, if such a requirement turns out to achieve a better ratio of successful deterrence to inducing wasteful effort in meeting requirements that are pointless in themselves" (Shaviro 2000).

To be sure, this approach is pervasive in U.S. income tax law (as well as that of any other country with a "generalized anti-avoidance rule" or GAAR). In particular, it commonly applies to transactions that ostensibly generate large tax losses. In that setting, however, anti-abuse rules reflect an unavoidable dilemma. True economic losses generally should be deductible, both to measure net income accurately and to avoid the discouragement of risk taking that would result from asymmetrically taxing gains but disallowing losses. By contrast, artificial tax shelter losses arguably should be disallowed in all cases, if one can properly identify them. The crux of the problem, however, is that the two are hard to tell apart in practice. Burdening taxpayers' loss claims with economic substance and business purpose requirements thus makes sense as a fallback. But no comparable dilemma applies in the foreign tax credit setting, if one regards offering a 100 percent MRR as less of a forced move than taxing net rather than gross income.

Inevitably, the foreign tax credit "abuses" that a 100 percent MRR invites are not limited to situations where economic substance requirements can be counted on to apply. Thus, the U.S. government periodically identifies new transactions that have sufficiently caught on in tax practice to make a targeted response necessary. One recent example is foreign tax credit arbitrage transactions, in which taxpayers exploit inconsistencies between countries' rules to permit the claiming of duplicative benefits with respect to foreign tax payments (see Sheppard 2008). The U.S. Treasury responded by issuing new proposed regulations that seek to prevent this from happening (see Peaslee, Duncan, and Berman 2008).

Likewise, consider the recent development of "splitter" transactions that briefly permitted U.S. taxpayers to claim foreign tax credits without having to include the associated income, which U.S. law attributes to a foreign taxpayer. The resulting "supercharged" credits (as they were known) could thus be used in full to reduce U.S. tax liability on other foreign source income. In 2010, after taxpayers had won a prominent case on the subject, Congress enacted a new "anti-splitting" statute to shut down this technique prospectively.[16] No doubt the future will bring a steady stream of new foreign tax credit planning tricks that either withstand initial IRS challenges or not, depending on the vagaries of legal interpretation, and that (either way) lead to the ongoing promulgation of new black-letter rules attempting to restrict or prevent them.

Indirect credits—To further illustrate the foreign tax credit rules' ineluctable complexity, consider how indirect credits work for foreign taxes paid by U.S. companies' CFCs. In the comparatively rare case of a U.S. company that acts abroad through foreign branches, FSI and creditable foreign taxes are recognized simultaneously. But when, for a period of years, CFCs accumulate FSI that benefits from deferral, while also paying ongoing foreign taxes, things may become considerably more complicated once repatriation actually occurs.

In principle, it may seem simple to identify the taxes paid on repatriated income, and thus the appropriate credit amount and income gross-up. Thus, suppose that Acme Sweden pays a $5 million dividend to its U.S parent, at a time when its E&P (as computed under U.S. rules) totaled $20 million and it had paid $8 million of Swedish taxes that the U.S. rules had not yet taken into account. Given that one-quarter of the E&P is being repatriated, the allowable credit presumably will be $2 million (barring further complexities), raising the amount deemed repatriated to $7 million. In practice, however, things are not always so simple. Indeed, the issues that may arise (see, e.g., Carr and Moetell 2007) include the following:

- the existence of distinct rules for repatriations of pre-1987 and post-1986 E&P,
- the treatment of dividends that are passed up the corporate chain through multiple tiers of intervening subsidiaries,
- the potential application of the anti-splitter rules,

- special rules limiting foreign tax credits that are associated with acquiring foreign assets that, due to the U.S. corporate tax rules for stock and asset acquisitions, can cause foreign assets to have a permanently higher basis for foreign than U.S. tax purposes,
- determining when distributions relate to income that was previously taxed to the U.S. parent under subpart F,
- determining how CFCs' losses may affect the computation of the ratio between their foreign taxes paid and their E&P,
- calculating U.S. companies' ownership percentage of particular CFCs when there are multiple owners and complex capital structures,
- determining the effect of changes in ownership status during the period before repatriation occurred.

Foreign tax credit limits—The rationale for having foreign tax credit limits is not as obvious as it may initially appear. Suppose Acme Products owes exactly a million dollars of tax on its U.S. source income, in addition to having foreign source income that is certain to be offset in full by foreign tax credits. The United States loses a dollar of tax revenue whether Acme's overall U.S. tax liability is declining (a) from $1,000,001 to $1 million or (b) from $1 million to $999,999. A dollar is a dollar. Nor can the two cases' incentive effects with regard to decisions to incur foreign tax liabilities easily be told apart. If one is attempting to discern the optimal MRR for the United States to provide with respect to foreign tax payments, it is hard to rationalize a sudden jump from 100 percent to 0 percent (ignoring the value of foreign tax credit carryovers) simply because the last dollar of U.S. tax liability on a given bundle of FSI has just been eliminated.

Accordingly, the best case for foreign tax credit limits is simply that their reducing the overall generosity of the rules both leans in the right direction and could not readily, as a political or administrative matter, be done by alternative means. Their discontinuous treatment of arithmetically equivalent reductions in U.S. tax revenues makes the limits hard to justify as any sort of a first-best approach, but does not rebut the view that simply eliminating them would be even worse.

A common line of argument holds that "the foreign tax credit limitation preserves U.S. sovereignty to tax U.S. source income" (Shay, Fleming, & Peroni 2002, 148). This is merely a semantic point, however, given that, in the absence of incentive and revenue problems, foreign tax credits could easily be made, not merely allowable against domestic tax liability, but refundable via a cash payment from the U.S. Treasury to the extent in excess thereof. Full refundability, however unwise, would make it clear that the tax on domestic source income was still being imposed, as "sovereignty" ostensibly requires. That tax would merely be getting offset, in the overall balance statement, by the distinct foreign tax credit refund program, while still, dollar for dollar, improving the government's bottom-line position. One is no less sovereign as a taxing authority merely because one chooses to make payments—as the foreign tax credit effectively does, from the very first dollar—in addition to levying taxes, and through an integrated delivery system.

As noted in chapter 2, one apparently gratuitous result of using foreign tax credit limits to cabin the overall U.S. revenue loss is that it divides U.S. multinationals into two distinct groups, each with its own distinct set of marginal incentives under U.S. law. Those with excess credits effectively operate in a different world than those that are "excess-limit" (i.e., that have foreign source income that is subject to U.S. tax and unsheltered by credits). The interest allocation rules provide a good illustration. Since the only effect of treating domestically incurred interest expense as foreign source is to reduce foreign source income and thus the foreign tax credit limit, the interest allocation rules only constrain excess-credit U.S. firms, and are irrelevant to any firm that is safely excess-limit. There is no good efficiency reason for thus dividing U.S. firms into two distinct groups that face distinct marginal incentives.

For firms with the potential to fall on either side of the line, foreign tax credit limits take on a dominant role in tax planning that almost guarantees an undesirably high ratio of tax planning and compliance costs to revenue actually raised. When U.S. multinationals have taxable repatriations in a given year (whether due to dividends paid or subpart F), they generally try to avoid being either excess-limit, which would cost them current year U.S. tax, or excess-credit, which would mean that particular credit claims were being deferred without interest. This, however, requires achieving exactly the right balance between repatriations from high-tax and low-tax countries (as defined by how the indirect credit rules work). Hence Edward Kleinbard's (2001, 14) point that, in practice "[f]oreign tax credit planning for ongoing international operations is like making fine Cognac, with the tax director as the master blender: deferral keeps the vats of differently-taxed and basketed foreign income secure until the master blender chooses to draw some down for the current year's blend. The low repatriation taxes noted by observers reflect the general success of these foreign tax credit planning techniques."

Cross-crediting—The mechanism for being neither excess-credit nor excess-limit is, of course, cross-crediting. U.S. companies' incentive to engage in cross-crediting is often condemned, and clearly there is no point, from an efficiency standpoint, to inducing them to balance high-tax against low-tax investments or repatriations. But there is nothing distinctive about U.S. companies' incentive to seek additional foreign tax credits when they would otherwise face a residual U.S. tax, and additional low-tax FSI when they would otherwise be excess-credit. Either way, they are simply acting on the incentives that foreign tax credits create more generally.

In illustration, consider the tax treatment of royalties that U.S. companies receive from their CFCs for the use abroad of intellectual property (such as valuable patents). Commentators such as Fleming, Peroni, and Shay (2009, 142) and Kleinbard (2011a, 1027) criticize the U.S. rules for permitting the U.S. parents to treat these royalty payments as yielding active business FSI, which can be sheltered by using unrelated foreign tax credits. They observe that the royalty payments generally are deductible by the CFCs in the source countries—thus eliminating source country taxation of the underlying intellectual property—and that, for this reason, territorial systems typically classify the royalties received by the home country parent as taxable domestic source income. In this sense, the nominally worldwide U.S. system can actually be better than exemption from the standpoint of U.S. multinationals.

This bottom line is important to understanding and assessing the current U.S. international tax system. It results from an aspect of the source rules—that is, how the U.S. rules define FSI—that is conceptually distinct from the question of how one should tax FSI once it has been defined. But given the mechanism that the above authors identify for the "better than exemption" result—using cross-crediting to eliminate the net U.S. tax on the royalties—they are no less critiquing foreign tax creditability than the existing source rules. After all, if offering a 100 percent MRR for foreign taxes paid is generally appropriate, it is hard to see where the problem lies. Only if we are rightly concerned about the foreign tax credit's over-generosity does applying more tightly defined limits become potentially appealing.

The difficulty in rationalizing the precise manner in which foreign tax credit limits respond to the underlying incentive problem created by a 100 percent MRR makes it difficult to assess the overall merits of particular approaches to impeding cross-crediting. However, one general disadvantage to having more separate "baskets" is that it is likely to increase taxpayers' administrative and compliance costs. More separately determined foreign tax credit limits means not only more record keeping with respect to particular credits that may be disallowed and carried forward, but also a greater need to determine how much of the taxpayer's overall FSI belongs in each "basket." But this does not tell us how having more separate baskets would affect deadweight loss overall. For example, even apart from the effect on how many dollars worth of foreign tax credits are claimed, limiting cross-crediting opportunities can potentially reduce the resources that U.S. companies devote to tax planning, in cases where the extra impediments induce giving up rather than trying harder.

The Obama administration in 2009 proposed a distinctive mechanism for impeding cross-crediting. Under this proposal, the foreign tax credits made available by repatriating CFC income would depend, not on the taxes paid with respect to the particular income that was repatriated, but on the overall ratio of foreign taxes to E&P for all of the taxpayer's CFCs. To illustrate this proposed "pooling" approach, suppose Acme-United States had two CFCs, each with $10 million of E&P. CFC-A had paid $3 million in foreign taxes, while CFC-B had paid only $1 million. Under current U.S. law, repatriating $1 million from CFC-A would trigger a foreign tax credit of $300,000, while repatriating $1 million from CFC-B would trigger a credit of only $100,000.[17] Under the proposal, repatriating $1 million from either CFC would trigger a foreign tax credit of $200,000, based on the aggregate ratio of foreign taxes paid to E&P for all of Acme's CFCs.

In short, the pooling approach would put an end to "fine Cognac-making" at the repatriation stage, by making it irrelevant which CFC's FSI comes home. Instead, cross-crediting could only be implemented through prior choices regarding where one invests and/or reports E&P. This might be harder to fine tune so precisely. U.S. companies might therefore more frequently fail to navigate right to the spot where they were neither excess-limit nor excess-credit. While this might result in their paying more U.S. tax per dollar repatriated, a consequence of this would be further discouraging repatriation. As we will see, however, this is just one illustrative instance of how foreign tax credits interact with deferral, which I discuss at the end of this chapter.

E. Deferral in Practice

The fact that publicly traded U.S. multinationals have an estimated $1.7 trillion of PRE (Linebaugh 2013) is eloquent testimony to the significance of lockout under current and expected future law, as well as current accounting practice. There are two main structural reasons, beyond simply having a lot of outbound investment, why U.S. companies may end up with a lot of PRE that, taxes aside, they would repatriate. First, business opportunities often have a natural life cycle. Suppose a U.S. company identifies a business opportunity abroad, such as a new production site from which it can serve nearby markets. To begin exploiting this opportunity, it may create a new subsidiary in the country where it will be conducting these operations, capitalized with enough equity to get the new business off the ground. The new subsidiary might start out relatively small, but gradually grow as its operations expand. During this stage, there might be no reason to repatriate its earnings to the U.S. parent, as they could conveniently be used to fund its growth. Eventually, however, its business may become mature (Hartman 1985)—that is, reach the point where, while it remains profitable, it has reached its optimal scale and no longer needs to fund further growth. Now is when repatriation would naturally occur, if not for its adverse tax and accounting consequences.

Second, trapped foreign earnings are a side effect of tax planning aimed at shifting the source of taxable income to low-tax foreign countries. Cisco Systems, Inc., the prominent consumer electronics and networking firm, provides a convenient illustration. As of 2010, three-quarters of its cash—$30 billion out of a $40 billion total—was offshore and could not be repatriated tax free. As Martin Sullivan (2010, 954) notes, "data showing disproportionate profitability outside the United States—combined with [a] large reduction in [its] effective tax rates due to foreign activity—strongly suggest that Cisco has aggressively shifted profits to low-tax jurisdictions," in particular through transfer pricing.

Companies with trapped foreign earnings may face two main disadvantages. The first is higher financing costs than they would otherwise incur, as in the case where costly third-party borrowing replaces the use of retained earnings. Second, they may end up using their retained earnings to invest less profitably than they could have if the repatriation tax were not an issue and the money could thus be invested at home.

It is frequently and plausibly asserted that, as firms' trapped foreign earnings rise relative to their overall assets, the costs of lockout increase more than proportionately (see, e.g., Grubert 2009a). This may help to explain the ongoing clamor, from U.S. multinationals that have tax planned themselves into having huge proportions of their global assets trapped offshore, for the adoption of another dividend holiday or else a shift to exemption.

F. Subpart F

As we saw in chapter 2, subpart F applies in two main settings, apart from its taxing quasi-repatriations via the investment of foreign earnings in U.S. property. The first is passive income, such as that earned by holding portfolio financial assets. The second involves arrangements suggestive of overseas tax planning, such as using a Luxembourg base company to divert taxable income either from the U.S. or from relatively high-tax countries such as France and Germany.

The common theme for both of these categories is mobility. Both types of subpart F income can relatively easily be placed in a low-tax country, for tax purposes, without any need for substantial economic activity in the claimed source country. However, subpart F aims to reduce or eliminate the advantages of doing this. Indeed, for income that a U.S. company would otherwise have shifted out of a foreign country, rather than out of the United States itself, subpart F can make the tax planning affirmatively disadvantageous. Thus, suppose that, but for subpart F, a U.S. company would have shifted certain FSI from a country where the corporate tax rate is 20 percent, to the Caymans, where there is no corporate income tax. This is clearly not worth doing if it causes the shifted income immediately to face a 35 percent U.S. tax.

In recent years, the difficulty of avoiding subpart F has greatly declined, by reason of the inadvertent and apparently unforeseen consequences of a regulatory change that was made for domestic tax policy reasons. In 1996, the U.S. Treasury Department issued what are known as the "check-the-box" regulations,[18] under which U.S. taxpayers can elect whether or not certain legal entities in which they own equity will be treated as distinct corporations for U.S. tax purposes. The check-the-box rule replaced prior law's cumbersome "corporate resemblance" test, thereby providing simplification and greater certainty.

The new rule turned out, however, to have rich tax planning applications for U.S. multinationals, for whom it facilitated the creation abroad of "hybrid entities," or those that U.S. tax law regards as merely undifferentiated branches of their sole owners (and thus, in tax lingo, as invisible or transparent), but that under foreign tax law are separate entities. This led to important erosion in the practical reach of subpart F. "Treasury officials [only] realized they had created a massive loophole when they noticed a spike in cross-border financing shortly after the rule took effect" (Drawbaugh and Sullivan 2013). The Treasury promptly moved to reverse the inadvertent aid to overseas tax planning, but a massive lobbying campaign forced it to stand down. Indeed, Congress soon passed legislation that effectively, although as yet only temporarily, embedded in the Internal Revenue Code a check-the-box-like rule that in some circumstances is of even broader scope.[19]

To illustrate how the check-the-box rules can be used to circumvent subpart F, suppose Acme United States' German subsidiary established a wholly owned entity in the Cayman Islands, qualifying under German law as a separate corporation but as to which the U.S. check-the-box rules apply. Acme-United States, by electing that the Caymans entity not be treated as a corporation for U.S. tax law purposes, can cause it to be a disregarded entity for U.S. tax purposes—in effect, a mere branch of the German CFC without separate legal existence. Thus, the interest payments from the German CFC to the Caymans entity, while still deductible for German tax purposes, will be ignored under U.S. tax law, and hence will not give rise to subpart F income.

The transaction works just as well if one places the transparent Caymans entity on top of the German one, since transactions between the two of them will still be ignored for U.S. tax purposes. Similarly, one can use hybrid entities to avoid the base company rules, since (in terms of the example from chapter 2), a transparent Luxembourg entity through which a U.S. company directs its European sales will be ignored, under the U.S. rules, even if fully effective for European tax planning purposes.

In 2009, the Obama administration proposed legislation that would have eliminated such uses of the check-the-box rules in international tax planning, by denying disregarded-entity status in circumstances such as the above. Thus, in the above example involving Acme-United States, transfers between its Germany subsidiary and the Caymans entity would be taken into account, for purposes of subpart F, even though the latter was not otherwise treated as a distinct entity for U.S. tax purposes.

This proposal, however, attracted widespread criticism. Potentially affected companies complained that, by effectively restoring the prior reach of subpart F, it would merely cause them to pay more foreign, as distinct from U.S. taxes. The administration responded by eliminating the proposal when, in 2010, it otherwise generally reiterated its support for a set of pro-worldwide international tax changes. At present, there appears to be no immediate prospect of legislative or regulatory action changing the check-the-box rules' effect on the prior status quo under subpart F—even though the change, whether good or bad as policy, undermines the evidently intended functioning of subpart F.

G. The Interaction between Deferral and Foreign Tax Credits

A final important topic regarding how the U.S. international tax rules currently operate concerns the relationship between deferral and foreign tax credits. In particular, four points are worth noting.

1. *Considered in isolation, each of the two rules creates bad incentives*—As we have seen, deferral leads to lockout of foreign earnings, which cannot be repatriated to the U.S. parent without adverse tax consequences, if repatriation can either be permanently avoided or postponed to a lower-rate future year. This may induce companies to engage in wasteful tax planning, raise their internal financing costs, and invest trapped foreign earnings in suboptimal ways. Likewise, foreign tax credits can make U.S. companies unwilling to spend as much as a (merely deductible) dollar to avoid a dollar of foreign taxes, leaving U.S. individuals poorer insofar as they own the U.S. companies. Where the effective MRR is indeed 100 percent, U.S. companies should be unwilling to spend even a penny to avoid a billion dollars of foreign taxes.

2. *Considered together, each of the two rules can reduce or even eliminate the other's bad incentive effects*—Suppose a given company would repatriate foreign earnings if not for the adverse U.S. tax consequences. With enough available foreign tax credits, the U.S. repatriation tax is zero, thus eliminating the lockout problem. Likewise, suppose that a company anticipates never repatriating its foreign earnings. Assuming that it cannot circumvent the anti-splitter rules and claim U.S. credits for the taxes on these earnings anyway, this means that the actual MRR for these taxes, just like the actual U.S. MTR for the earnings, is 0 percent. Accordingly, the company should be willing to spend up to a dollar to avoid a dollar of foreign taxes.

3. *This interaction creates a dilemma in assessing international tax reform proposals*—Given the inverse relationship between the bad incentive effects created by deferral on the one hand and foreign tax credits on the other, proponents of international tax reform can face a dilemma. For example, as noted above, the Obama administration's pooling proposal for foreign tax credits, by reason of its impeding cross-crediting, would have worsened the lockout problem, thus supporting the critique that it was an inefficient "new tax penalty" on repatriations (Sullivan 2009). Likewise, proposals to eliminate deferral (such as in Grubert and Altshuler 2008; or Kleinbard 2011a, b, and c) would cause the MRR for foreign tax credits actually to be 100 percent in all cases where foreign tax credit limits did not apply.

   Given this tradeoff, one cannot credibly assess the overall merits of a proposal to reduce the distortions caused either by deferral or by foreign tax creditability simply by noting the incentive effect at the margin one is addressing directly. Both margins need to be considered, along with any other relevant margins (such as those pertaining to the average and marginal tax rates on U.S. companies' FSI). And more generally, efforts to improve (without eliminating) our worldwide system for taxing resident corporations are stuck in an "iron box," where improving incentives at one of the two main margins created by deferral and the foreign tax credit inevitably worsens them at the other. So long as we remain trapped inside the iron box, a distressing level of overall inefficiency is guaranteed, and significant progress is hard to make or even assess.

4. *Even though deferral and the foreign tax credit reduce each other's adverse incentive effects, a system with both is likely to be extremely inefficient*—As I noted near the start of chapter 1, there is a widespread consensus that the U.S. international tax rules result in tax planning and compliance costs that are "extremely high relative to the revenue raised by the U.S. government on this income" (Blumenthal and Slemrod 1996, 48). This problem has only gotten worse since those words were written, given the subsequent explosion of tax planning technology, exacerbated by legal changes such as the check-the-box rules. Its scope is both exemplified and increased by the stunning rise in U.S. companies' "permanently reinvested" foreign earnings, which not only reflect underlying tax planning, but themselves give rise to significant tax planning costs (Clemens 2009). We are now in a good position to see why U.S. companies' tax planning and compliance costs are so high.

U.S. companies face a 35 percent marginal tax rate on their FSI, but a much lower average rate due to foreign tax credits and deferral. They are thus willing to devote a lot of resources to tax planning where this is necessary at the margin, and yet the United States is not collecting very much tax on FSI (relative to the size of the base). Both the foreign tax credit rules and deferral can induce very costly tax planning relative to the revenue that ends up being raised. As noted above, foreign tax credit issues are a significant time sink for lawyers and accountants, while the prospect of benefiting from deferral makes companies willing to spend a lot on transfer pricing. With the two being manipulated in unison, one ends up with Kleinbard's (2001, 14) makers of "fine Cognac," whose "low repatriation taxes... reflect the general success of... [their] planning techniques."

To be sure, one could eliminate both sets of problems by repealing deferral and making foreign taxes merely deductible. Under such a regime, virtually all of the rules discussed in this chapter, apart from those for determining corporate residence, could be eliminated so far as U.S. companies were concerned. (One would still, however, need to apply source rules to non-U.S. companies, unless the source-based corporate tax was also repealed.) But this, by greatly increasing the tax costs associated with U.S. corporate residence, would run into the problems associated with U.S. corporate residence electivity.

This is yet a third aspect of the iron box, if the statutory tax rate on FSI, other than in the case of exemption, must equal that for domestic source income. Is there a way out? Perhaps so, but before considering it further we must turn to the broader normative issues in international tax policy.

Endnotes

1. Where applicable tax rates differed between years, however, taxpayers might want to shift loss realization to high-rate years and gain realization to low-rate years.

2. Kane and Rock, due to their interest in the issue of international charter competition, restrict the term "corporate surplus" to governance-related factors resulting from the choice of substantive corporate law. I use the term more broadly, given my interest here in factors affecting electivity generally.

3. I assume that either investor would pay Chinese tax at the same rate, thus leaving only residence-based taxation as a potential source of disparity.

4. On the tax electivity that may be associated with headquarters rules, see Voget 2011, finding that about 6 percent of multinationals moved their headquarters between countries between 1997 and 2007, and that increasing the repatriation tax or introducing controlled foreign corporations legislation tended to increase relocations out of a given country.

5. For a recent version of the Stop Tax Haven Abuse Act, see S. 1346, introduced by Senator Levin on July 12, 2011. The Act has a special exception that would prevent the extension of domestic resident status to U.S.-managed foreign CFCs of U.S. companies. This presumably reflects that treating such CFCs as U.S. companies, and thus causing them to lose the tax benefit of deferral, would mainly address an issue that is quite distinct from that of which multinational groups should be treated as United States headed.

6. Bausch & Lomb, Inc. v. Commissioner, 933 F.2d 1084 (2nd Cir. 1991).

7. LIBOR, or the London Interbank Offered Rate, is a widely accepted floating interest rate benchmark.

8. For an even more aggressive total return swap transaction, suppose a foreign investor holds Acme stock, on which a dividend had been declared. Three or four days before the dividend record date, the investor enters into a one-week swap with a U.S. bank, and sells its Acme stock to the bank for the contemporary market price. A week later, when the swap is settled, the investor repurchases the same shares for the new market price. The net effect, given the swap, is that (a) the bank, rather than the investor, receives the dividend; and (b) the bank effectively pays the dividend amount to the investor (minus its fee and a week's worth of the LIBOR interest on the initial purchase prices), but without there being any withholding.

9. See Treasury Regulation Section 1.871-1(b)(2). Some taxpayers argued, however, that IRS Notice 97-66, 1997-2 C.B. 328 (1997) supported the claim that no withholding tax was due.

10. Quoted in Young 2007.

11. As Shaheen (2013) notes, if foreign pre-tax rates of return are the same in high-tax and low-tax countries, causing after-tax rates of return to be higher in the latter, then U.S. companies that benefit from deferral have good reason to be foreign tax adverse.

12. IRS Notice 98-5, 1998-1 C.B. 334, Example 1, subsequently withdrawn by IRS Notice 2004-19, 2004-1 C.B. 606. In the same year that it withdrew Notice 98-5, the IRS issued a separate notice announcing that it would not consider particular transactions to be "listed" ones (i.e., presumptive tax shelters for certain reporting and penalty purposes) "solely because they are the same as or substantially similar to the transactions or arrangements described in...Notice 98-5." IRS Notice 2004-67; 2004-2 C.B. 600. This does not, however, necessarily imply that the IRS now thought Example 1 was non-abusive and legally valid.

13. 253 F.3d 350 (8th Cir. 2001), rev'g 113 T.C. 214 (1999). I discuss the *Compaq* case at length in Shaviro (2000) and Shaviro and Weisbach (2002).

14. Compaq's after-tax profit from the transaction would have been $1.9 million except for the fact that the Dutch withholding taxes, since they were being claimed as credits, could not be deducted. Thus, the transaction gave Compaq positive taxable income for U.S. purposes that reduced its overall profit from the transaction to about $1.25 million (Shaviro 2000, 225).

15. Code section 901(k), which was initially enacted in 1997.

16. Code section 909.

17. In each case, I assume that the amount deemed repatriated reflects grossing up the pre-tax repatriation by the amount of associated deemed foreign taxes paid, as required by U.S. law.

18. U.S. Treasury Regulations sections 301.7701-1 through 301.7701-3.

19. The operative provision, Internal Revenue Code section 954(c)(6), is scheduled at this writing to expire at the end of 2013. It differs from the check-the-box rule in not requiring the use of hybrid entities. Rather, it provides a "look-thru rule" under which certain payments (such as interest and royalties) that are made between related party CFCs generally do not give rise to subpart F income insofar as they involve active business income of the payer. This effectively yields the same result, under subpart F, as that from disregarding the payment due to the use of a hybrid entity as either payer or recipient. Thus, Code section 954(c)(6), while it remains on the books, makes it even easier than under the check-the-box rules to shift active business income from high-tax to low-tax foreign countries without creating subpart F income.

II Developing and Applying a Policy Framework

TO THE INTERNATIONAL tax policy novice—and more than a few experts—the common terms of policy debate in the field can look very strange. Legal and economic analysis of domestic tax policy issues typically relies on efficiency and equity in evaluating proposed alternative approaches and rules. These are broad concepts of general application. Efficiency is about minimizing deadweight loss, or instances in which someone loses and no one gains. Equity is about who gets what, and often is interpreted as motivating progressivity, or the shifting of resources from better-off to worse-off individuals. When the analysis of efficiency and equity is done right, all considerations relating to how a given policy choice would affect people's welfare are raised, and if necessary can be explicitly traded off against each other.

International tax policy debate often looks very different. Rather than attempting comprehensive valuation, it typically plunges the reader into a veritable alphabet soup of rival efficiency norms. The leading examples include (1) CEN (capital export neutrality), (2) CIN (capital import neutrality), (3) CON (capital ownership neutrality), (4) NN (national neutrality), (5) NON (national ownership neutrality), and (6) GPN (global portfolio neutrality). Each of these efficiency norms describes a single margin of choice at which the tax system ostensibly ought to be neutral, so taxpayers will make choices based on pre-tax profitability (reflecting that taxes are socially transfers, rather than costs). None purports to address the whole picture. Yet it is common to assume (or even expressly state) that whichever norm one likes best should be used as the exclusive basis for answering a whole set of international tax policy questions. So the analysis often devolves into a simple "battle-of-the-acronyms"—one decides which of the competing norms one likes the best, and then simply applies it without further inquiry into tradeoffs or underlying objectives.

An immediate mystery is why one would choose a single margin and then let it do all the work, rather than generally analyzing tradeoffs. Perhaps an even greater mystery, however, arises from the fact that the first three of the above neutrality norms—in practice, those that are discussed the most—are about *global* efficiency or economic welfare, rather than that of the particular nation that is setting its international tax rules. They raise the question, therefore, of why one would expect a country to make tax policy decisions under the disinterested premise that the economic welfare of all people in the world, without limitation to its own residents, counts equally. This is not how national policy making is usually done.

A further mystery is where and how distributional or equity considerations are supposed to figure in the analysis, if it is confined to choosing and implementing a particular neutrality norm. To be sure, ignoring distributional considerations in tax policy analysis is not inherently inappropriate, even if one believes they are extremely important, since they need not be raised in all settings so long as they duly influence the overall bottom line. Thus, in the domestic arena, one could endorse comprehensive tax reform, defined as broadening the tax base to eliminate various preferences, purely on efficiency grounds, under the view that distributional issues are best handled through the rate structure that applies to the base.

However, while this type of reasoning logically could explain the frequent international tax policy focus on neutrality norms to the exclusion of all else, one wonders if it really does. Consider, for example, that Democrats often favor expanding worldwide taxation of U.S. multinationals, while Republicans tend to favor shifting toward an exemption system. With suspicious fortuity, this turns out exactly as one might expect, based on the parties' distributional preferences, if high-income individuals (such as shareholders) are assumed to bear the companies' U.S. taxes on outbound investment.[1] Yet frequently neither side in the debate, even if it is implicitly relying on the distributional preferences that its favored policy appears to advance, seems eager to emphasize this angle (Shaviro 2007).

In fairness to the traditional approach to international tax policy analysis, it offered a major advance when introduced, and it has played an invaluable role in framing several of the principal issues. However, the time has long since come to move beyond it. At present, it critically impedes clear thinking, not just about how to evaluate important choices, but even about what the choices are. And this is true whether people actually rely on global welfare norms or instead are merely using them, be it pretextually or just lazily, as the go-to rationales for policy conclusions that they actually favor on different grounds.

Even if the global welfare norms are just window dressing much of the time, clearing them away may lead to clearer discussion of people's actual concerns.

With the aim of moving toward a better foundation for international tax policy discussion, chapter 4 examines the question of what role global welfare analysis should play. It concludes that, contrary to the assumptions underlying CEN, CIN, and CON, the role that it can constructively play is actually quite small. This is so despite an initially appealing analogy to international trade policy, in which global and national welfare considerations have indeed jibed nicely in support of multilateral trade agreements that support free trade by barring the use of instruments such as tariffs and export subsidies.

Chapter 5 then examines unilateral national welfare. It explains why, on the one hand, a country such as the United States may reasonably be reluctant to abandon either residence-based or source-based taxation, yet on the other hand there is little danger of either's being pursued so rigorously as to pose a serious threat of full-scale double taxation that would significantly discourage cross-border activity. Once again, however, the battle of the acronyms fails to illuminate the relevant issues, which turn on countries' degree of market power to use residence-based and source-based taxation to pursue underlying objectives that they may have.

Finally, chapter 6 discusses the overall implications of the preceding analysis for U.S. international tax policy. After examining whether large-scale changes to U.S. income taxation (not just in the international realm) might permit us to escape some of the underlying dilemmas, it sketches out possible improvements (and how to think about the tradeoffs) that vary in ambition, depending on how constrained we are to retain the current system's key features.

Endnotes

1. The incidence of the U.S. corporate tax, which newly exempting foreign source income would reduce (all else equal), is a topic of much dispute. Some argue that, in the long run, the tax is borne by workers and consumers, rather than shareholders or investors generally. However, U.S. companies' shareholders would likely reap the short-term transition gain from an unexpected reduction in the companies' tax burdens. See Shaviro 2009a, 60–61 and 68–71.

4   The Global Welfare Perspective

TODAY WE LIVE in, not just a cynical age, but a tribal one. Governments and elites inspire mistrust. People who state high ideals face the suspicion, often all too rightly, that they are actually con artists looking out for themselves. The one broader "moral" sentiment (if one can call it that) that seems to resonate widely is tribal identification with one's own group, often inseparably intertwined with hatred for rival groups. Whether it is the U.S. culture wars, the supposed post-9/11 "clash of civilizations," or ethnic and religious conflict in an ever-changing array of hot spots around the world, ours is not an era in which the big problem is an excess of misdirected compassion and idealism. Epitomizing where we are today, the word Kumbaya, once the chorus of a "petition for balm and righteousness," has become the "all-purpose put-down of the political moment," used as "snarky shorthand for ridiculing...idealism [and the] quest for common ground" (Freedman 2010).

Against this background, there may initially seem to be something refreshing, and indeed almost touching, about the idea that international tax policy should be based on global welfare. This chapter, however, will demonstrate two main things. The first is that the motivation for a global welfare approach to international tax policy is, at least potentially, a lot more hardheaded than it sounds. But the second is that the approach is nonetheless largely misguided, because the potential gains that are available through global cooperation are much more limited here than, say, in the field of international trade. Avoiding destructive interactions between countries' tax systems depends more on countries' unilateral incentives (discussed in chapter 5) than on the prospects for mutual forbearance in pursuit of a greater common good.

A. Why Global Welfare?

The surprising prominence of appeals to global economic welfare in U.S. international tax policy debate has multiple causes. In particular, a global welfare standard (1) is in principle normatively appealing; (2) could be viewed (and not entirely indefensibly) as actually a key influence on prevailing international tax practice; and (3) could conceivably point the way to improving all nations' welfare, compared to the case where each unilaterally (and thus noncooperatively) pursued its own national welfare. Each of these points merits further elaboration.

The normative appeal of a global welfare standard—If modern social morality has one central tenet, it is that we must treat other people as equal in importance to ourselves, in whatever is the relevant moral sense. A version of this broader principle governs whether one endorses the Golden Rule, which counsels treating others as we would like them to treat us; or libertarianism, which grounds morality on a set of claims about the need to respect all individuals' distinct rights; or utilitarianism, which calls for counting everyone's welfare equally and maximizing overall utility.

Under my approach in this book, which is based on welfare, one cannot ultimately justify limiting the reach of the principle that everyone counts equally to people in one's own country. Just as I must accept that my neighbors' welfare matters ethically just as much as my own, notwithstanding that I do not group them emotionally with myself or the members of my family, so people on the other side of a national border, or even across the ocean, must count the same as well. Our shared humanity, not my emotional affinity for them, makes this conclusion inescapable once I have accepted the ethical necessity of taking the first step beyond myself.

Without more, this might suggest that international tax policy should, and indeed must, be based on global welfare, not just that of the particular country that is deciding on its rules. But let's take the analogy between personal and national decision making a step further. Suppose I regarded the conclusion that everyone's welfare counts equally as necessarily governing my own private behavior in all respects. Then I would consider myself morally compelled to live a very different sort of life than anyone I have ever met actually does. For example, I would have to direct each dollar within my grasp, and every minute of my time, to benefiting whichever individual, in all the world, it would do the most marginal good. There would be no presumption that I and the members of my family should come first.

In practice, almost no one lives this way. What is more, "the failure to engage in such saintly behavior is not generally taken to be morally wrong, subjecting the transgressor to disapprobation" (Kaplow and Shavell 2002b, 5). While utilitarian writers have at times wrestled with the question of why predominantly self-directed private behavior might be morally defensible, for present purposes we can take it as given. Individuals are expected to live their daily lives chiefly with an eye to their own benefit and that of loved ones. We understand, moreover, that aiming for sainthood would make most people exploitable and unhappy.

If such predominantly self-directed behavior is accepted for individuals, then surely it is permissible as well for countries. What is more, in the national setting, any effort to impose policies that reflected global altruism in excess of that favored by the public would raise principal-agent issues. As Michael Graetz (2000, 279) has observed, U.S. government actors' "higher obligation to U.S. citizens and legal residents" implies caring about "where enhanced economic output occurs, whom it benefits, and what national treasury obtains the tax revenues," and thus seeking primarily to promote domestic economic output and well-being, rather than that of the entire world.

Despite all the global welfare talk that one hears in international tax policy debate, this conclusion is actually little disputed. Proponents of global welfare-based approaches to international tax policy generally do not take the next step and urge that the United States give trillions of dollars away to poorer countries. No one argues that road repair or school construction in the United States should cease until we have exhausted all opportunities to do more good overseas. Thus, unless one can find other explanations for using a global welfare-based approach to U.S. international tax policy, its proponents are guilty of unexplained intellectual inconsistency, or else of failing to express clearly what they actually believe.

The claim that global welfare actually influences prevailing international tax practice—If the only rationale for basing international tax policy on global rather than national welfare was the moral case for universalistic altruism, the approach would never have gotten off the ground. Its evident naïveté, in this scenario, would have prevented it from garnering serious attention. Sardonic and dismissive references to the spirit of Kumbaya would no doubt long since have become standard fare in discussions of international tax policy, if this were all that was going on.

But when countries that are taxing foreign source income routinely grant a 100 percent credit for foreign taxes paid, the prominence of appeals to global welfare in policy debate becomes a lot more understandable. The allowance of foreign tax credits arguably suggests that a focus on global welfare is actually descriptive, not just aspirational. Moreover, if promoting global welfare is indeed the prevalent approach, a country as potentially influential as the United States might rightly be reluctant to disrupt it, on the view that defecting to pursue unilateral national welfare might influence other countries to shift gears as well.

But does the allowance of foreign tax credits actually bespeak the pursuit of global, rather than national, welfare? From the standpoint of Occam's Razor, which holds that the simplest explanation of a phenomenon is usually the correct one, it may seem that only actual indifference to whether we or some other country gets the money—suggesting a global welfare perspective—could explain the apparent indifference that foreign tax credits manifest. Indeed, many "modern analysts seem to think [that the foreign tax credit was] enacted to advance the goal of worldwide economic efficiency" (Graetz and O'Hear 1997, 1027). Seemingly adding to the plausibility of such a view, two obvious alternative explanations of foreign tax creditability appear not to hold water.

The first would be a reciprocity theory. There need not be anything altruistic about crediting other countries' taxes in exchange for their agreeing to credit one's own. But as a historical matter, the United States enacted foreign tax credits unilaterally in 1918, without any effort to use them as a bargaining chip dependent on other countries' willingness to credit our taxes, and in the face of the critique that, as leading tax policy expert E.R.A. Seligman noted, we were "making a present of the revenue to other countries" (Graetz and O'Hear 1997, 1047). Use of the foreign tax credit then spread around the world through similar unilateral action. Bilateral tax treaties generally do not require foreign tax creditability to be reciprocal, since one can instead eliminate overlapping double taxation via exemption (with its 0 percent MRR). In the United States, even other countries' recent shifts toward territoriality, while exciting anxiety about the continuing feasibility of our at least nominally worldwide system, have not prompted much concern that our offering foreign tax credits is too generous. Instead, the concern emphasizes the "competitiveness" of U.S. multinationals.

A second alternative explanation of foreign tax creditability might rest on interest group politics. Many U.S. multinationals are politically active and wield significant influence in Washington, and obviously such companies prefer foreign tax creditability to deductibility (all else equal). However, they generally would like exemption of their foreign source income better still. Thus, if one were to attribute creditability to U.S. multinationals' political clout, one would have to explain why, since the earliest days, their "argument that... [any U.S. tax on outbound investment would] disadvantage [them] in foreign markets... was rejected, but the argument based on the burden of double taxation was persuasive" (Surrey 1956, 818).

Does the allowance of foreign tax credits therefore show that U.S. international tax policy is driven by the goal of promoting global, rather than domestic, economic welfare? This would be a surprising story, if true, given the implausibility of an account in which one-worlders, bleating that all human welfare matters equally, could ever have persuaded the U.S. Congress to make unilateral gifts of our tax revenue to other countries. In fact, however, as Graetz and O'Hear (1997) demonstrate, the actual story is quite different.

As they recount, foreign tax credits were the brainchild of T. S. Adams, a leading Treasury economist in the early years of the U.S. federal income tax, who persuaded the Wilson administration to propose them in 1918. At the time, Adams was skeptical that a proposal so "extraordinarily generous" would go anywhere in Congress. Thus, he was quite surprised when it easily passed (1046). Adams might have been even more surprised had he gotten to witness the provision's almost unchallenged intellectual and political entrenchment during the more than ninety years since its enactment (Shaviro 2011a, 170).

The reason the case for foreign tax credits has proved so politically potent is that it addresses what is "perceived as the manifest injustice of double taxation" (Graetz and O'Hear 1997, 1047). Taxing foreign profits, it is widely felt, create what verges on a moral compulsion to grant foreign tax credits, so as to mitigate double taxation's "essential unfairness" (1109). This is not, at least primarily or directly, a global welfare story at all.

Rather, it concerns acting unilaterally to avoid perceived unfairness toward a group of domestic taxpayers.

While aversion to the "unfairness" of double taxation is a unilateral and domestically directed political sentiment, it arguably has a globally cooperative element. After all, residence-country proponents of using foreign tax credits (or exemption) to avoid double taxation do indeed take on the responsibility for addressing it, rather than dismissing it as the source countries' fault. In addition, when residence countries so act, they reduce the discouragement of cross-border economic activity that would result if, instead, full double taxation applied. And such discouragement, if unmitigated, could potentially reduce global welfare (and each country's welfare) relative to the case where they generally cooperated to abate it. This, however, brings us to the third rationale for basing international tax policy on global rather than national welfare.

The cooperative pursuit of global welfare as a means of advancing national welfare—The final, and perhaps most important, ground for international tax policy analysts' often predominant focus on global welfare follows from their observing that countries do not generally impose full double taxation on cross-border economic activity. If we were to assume that, from a unilateral national welfare standpoint, countries ought to do this, two conclusions would immediately follow. The first would be that they must be cooperating, rather than pursuing unilateral national welfare. The second would be that we should be glad they are doing so, given that all countries would likely be worse off otherwise.

As we will see in chapter 5, it is not actually the case that unilateral national welfare dictates applying full residence-based and source-based taxation to cross-border activity. However, a broader and more general point clearly is correct. Whenever countries could increase global welfare by cooperating, in lieu of pursuing unilateral national welfare, in theory such cooperation could leave everyone better off, or at least no one worse off (i.e., it could lead to a global Pareto improvement). All this requires, beyond the cooperation itself, is that the winners from global cooperation compensate any losers. After all, by definition, if there is global welfare gain, the winners must have gained more than the losers lost.

Given the compensation idea, whichever set of policies around the world would create the very greatest level of global welfare can in principle be made Pareto superior to anything else. All this would take is full global cooperation plus the requisite compensatory side payments. Thus, if making and honoring the deals is sufficiently feasible and indeed easy, there is really no need for international tax policy analysts to spend any time thinking about unilateral national welfare. All they need to ask is how countries could achieve the global optimum, and national negotiators can take care of the rest.

This intuition may provide the (generally unstated) motivation for paying so much attention to the single-bullet global welfare norms, such as CEN, CIN, and CON. Analysts apparently think that all they need do is determine which of the approaches is globally best, so that countries seeking guidance on how best to cooperate will have the information they need. Unfortunately, however, while the question of how best to achieve the global optimum is indeed relevant, in practice it proves wholly inadequate. The possibility that countries might benefit from cooperation is an important input to national welfare analysis. But it most definitely does not mean that all other (such as unilateral) analysis of national welfare is unnecessary.

The problem lies in the fact that the transaction costs which countries would have to surmount, in order to make Pareto deals based on the global welfare optimum, are formidable or even prohibitive (see generally Shaviro 2007). There are dozens of governments around the world. Each presumably wants to capture as much of the surplus as possible, and may have its own views about how best to achieve the global optimum. Arranging compensatory side deals is notoriously difficult. Monitoring compliance with the terms of an agreement may be impossible. Finally, countries may be unable to pursue national self-interest effectively in complicated settings, such as in executing effective strategic responses to what other countries do, given their internal political constraints, which reflect domestic conflicts of interest and the difficulty of arranging their own internal Pareto deals between constituencies.

To be sure, the extent to which one should think in unilateral, rather than global, terms may vary with the country. The U.S. Treasury has argued against our adopting international tax policies that "promote national short-term interests at the expense of global economic welfare," not just because other countries may reply in kind, but also because the United States "is often looked upon to provide global leadership in the policies it adopts" (Office of Tax Policy 2000, 25–26). Insofar as others will follow our lead, we may indeed find it in our national self-interest to give more weight than other countries would to cooperative and strategic considerations, as distinct from those that are purely unilateral.

The degree to which this is so, however, can easily be overstated, and appears to be declining over time. Other countries followed our lead after we enacted the foreign tax credit in 1918, and also after we enacted the subpart F rules in 1962. The Tax Reform Act of 1986, in which the United States lowered its statutory corporate rate from 46 percent to (initially) 34 percent, also appears to have stimulated responsive corporate tax rate-cutting in other countries. And even if this was pure tax competition, rather than emulation, it still supports viewing U.S. policy choices as more broadly influential. But in more recent years, other countries have not waited for American action before moving toward territoriality (and thus away from granting foreign tax credits), or before reducing their statutory corporate tax rates. Thus, while the United States may continue to face somewhat different overall incentives than does, say, Mexico or Belgium, it certainly is no longer in a position to dictate rules that others will generally follow.

Three conclusions follow from all this. First, in practice countries' self-interest in international tax policy must and will be pursued at least partly unilaterally. Strategic or other responses by other countries to one's own international tax policy choices may be relevant, but are likely to be limited. Second, while U.S. international tax policy choices may have greater ripple effects abroad than those made by many other countries, the United

States nonetheless (and perhaps increasingly) operates in a setting with substantial unilateral elements. Third, insofar as cooperation would yield greater global welfare, one has to consider, not just the global optimum, but the feasibility of cooperative mechanisms.

B. If Cooperation Is the Answer, What Is the Question?

If countries are deliberately to cooperate with the aim of achieving greater global welfare than would result if each acted unilaterally, it helps if they have a sufficiently common view regarding how, and toward what ends, they are cooperating. Otherwise, cooperation is just a nice idea that offers no specific counsel. As it happens, at a very general level the objectives that international tax cooperation might serve are clear. Countries may mutually benefit from limiting tax-induced distortion of cross-border investment decisions, and/or from helping each other to address undesired tax avoidance. Unfortunately, however, the more precise terms around which cooperation might best be organized have proven elusive, in both theory and practice.

This difficulty may initially seem surprising, for at least two reasons. First, one actually can discern a prevailing international tax policy objective, reflected in dozens of bilateral tax treaties between nation pairs around the world: that of avoiding double taxation (along with double nontaxation). Why can't this norm do the job? Second, one might wonder why international tax policy should be any harder to coordinate than international trade policy. In the latter realm, a prevailing norm—that of supporting free trade, by discouraging such instruments as import tariffs and export subsidies—has been enshrined for decades, and is enforced on a multilateral basis by the World Trade Organization (WTO), which has the power to respond to members' free trade violations by authorizing countervailing measures by other members. As we will see, however, neither of these considerations prevents international tax coordination, on a global basis, from remaining quite limited.

1. Is the Problem Double Taxation?

What could be more intuitive than the idea that multinationals' income should be taxed exactly once? Hence, the predominance of this approach in bilateral tax treaties comes as no surprise—although the absence of WTO-like global tax institutions, with authority to ensure, via consistent income definition and source rules, that every dollar of a multinational's income is taxed exactly once, is noteworthy as well.

There are a number of good explanations (indeed, almost too many) for the ongoing failure to achieve fuller coordination. One is that income taxation's central role in economic policy making and revenue raising makes it an area in which governments especially value retaining their own independent discretion. A second is that the most obvious route to ensuring that all income is taxed exactly once—requiring that source be defined "correctly"—is unavailable, given that often there is no correct answer to the source question. A third key problem, however, is that the principle of taxing all income once lacks any clear relationship to the goal of advancing global efficiency. Thus, it has no obvious capacity to serve as a mechanism for achieving global Pareto improvements.

To illustrate this last point, suppose initially that all countries' tax rules were identical in all respects, including tax rates and how they treated cross-border income, which was taxed exclusively on either a residence basis or a source basis, but not both. All income would therefore be taxed the same, no matter who earned it or where it was earned. Under these conditions, the fact that all income was being taxed exactly once would indeed yield global economic surplus in certain respects. For example, it would increase global production efficiency, by causing locational decisions to depend purely on pre-tax rather than after-tax profitability. Likewise, it would make economic actors indifferent, so far as taxes were concerned, to who made a particular investment or owned a particular asset, thus allowing these decisions as well to rest entirely on nontax considerations.

The picture changes, however, once we allow for tax rate differences between countries. Now taxing all cross-border income exactly once does *not* necessarily promote global efficiency at any of the above margins. Taxpayer incentives depend on bottom-line tax liability, which varies with the tax rate and does not depend on the formalistic question of how many separate times a particular item has been included.

If we shift to the context of a single country's tax rules for domestic source income, no one would seriously maintain that taxing everything exactly once, even if at varying rates, was a magic formula for increasing economic efficiency. Thus, suppose Assyria had two industries, farming and shopkeeping, the former of which was tax-favored relative to the latter. If shopkeeping was taxed at 40 percent, it would make no difference whether farming income was (a) 50 percent excludable, with the remainder being taxed at 40 percent; or (b) fully includable, but taxed at only 20 percent. Unfortunately, the principle that everything should be taxed exactly once reaches instead the fallacious conclusion that (a) is bad while (b) is acceptable.

Analogously, in the international tax realm, if Assyria's tax rate is 40 percent while that in Babylonia is 20 percent, taxpayer decisions are going to be distorted, from a global efficiency standpoint, even if everything is taxed exactly once by one country or the other. Indeed, it is possible that partly double taxing income that faces the Babylonian rate, or allowing partial exclusion of income that otherwise faces the Assyrian rate, would end up increasing global efficiency.

Where taxing everything exactly once fails to yield global efficiency gain, the Pareto rationale for focusing on global rather than unilateral national welfare cannot apply. Even without transaction costs, an absence of overall gain might prevent pre-deal "winners" from retaining any surplus after they fully compensated the "losers" who had receded on overlapping tax-jurisdictional claims.

This leaves the question of why bilateral tax treaties so strongly emphasize the principle of addressing double taxation and double nontaxation. The answer may lie in the fact that this principle can actually work very well as between peer countries, or more precisely those that are sufficiently similar for mutual concessions to work out reasonably symmetrically in practice.

In illustration, suppose Assyria and Babylonia are similar countries—having, in particular, the same tax rates and equal cross-border capital flows in each direction that yield the same rates of return (and thus the same overall FSI) to outbound investors. In addition, suppose that, in the absence of a treaty, each would benefit from exercising in full both its residence-based and its source-based tax jurisdiction, leading to unmitigated double taxation if they did not cooperate. (As we will see in chapter 5, however, this probably is not the case.) A conventional bilateral tax treaty, in which each reciprocally surrendered a given jurisdictional claim in cases of overlap, would clearly offer mutual gain.

Given the equal tax rates, avoiding double taxation does indeed promote global efficiency, by ensuring that there will be no difference between the global tax burdens on one-country and cross-border income. Thus, the arrangement creates economic surplus that makes mutual gain possible. In addition, the compensation scheme seems likely to work, in the sense that each country gets fair consideration for its own willingness to recede where there was tax jurisdictional overlap. For example, while Assyria surrenders the opportunity to tax Babylonians who make passive investments in Assyria, it gets in exchange Babylonia's agreement to offer the same benefit to Assyrians. Likewise, while Assyria allows its residents to escape the source-based domestic tax by investing in Babylonia rather than at home, in exchange Babylonia offers its own residents an identical incentive to invest in Assyria. And the assumption that the two countries are relevantly identical suggests that each country's benefits received will equal the value surrendered, presumably ensuring that some of the global surplus will redound to each.

In short, with homogeneity between countries, the principle that everything should be taxed exactly once combines attractive global efficiency features with a ready-made cooperative mechanism that can assure mutual gain. But heterogeneity undermines and may eventually destroy both elements. Again, if countries' tax rates differ, taxing everything once may not yield global efficiency benefits. And if the cross-border capital flows, income amounts, or tax rates are sufficiently dissimilar, one of the two countries may find (if full residence-based and source-based taxation would be unilaterally optimal) that its detriment from the mutual agreements to recede exceeds its benefit. Indeed, even in the bilateral treaty setting, modest heterogeneity apparently is enough to discourage agreement to uniform source rules (such as with regard to interest deductions), reflecting that there is no opportunity for direct reciprocity if the choice of rule affects each country's share of the available tax base.

Unfortunately, the biggest problems in international taxation are those reflecting heterogeneity, such as the existence of tax havens. For example, U.S. multinationals would not be able to reduce their global tax burdens through income shifting if everyone charged the U.S. rate. Heterogeneity creates problems even with respect to countries that have relatively similar tax systems. For example, once there are tax havens, U.S. companies may raise competitiveness complaints regarding German companies, even if the U.S. and German tax rates are the same, if the German companies can benefit more from income shifting to the havens. So the principle that everything should be taxed exactly once falls well short of the mark—solving certain easy problems in international tax policy, but failing to address adequately the hard ones that actually matter.

2. The Analogy to Trade Policy

While double taxation is too formalistic a concept to be useful in achieving multi-lateral optimization, one could think of it as an imperfect proxy for something that clearly does matter: relative overtaxation of cross-border economic activity. After all, such activity surely would be unduly tax discouraged, to general detriment, if all countries taxed their residents' FSI at the full domestic rate while treating foreign taxes as merely deductible.

Given that a similar concern about cross-border activity also critically underlies international trade policy, a natural question is why devising a precise or well-specified cooperative framework for international tax policy should be so challenging. In the trade realm, while we have not achieved nirvana, there is both widespread expert agreement about how global welfare can best be promoted, through the promotion of free trade, and a set of real-world institutions (such as the WTO) that use this approach as a lodestar guiding conflict resolution in particular cases. Why has international tax policy been unable to achieve similar results, either intellectually or institutionally?

Let's proceed by asking what makes international trade policy as intellectually and institutionally tractable as it is, and then consider the key considerations' applicability to international taxation. Above all, free trade has three great advantages that help make it the widely accepted focus on international trade policy: (1) it relies on a straightforward global welfare analysis, (2) there is a simple way to advance the chosen global welfare norm through international trade policy, and (3) countries' unilateral incentives are highly compatible with their cooperating to advance it. Each of these preconditions is at best much more tenuously satisfied in the international tax policy realm, and at worst not satisfied at all.

Straightforward global welfare analysis—As Joel Slemrod (1995, 472) notes, "[t]he case for free trade is that the gains from trade, and therefore national income, are maximized when domestic consumers and producers face world prices that are undistorted by import tariffs, export subsidies, and the like." This advances what one could call global consumption efficiency, since all countries' "[c]onsumers are made better off by the opportunity to exchange at world prices domestically produced goods for goods that can be obtained from abroad." It also advances global production efficiency, since "[t]he benefit from this exchange will be maximized if [all countries'] domestic producers produce the goods and services that have the greatest possible value on world markets, which they will do in their own interest if they are free to trade at world prices."

For international tax policy, the issue is coordinating countries' income taxes. Since income taxes are levied on the value of production, they inevitably raise issues of production efficiency (see, e.g., Diamond and Mirrlees 1971). Unsurprisingly, then, global production efficiency[1] is indeed an important issue in international tax policy. In order for it to be satisfied in the international setting, the tax rate that producers face must not depend on the country in which they locate their activity, or on the question of whether they have used cross-border capital flows to fund the underlying investment (see Slemrod 1995, 475–476).

So far, so good. The fact that global production efficiency matters in both the tax and trade realms might seem to indicate that the global welfare analysis will play out similarly, even if it indicates adopting different specific measures in each. There is a problem, however. Income taxes implicate not only production and consumption decisions, but also the decision to save, which they tax penalize by imposing a tax on the time value returns earned by savers. In addition, real-world corporate income taxes are levied at the entity level, and may depend in part on corporate residence, which is generally a much more tax-elastic attribute than individuals' choice of residence. Accordingly, as we will see later in this chapter, the savings and corporate residence margins raise additional global efficiency issues that can compete with focusing on locational production efficiency. Thus, the global efficiency analysis for international tax policy is more multidimensional, leaving greater ambiguity and potential for disagreement with regard to its proper bottom-line focus, than that which is widely accepted in the field of international trade.

Ease of advancing production efficiency—In international trade policy, once free trade has been adopted as the goal, the rest is fairly easy. Import tariffs distort domestic consumers' choices between foreign and domestic products. Likewise, export subsidies cause domestic producers to act as if foreigners valued exportable commodities more than the foreigners actually do. Banning import tariffs and export subsidies makes these problems go away—at least, leaving aside the second-best argument that the trade distortions they create might fortuitously offset other distortions and thereby increase efficiency (Slemrod 1995, 473).[2]

To be sure, there are cases of mixed motivation and effect to worry about. For example, suppose the U.S. Congress bans the domestic sale of tuna that has been caught through techniques that kill dolphins. Is this bona fide environmental policy, or a subterfuge to exclude tuna caught by foreign operators that happen to use less dolphin-friendly techniques? Or suppose Germany has beer purity laws that happen to disfavor imported brands, ostensibly for health or cultural reasons. Should this be taken at face value and therefore allowed, or struck down due to its functioning as an import barrier? Still, the problems that such disputes present are relatively limited, given that tariffs and export subsidies both are often reasonably identifiable and have widely been accepted as undesirable.

In international taxation, things are not so easy even if we adopt production efficiency as the core goal. Suppose that there was no entity-level corporate income taxation, and that all income earned through a corporation was taxed directly to individuals at the owner level, with the residence-based tax (if any) that was imposed depending purely on the individual's place of residence. In that scenario, production efficiency would be in principle just as easy to achieve through corporate income taxation as it is through trade policy. Only two things would be necessary (leaving aside the same sorts of second-best arguments that we generally ignore in international trade). First, to avoid the equivalent of import tariffs, countries would have to forgo imposing source-based taxes on inbound capital. Second, to avoid the equivalent of export subsidies, countries would have to impose full residence-based taxes on resident individuals' outbound capital.

There are just two problems. The first is that corporations are taxed directly on their own income, based on entity-level residence determinations. Accordingly, the universal application of pure residence-based, without source-based, income taxation may fail to address actual cross-border capital flows, which the system may pervasively fail to observe accurately. For example, if I, as an American, use a French company to invest at home, the international tax rules misclassify this as inbound rather than home country investment, whereas if a French individual uses a U.S. company to invest in France, the rules misclassify this as outbound U.S. investment.

Suppose, at the extreme, that individuals' corporate residence choices were wholly elective and independent of where they themselves lived. That is, suppose the choices had zero nontax implications and that there was no home equity bias. Then all that the global residence-based system would do is encourage investment through companies that are treated as residing in tax havens. All corporate investment would therefore face the same tax rate (zero). Within the corporate sector, this would create production efficiency, but noncorporate investment would be inefficiently disfavored. Even just within the corporate sector, however, relaxing the above assumptions about corporate residence choice causes the picture to worsen. In particular, if one's choice of corporate residence may affect production costs, then inducing investment through companies that reside in tax havens undermines production efficiency. In addition, if investment choices differ in their compatibility with incorporating overseas, then the system further undermines production efficiency by creating a tax preference for those choices that are more compatible therewith.

This brings us to the second problem with achieving production efficiency in international income taxation. Countries (other than tax havens) are simply unwilling to forgo source-based taxation. As we will see in chapter 5, there are several good rationales for this, not limited to the tariff-like motivation of wanting to impose a tax hit at the border on foreigners. (Indeed, one of the rationales pertains to the concern that resident individuals can avoid residence-based taxation of home investment by round-tripping their capital through foreign companies.) But even if there were no such rationales, the prevalence of source-based taxes would be a brute fact impeding the achievement of production efficiency in international taxation.

With ubiquitous source-based taxes, the only way to achieve production efficiency in international taxation is through the provision of unlimited foreign tax credits. As Slemrod (1995, 479) notes, "[i]t's as if, faced with tariffs imposed by all nations importing a certain good, all the exporting nations imposed exactly offsetting export subsidies." Given the universality of foreign tax credit limits in credit-granting countries, this evidently is a policy that no one in the world is willing to push beyond a given, arbitrarily defined point.

Countries' universal unwillingness to provide unlimited foreign tax credits, even though this would be globally optimal if one focused exclusively on production efficiency and ignored the corporate residence problem, is unsurprising from a unilateral standpoint. As the history of trade disputes reveals, countries sometimes are willing to offer export subsidies, which distort international trade if they are not offsetting other countries' import tariffs. This may either be at the prompting of domestic producers, or else out of adherence to mercantilism (the largely discredited doctrine that treats penetrating foreign markets and having a positive trade balance as inherently in the national interest). At least one commentator has therefore described the policy of offering foreign tax credits as "backdoor mercantilism" (Schmidt 1975). But even countries that would be willing, for mercantilist domestic political reasons, to consider export subsidies that the international trade rules permit might be put off by the structure of this particular one. After all, the export subsidy that the credits provide depends on the amount of foreign tax paid, and is thus "essentially... a transfer payment to the foreign government" (Slemrod 1995, 479), which thereby acquires an incentive to levy high source-based taxes on one's residents.

In sum, even if one were to select production efficiency as the predominant global efficiency issue raised by international tax policy, advancing it through coordinated national policies would be much harder than in the case of international trade. Rather than simply focusing on certain relatively easily identified instruments (i.e., import tariffs and export subsidies), any effort to pursue production efficiency in international taxation must cope with the problems stemming from the prevalence both of entity-level corporate taxation and of source-based taxes. However, the fact that the latter set of problems could indeed be addressed by unlimited foreign tax credits, if only countries were willing to offer them, suggests turning our attention to a third key difference between the fields of international trade and international tax, which is the degree of tension between countries' cooperative and unilateral incentives.

Compatibility of countries' unilateral incentives with the dictates of global production efficiency—A final important distinction between international trade and international tax policy pertains to countries' unilateral incentives to behave consistently with international cooperative norms. In general, it seems likely that, the smaller the departure from unilateral national self-interest that cooperation in advancing global welfare would require, the greater the feasibility and likelihood of such cooperation in practice.

Although I will postpone until chapter 5 a full examination of countries' unilateral incentives in either realm, the really striking point, in international trade, is how little tension there is between the unilateral and global perspectives. Accepted economic wisdom holds that tariffs are generally bad for the countries that impose them, and thus generally should not be used when countries pursue their national self-interest unilaterally. Indeed, even if other countries are imposing tariffs, responding with one's own—other than in the case where they are used strategically to induce general tariff reduction— makes no more sense than "drop[ping] rocks into our own harbors because other nations have rocky coasts" (Robinson 1947, 192). As for export subsidies, Paul Krugman (1984, 79) has noted that the optimal response by other countries may be to send a "note of thanks" for the special discount on export goods.

As we will see in chapter 5, there are special cases where these general principles do not hold, and import tariffs or export subsidies actually may advance unilateral national self-interest, and thus be worth adopting in the absence of WTO sanctions or other retaliation. These cases appear to be considerably rarer, however, than those in which domestic interest group politics creates a predilection to use anti-free trade measures that benefit particular industries while imposing greater, but more diffuse (and hence politically under-appreciated), harm on domestic consumers or taxpayers. Accordingly, free trade agreements serve, at least to a considerable degree, as internal precommitment devices that countries use to address their own anticipated internal political problems, by reciprocally promising to forgo hurting both themselves and each other. This may greatly ease the path to greater cooperation, or at least to global acceptance of broad cooperative principles that remain subject to being violated in particular cases.

In international taxation, while chapter 5 will show the parallels between countries' unilateral incentives in tax and trade policy, there are significant differences. In particular, the widespread use of source taxation, despite its being in tension with global production efficiency, strongly (and, as we will see, correctly) suggests that the appeal of using it goes well beyond that of imposing tariffs or subsidizing exports. And negating others' source taxes by offering unlimited foreign tax credits clearly is not optimal as a unilateral policy (see Shaviro 2010; Slemrod 1995, 479).

So the third key factor that underlies the international trade consensus—its urging countries to follow policies that, even if they were acting unilaterally, would for the most part be optimal anyway—does not carry over to international income taxation. Only on some other, perhaps different, less self-evident, and certainly more contested, basis could grounds for global cooperation potentially be discerned. But if one question has preoccupied international tax policy writers for the last fifty years, it is what that best of all conceivable organizing principles for global cooperation—reflexively assumed to exist—could possibly be.

C. Global Alphabet Soup: Capital Export Neutrality versus Capital Import Neutrality versus Capital Ownership Neutrality versus None of the Above

The modern international tax policy literature was almost single-handedly launched by Peggy Richman (1963), with further elaboration under her married name of Musgrave (1969). As we will see, the mystery is not that she chose to identify and emphasize particular global welfare norms, which very usefully helped to orient the field. Rather, it lies in the widespread assumption, for decades thereafter, that choosing which global welfare norm to implement was the right way to go about international tax policy making. Indeed, even when the contemporary usefulness of Musgrave's analytical structure finally began to attract prominent criticism, such as in the work of Michael Graetz (2000) and Mihir A. Desai with James R. Hines (2003, 2004), this did not invariably translate into recognizing the need to go beyond one-stop shopping for welfare norms. Instead, Desai and Hines—though not Graetz—advocated adding new global (as well as national) welfare norms to the list, as distinct from shifting to a new approach altogether. To this day, the duly modified and expanded Musgrave-Desai-Hines approach, under which the core question is which global welfare norm would yield the best results if everyone adopted it, remains startlingly prominent, albeit more in legal than economic circles.

1. The Rise of Capital Export Neutrality and Capital Import Neutrality

In her pathbreaking 1960's work, Musgrave analyzed international tax policy from both a global and a unilateral national efficiency perspective, while also relying on equity concepts such as that of "inter-nation equity" (Musgrave 1969, 130–133). Under her approach, however, global efficiency played a central role in shaping good international tax policy. This reflected that, under her view of national welfare (which I discuss in chapter 5), countries that were acting in their unilateral self-interest would tax all of their residents' worldwide income at the full domestic rate, while permitting only deductions for foreign taxes paid. Cross-border investment would therefore generally face much higher worldwide tax rates than purely domestic investment. That this would be highly undesirable appeared to suggest that a global welfare perspective was necessary. That in practice it was so rare appeared to suggest that a global perspective must indeed be prevalent, and thus entirely practical rather than a pipe dream.

Musgrave started from the well-accepted idea that, since taxes are costs to the taxpayer but socially are transfers, efficiency dictates that taxes be neutral as between alternative choices. From the standpoint of global welfare, this required counting all countries' taxes, since someone somewhere always gets the money. What made the problem interesting was the unavailability of the familiar conclusion in one-country cases, which is that everything should be taxed the same. Once we are looking internationally at countries that apply different tax rates, this alternative has been ruled out up front, so the only remaining question is what, short of everything, we should equalize.

A simple 2-by-2 grid can help one to visualize the problem that Musgrave was analyzing. Suppose the United States has a 35 percent domestic rate, while China has a 25 percent rate. We know, therefore, that U.S. taxpayers who are investing at home will face the U.S. rate, while Chinese taxpayers who are investing at home will face the Chinese rate. This leaves us, however, with the two cross-border investment cases to think about, as we can see in Table 4.1:

TABLE 4.1
THE NATURE OF THE PROBLEM

		SOURCE OF INCOME	
		U.S.	China
RESIDENCE OF TAXPAYER	U.S.	35%	?
	China	?	25%

Again, we cannot achieve full global neutrality because the tax rate in the upper left-hand box differs from that in the lower right-hand box. We can, however, align the two missing tax rates either horizontally, so that a given taxpayer faces the same tax rate in both countries, or else vertically, so that an investment in a given country faces the same tax rate no matter who makes it. In other words, one choice is to do this:

TABLE 4.2
EACH TAXPAYER FACES THE SAME TAX RATE NO MATTER WHERE IT INVESTS

		SOURCE OF INCOME	
		U.S.	China
RESIDENCE OF TAXPAYER	U.S.	35%	35%
	China	25%	25%

The other choice is to do this:

TABLE 4.3
EACH INVESTMENT FACES THE SAME TAX RATE NO MATTER WHO MAKES IT

		SOURCE OF INCOME	
		U.S.	China
RESIDENCE OF	U.S.	35%	25%
TAXPAYER	China	35%	25%

Musgrave labeled the Table 4.2 approach capital export neutrality (CEN), because, under it, a given taxpayer will face the same tax rate whether it exports its capital or keeps it at home. Thus, the U.S. taxpayer, assured of facing a 35 percent tax rate no matter where it invests, presumably will make whatever investment choice offers the highest expected pre-tax return. And given the global welfare perspective, it makes no difference to the analysis (any more than it does to the firm) what share the United States, as opposed to China, gets of the tax revenues in any instance. Thus, under CEN one can ignore the question of whether taxes are exclusively residence based, or instead reflect source-based taxation plus foreign tax credits (although, in that case, to keep the Chinese tax rate at 25 percent no matter what, China would have to forgo foreign tax credit limits).

As for Table 4.3, in which everyone investing in a given country faces the same tax rate, Musgrave labeled its approach capital import neutrality (CIN), because, under it, capital that is imported to a given country faces the same tax rate as that which is already there. CIN presumably requires the application of source-based taxation only. While in principle one could imagine (à la CEN) source countries offering unlimited credits for foreign taxpayers' residence-based taxes on inbound investment, this appears prohibitively unlikely in practice.

Why might one favor either CEN or CIN as a global welfare approach with respect to cross-border activity? The case for CEN is relatively straightforward. It is simply global production efficiency, albeit as separately determined for the residents of each country (a qualification that, as we will see shortly, ends up being extremely important). Again, if your tax rate is the same everywhere, presumably you will look for the highest available pre-tax return, which should be the "best" investment if markets are functioning properly.

Motivating support for CIN in a global welfare framework is a bit trickier. For U.S. multinationals that are complaining about the burden imposed on them by U.S. worldwide taxation, the rationale for it is clear. They argue that they cannot compete overseas with local businesses abroad that face only the lower local rate, or indeed with other multinationals from countries with milder (or no) worldwide taxation. CIN, therefore, ostensibly is needed to provide them with a level playing field.

This may sound like an argument about national self-interest in favoring (or at least not disfavoring) the "home team." However, there would also be global efficiency implications if tax rate differences permitted less efficient producers to win market share from those that were more efficient. Thus, the argument can be adapted to a global welfare setting in which one has no a priori reason to root for one country's firms against another's.

However, as Musgrave (1969, 82–85) noted, the global welfare argument for competitiveness via equal tax rates proves considerably less powerful upon close examination than it may initially seem. Suppose we start with a clear-cut case of unequal competition, such as that which would arise if U.S. law required U.S. firms, when operating in China, to pay higher wages than Chinese firms would owe the same workers for the same work. Assuming perfect competition and equivalence between American and Chinese firms in all other respects, this would make it impossible for the former to compete with the latter with respect to production in China. (And even with imperfect competition, it would be a handicap.) U.S. firms would have to set higher prices to recover their costs, and the

Chinese firms would therefore be able to underprice their U.S. rivals without any whiff of predatory price manipulation.

A higher income tax rate is entirely different from this, however, because it falls on the net profit earned, rather than being an input to the cost of production. A U.S. firm that faces a 35 percent rate in China should still set its prices in exactly the same way as it would if it faced only a 25 percent rate. After all, the higher the pre-tax profit, the more is left after-tax under any applicable tax rate below 100 percent.

Suppose that, absent income taxes, an American and a Chinese investor would each earn a 10 percent return on the investments in China that they are considering. In a CEN world, the American ends up with only a 6.5 percent return after-tax, while the Chinese investor clears 7.5 percent. Obviously, one would rather be the Chinese than the American investor, all else equal, but this is not a choice that people have if their residence is fixed. Even with only a 6.5 percent after-tax return, the American can meet all of her financial obligations from the investment in China and stay in business. What is more, if 10 percent is the best pre-tax return available to her, then she cannot earn more (in a CEN world) by pulling the money out and investing someplace else instead. And again, the American investor has no direct competitive disadvantage. For example, if the two companies otherwise have the same cost structure, one would expect them to set the same prices despite the difference in after-tax yield.

The picture may get cloudier if we add in second-order, more speculative considerations. Suppose both the American and the Chinese investor have profitable expansion opportunities that would require an upfront cash outlay. With perfect capital markets, each could easily finance the expansion with outside cash, if needed, by simply demonstrating the merits of the investment. In practice, however, capital markets suffer from information asymmetries, such as the fact that firms seeking capital may know more than do the suppliers of capital about their true prospects, and thus cannot be entirely be trusted when they paint a rosy picture (even if in fact it is accurate). Thus, internally generated funds, such as from retained earnings, may play an important role in financing growth.

Insofar as this consideration applies, the Chinese firm that pays tax at only 25 percent may have a genuine, tax-generated, competitive advantage over the U.S. firm, because it gets to keep more out of each dollar of pre-tax profits. Thus, it may be able to grow faster, and might even conceivably chase the U.S. firm out of a given market if the payoff to being the first mover or achieving a particular scale is great enough.

While one therefore cannot rule out the possibility that the neutrality margin identified by CIN can have important practical implications relating to business competition, the argument would have to rely on special circumstances that may not be widely applicable. Accordingly, one can readily understand why Musgrave viewed the case for CEN as stronger, if we view immobile individuals as the resident actors and if competitive concerns offer the only counterbalance in favor of CIN.

Might there be other global welfare arguments for it, however? To this day, CIN remains to some extent "a neutrality property in search of a rationale" (Devereux 2008, 13).

However, Thomas Horst (1980) supplied one that has proven academically, if not politically, influential. Under the continuing assumption that resident individuals are the relevant actors, his analysis showed that, just as CEN prevents misallocation of investment, CIN may prevent misallocation of the underlying saving that is needed to fund investment.

To illustrate this rationale for CIN, suppose the question is whether an American or a Chinese individual will save $100 in order to invest that amount in China. Unless both individuals face the same tax rate on this saving, they will anticipate different after-tax returns from it even if they would earn the same amount before tax.

Why would this matter? People who are considering saving, which provides the funds for future consumption, commonly are viewed in economic models as comparing the subjective value of their present and future consumption opportunities, where the latter would be greater in absolute amount if the saving earns a positive return. If they otherwise would rather consume now, however, they presumably will apply a discount rate in determining the present value to them of the future consumption. Thus, only if the after-tax return to saving exceeds the discount rate will saving, in lieu of immediate consumption, appear worthwhile.

Against this background, suppose that the American who is considering saving $100 to fund an investment in China has a discount rate of 6.8 percent, while the Chinese individual has a discount rate of 7.2 percent. Thus, the American won't save $100 unless she ends up with at least $106.80, whereas the Chinese individual, who evidently is a tad more impatient or present oriented, would require $107.20. With a 10 percent pre-tax return to either of them but a CEN-based tax policy, the American would retain only $106.50 after paying the 35 percent U.S. tax, while the Chinese individual would retain $107.50. Thus, only the Chinese individual will be able to satisfy her discount rate, and the "wrong" individual—the one who was more present minded and thus lost greater utility from deferring consumption—will be the one who ends up saving.

Under the hypothetical's terms, this creates a global efficiency loss, no less than would violating CEN and thus causing investments to be made in the wrong place (where they earned less, rather than psychologically costing more, before tax). To avoid it, one needs to follow CIN, and thereby provide that all prospective savers would face the same tax rate with respect to a given investment.

This argument for CIN is far too esoteric for it ever to have had significant political traction. Its relying on the psychic costs associated with discount rates makes it much less tangible to the naked eye than either the case for CEN, which relies on pre-tax cash returns, or the standard competitiveness rationale for CIN. Nonetheless, the savings-based argument for CIN was long accepted in the academic literature as needing to be weighed against the investment-based argument for CEN.

Horst (1980, 798) suggested that international tax policy "strike a balance between these two competing objectives." This might, for example, involve the United States' imposing a tax rate on Americans' investment in China (on top of China's 25 percent tax) that was below the supplementary 10 percent rate suggested by CEN, but greater than zero. Exactly where this intermediate rate should fall might depend on the relative elasticity of investment choices on the one hand and savings choices on the other.

A more commonly followed approach, however, was to seek "primacy of one principle over the other" (Keen 1993, 29), with the outcome "depend[ing] on the relative importance of the distortions induced in production [by violating CEN] and consumption [by violating CIN]" (Giovannini 1989, 367). Under this horse race-style approach to the choice, the verdict of most analysts was fairly clear. The tax elasticity of saving, though widely disputed in the literature, is often deemed low, whereas in today's world investment capital clearly is highly mobile and tax responsive. Hence, CEN generally captured the gold medal, on the ground that violating it would lead in practice to greater departures from the efficient pre-tax benchmark (Shaviro 2009a, 127).

There also were several other reasons why CEN largely prevailed in the academic literature. In particular:

1. Countries can unilaterally achieve CEN as to their residents if they grant unlimited foreign tax credits. While the "unlimited" aspect of this policy prescription plainly was politically unrealistic, the prospects for unilaterally achieving CIN appeared to be even worse. Given the existence of residence-based taxes, source countries would have had to grant unlimited tax credits, offsetting those taxes, to inbound investors if they wanted to ensure that everyone faced the same marginal rate on local investment. This seemed highly unlikely, even without regard to the problem of credit limits.

2. The source-based taxation that achievement of CIN would require runs into the incoherence of income source as an economic concept. In practice, source-based taxes inevitably lead to the distortions and manipulations associated with transfer pricing (Keen 1993, 30), as well as to such games as using intra-group borrowing to shift net income out of high-tax countries. Residence, by contrast, is a well-defined idea and easy to apply in most cases, if one continues to ignore (for now) the difficulty of applying it to legal entities rather than just to individuals.

3. Source-based taxation leads to tax competition between jurisdictions for mobile capital (Giovannini 1989, 368). Residence-based taxation of individuals, by contrast, avoids such tax competition because investors will pay the national rate no matter where they invest. While it creates tax competition for residents, this remains muted if people are relatively immobile as between countries.[3] Accordingly, if one dislikes tax competition, one has a further reason for preferring residence-based tax policies that advance CEN rather than CIN.

4. Income taxes inherently discourage saving, leading to distortion of people's decisions regarding when to consume. For this reason, many academics believe that a suitably progressive consumption tax (little found in practice, but extensively

explored in recent literature) could reduce the efficiency costs of taxation without reducing progressive redistribution.[4] This seems unlikely to happen any time soon, but it affects CIN's apparent merits.

Against an at least implicitly pro-consumption tax background, CIN's particular angle on how to address the income tax's discouragement of saving may seem a bit odd. In effect, a CIN-based analysis treats as fixed the overall extent to which income taxes around the world inefficiently discourage saving, and merely suggests avoiding the scenario where the discouragement is uneven across countries, in the circumstance where prospective savers in different countries happen to be considering setting aside funds for the same investment. Arguably, this is a labored and indirect way of addressing income taxation's inefficiency at the savings margin—as compared, for example, to simply reducing the tax burden on saving (which any country can do unilaterally as to its own residents).

In sum, the traditional analysis seemed to lead in a definite direction, suggesting that global welfare would be highest if all countries followed CEN. And if there was any reason to doubt that this led straight to the conclusion that the United States should follow CEN—apparently, without insisting on reciprocity, or even on evidence that CEN was being widely followed elsewhere—one could not have discerned this from the literature. Indeed, the literature's silence on the need for any particular bridge from the global welfare conclusion to the making of definitive domestic policy recommendations seemed to imply that the connection must somehow be entirely self-evident.

With time, however, it has become clear that the traditional global welfare analysis—extending not just to its pro-CEN conclusion, but to the entire terms of the debate—was seriously flawed, despite the elements of sound internal logic that help to explain its longstanding appeal. Indeed, the problems relate both to the purely global analysis and to the unexplained leap from global to national optimality. I examine these problems next.

2. Global Welfare Problems with CEN and CIN

By awarding the gold medal to CEN, the traditional literature opted for global production efficiency, based on the consensus that, in the end, one can properly overlook the fact that (as evinced by CIN) income taxation also distorts decisions about saving. But even just considered as a global welfare benchmark (i.e., without regard to whether this is the right mode of analysis), CEN turns out to have two key shortcomings. One is its potentially limited capacity to increase global production efficiency if not all countries follow it, by reason of what are called clientele effects. The other is its ignoring the issues raised by entity-level corporate income taxation.

Clientele effects—In explaining this issue, once again a comparison to international trade may help. Suppose two countries enter into a bilateral free trade agreement, while the rest of the world engages in protectionism. One may reasonably hope that the agreement will increase global production efficiency (as well as the economic welfare of the treaty partners), even though the rest of the world stands outside it, because it permits people in the two countries to make mutually advantageous deals that tariffs or export subsidies would have impeded. Any adverse effects on others, such as those in countries that stand outside the agreements, are easy to overlook, even if in principle they should be kept in mind.[5] And even if they are kept in mind, they arguably are best addressed by further extending the agreements in an iterative process.

If we turn to international taxation, and more particularly to the effect on global production efficiency if only a few countries sign on to the program, such optimism may be harder to motivate. CEN addresses the global allocation of capital, which can flow freely between multiple countries, as distinct from emphasizing particular bilateral trade opportunities. In consequence, there are realistic scenarios in which the fact that not everyone is following CEN ends up substantially undermining, or even eliminating, the gains in global production efficiency that one might have hoped would result if even just a few countries embraced it. Nor may one have much reason to hope that the range of CEN will keep on extending, in the manner of free trade under an optimistic scenario.

Suppose that taxpayers who hold capital that they are willing to export can invest either in Assyria, where the tax rate is 50 percent, or in Babylonia, where it is 25 percent. If everyone had a worldwide system with unlimited foreign tax credits, then all investors who were seeking to maximize their after-tax returns would ignore the difference in source tax rate, and invest in whichever country offered the higher expected pre-tax return. By contrast, if everyone had a territorial system, investors would demand that pre-tax returns in Assyria be 150 percent of those in Babylonia, all else equal. For example, earning 12 percent before tax in Assyria leads to the same 6 percent after-source-tax return as earning 8 percent in Babylonia.

Just for descriptive convenience, suppose that initially everyone has a territorial system, and that the pre-source-tax rates of return available at the margin are indeed 12 percent in Assyria and 8 percent in Babylonia. Thus, global production efficiency is being impaired by the failure to increase such returns by shifting capital from Babylonia to Assyria until the pre-source-tax rates of return that are available at the margin have been equalized. Then, the United States enacts a CEN-based system, featuring worldwide taxation of U.S. residents and unlimited foreign tax credits. (To avoid conflating this issue with the separate one of how CEN is undermined by entity-level corporate taxation, suppose for now that all income taxes are imposed directly on individuals, based on their own residence.)

Under these circumstances, U.S. investors would be expected to respond by shifting capital from Babylonia to Assyria. Indeed, leaving aside diversification concerns and location-specific opportunities to earn more than the marginal rate of return in Babylonia, they will shift all of their capital from Babylonia to Assyria (if these are the only two choices) until the two jurisdictions' marginal pre-source-tax rates of return are equalized.

If U.S. investors were the only ones who could provide capital to fund Assyrian and Babylonian investments, one would indeed expect the two jurisdictions' marginal pre-source-tax rates of return to be equalized. This would increase global production efficiency, as investments in Assyria that were more profitable supplanted those in Babylonia that would have been less profitable. But when there are also investors in the market who, due to their own countries' territorial systems, care about the after-source-tax, rather than the pre-source-tax, rate of return, things are more complicated. Initially, as U.S. investors try to sell Babylonian investments that earn 8 percent before tax and buy Assyrian assets that pay 12 percent, they may conceivably find all of the willing counterparties that they need from other countries. After all, the fact that these are equilibrium rates of return suggests that there are willing buyers and sellers at the prevailing prices.

Depending on market conditions, including the overall extent to which global capital is held by U.S. residents, it is possible that there will be *no* change in Assyrian versus Babylonian pre-source-tax rates of return. Instead, there might simply be ownership shifts—known as clientele effects, because the U.S. investors' domestic tax situation makes them a "clientele" that is especially interested in holding Assyrian investments. If this were to happen, global production efficiency would not have increased at all. Indeed, it is possible that the clientele effects would themselves have efficiency costs, by reason of their distorting what would otherwise have been the optimal ownership patterns, although this would require supplementing, in some fashion, the story as it stands so far.

Now suppose instead that U.S. investors still wanted to shift capital from Babylonia to Assyria but had run out of counterparties. Now there really would be a shift in overall capital from Babylonia to Assyria, increasing global output. But as soon as marginal pre-tax rates of return converged at all, clientele effects would drive non-U.S. investors in the opposite direction, from Assyria to Babylonia.

In a conventional "marginal investor" model, the only question would be whether U.S. or non-U.S. investors were setting relative prices at the margin. Thus, either the two countries' pre-tax rates of return would remain at their prior ratio, or else they would be fully equalized. But in more sophisticated models where investors are maximizing expected utility, not just expected after-tax rates of return, based in part on risk aversion and a resulting preference for diversification, intermediate outcomes are possible as well (Desai and Dharmapala 2009, 15–18). If this is what happens, then there is some increase in global production efficiency by reason of U.S. adherence to CEN, but it still is reduced by the occurrence of mere clientele effects, which also (in a fuller story) may indicate countervailing efficiency issues.

The significance of entity-level corporate income taxation—Despite continuing home equity bias, these days one really cannot reasonably ignore cross-border shareholding. Domestic individuals own stock in foreign corporations, while foreign individuals hold stock in domestic corporations. Either group can respond to tax differentials between the treatment of domestic and foreign companies by adjusting where they incorporate, where they contribute capital for new equity, and where they buy existing stock.

With corporations being treated as separate taxpayers, leading to entity-level residence determinations that may not match the residence status of the owners, both CEN and CIN are, at a minimum, badly undermined as global efficiency norms. Thus, suppose that a U.S. company making a given investment in China would face the full U.S. rate, while a German or Chinese company that made the same investment would face only the lower Chinese rate. The global efficiency rationale for CEN fails to apply if, say, U.S. individuals who want to make the investment respond by doing it through a German or Chinese company, rather than a U.S. company. As for CIN, while its savings rationale may end up being satisfied if potential savers and investors in the world can all alike elect into territoriality through their corporate residence choices, it is focused on the wrong variable if it treats, say, U.S. taxpayers (including resident companies) as a proxy for individuals living in the United States who are deciding how much to save.

3. Capital Ownership Neutrality (CON) as an Alternative Global Welfare Norm

While cross-border shareholding greatly limits countries' ability to advance global production efficiency through CEN, this fact does not alone tell us whether its existence raises other global efficiency issues. Mihir Desai and James R. Hines (2003) were among the first to notice that it does.[6] In an influential article concerning the prevailing global and national welfare norms, Desai and Hines, after briefly describing the CEN versus CIN debate and suggesting that it has become outmoded, turn to the question of why we observe foreign direct investment (FDI) by multinational firms. They note that economists, after initially explaining FDI as merely a device to shift global net saving from wherever it arose to the countries with the best investment opportunities, now "emphasized a transaction-cost approach whereby multinational firms emerge because of the advantages conferred by joint ownership of assets across locations" (488). For example, McDonald's and Microsoft might find that owning their intangible assets, such as brand names, production processes, and patents, was crucial to exploiting these assets efficiently around the world in the face of agency costs. This, in turn, suggests that ownership arrangements are crucial in explaining FDI, and that "ownership is likely to be associated with significant productivity differences" (489).

From this, Desai and Hines draw the conclusion that it is not enough to ask the CEN question of how taxes affect where investments are made, or the CIN question of how taxes affect who saves. One also has to ask how taxes affect the ownership of assets. This leads them to a new global efficiency benchmark, capital ownership neutrality or CON, which requires that tax systems not distort ownership patterns. Where CON is satisfied, "it is impossible to increase output by trading capital ownership among investors" (495).[7]

CON, like CEN, relates to global production efficiency, albeit at a different margin of choice—asset ownership, rather than investment location. As Desai and Hines define CON, it might be relevant even in the absence of cross-border shareholding and entity-level residence determinations. For example, it might be violated if the imposition, by some but not all countries, of worldwide residence-based taxation of individuals (including on the income that they earned abroad through corporations) led to clientele effects. Thus, in the earlier example where the unique U.S. imposition of such taxation led U.S. individuals to favor high-taxed Assyrian assets while other investors favored low-taxed Babylonian assets, CON would be violated if this ownership pattern reduced global output.

However, the Desai-Hines definition is too narrow to capture all of the potential global production efficiency consequences of cross-border shareholding, multinational economic activity, and entity-level corporate taxation. In particular, their focus on whether one can "increase output by trading capital ownership among investors" fails to capture the full set of phenomena that may be of interest here. It pushes one toward looking just at fixed amounts of corporate equity in each jurisdiction, the owners of which are participating in a global asset auction, to the exclusion of broader corporate ownership-related phenomena.

Under the Desai-Hines analysis, universal exemption of foreign source income would satisfy CON, because then "the tax treatment of foreign investment income is the same for all investors, and competition between potential buyers allocates assets to their most productive owners" (494). This is a statement about idealized, rather than actual, territoriality. After all, in practice, being a multinational may affect source determinations, by creating income-shifting opportunities, and by inducing source countries to apply inevitably imperfect rules that look at global operations in the course of measuring domestic income.

Thus, in a territorial world, multinationals may have a tax advantage over purely domestic businesses, given the opportunity to use commonly owned operations in low-tax jurisdictions as a magnet for reported taxable income. One might therefore expect multinationals to outbid purely domestic owners for the ownership of assets that would offer especial income-shifting synergies, even if this reduces global output. Adverse effects on output could result, not just from multinationals holding the wrong assets, but from excessive multinational activity in response to the availability of sourcing-based tax synergies. Thus, suppose that two separate businesses, one in a high-tax country and the other in a low-tax country, would reduce their output by merging, because common ownership would actually worsen managerial incentives and oversight in each location. They might nonetheless decide to merge for tax reasons if they could reduce their combined tax burden by shifting the reported source of income from the high-tax to the low-tax jurisdiction.

Further issues lying outside the context of a global asset auction arise when Desai and Hines turn their attention to worldwide residence-based taxation. They assert that such taxation (whether achieved by eliminating source-based taxes or through the universal allowance of unlimited foreign tax credits) can also be consistent with satisfying CON. Their argument goes as follows. Suppose that, because all countries follow CEN, each company will face the domestic rate no matter where it invests. For example, a U.S. company will face a 35 percent rate whether it invests at home, in China, or in the Cayman Islands, whereas a Caymans company always will face a o percent rate.[8] Where this is the case, neither company will have any tax reason for preferring one asset to another. They will merely (and in common) want to maximize their pre-tax returns, which correlates with maximizing after-tax returns given that the same overall tax rate will apply no matter where one invests. In consequence, the difference between the two companies' residence-based tax rates should have no effect on what they are willing to bid in the global asset auction.[9]

While this argument is correct as far as it goes, the claim that universal adherence to CEN will not distort ownership is mistaken, once one looks beyond asset auctions to broader ownership issues. Suppose Acme United States is considering acquiring Lithco, a company that operates in Lithuania and is entirely owned by Lithuanians, and that Lithuania's corporate tax rate is 20 percent. The acquisition would involve Acme's giving Lithco's owners shares of Acme stock in exchange for all the Lithco stock. The acquisition would permit Acme to integrate Lithco's operations with its own, raising Lithco's expected annual yield by 10 percent, from $1 million to $1.1 million. Given, however, the 35 percent U.S. corporate tax rate (and the assumed absence of deferral in a CEN world), the merger would reduce Lithco's after-tax profits from $800,000 to $715,000. Thus, the merger would not occur under a universal global regime featuring worldwide taxation that was based on corporate residence, and that treated a commonly owned corporate group as a single taxpayer.

To the same effect, suppose I am considering contributing cash for new equity to an existing company, incorporated either in the United States or the Caymans, that will use the money to fund a new investment someplace. Even if the U.S. company could earn greater pre-tax profits if it were the owner and operator, I will invest through the Caymans company—causing the new assets to have the wrong owner, from the standpoint of maximizing global output—if the U.S. firm's pre-tax advantage is not great enough to make up for the difference between the firms' residence-based tax rates.

A further global production efficiency issue that relates to corporate residence and ownership, although outside the scope of CON as defined by Desai and Hines, arises when business owners are deciding where to incorporate. Thus, suppose I can locate the corporate entity through which I run my business either in the United States or in the Caymans, and that the former choice would lead to higher output, taxes aside. For example, it might lower my legal costs by permitting retention of local counsel. Moreover, if investors preferred U.S. corporate law from a governance standpoint, using it might lower my financing costs. Once again, under worldwide residence-based taxation but not under territorial taxation, I might end up making the lower-global-output choice for tax reasons.

Not having such examples in mind, Desai and Hines conclude that, in principle, CIN-compatible and CEN-compatible systems of taxation, if followed by everyone, would each lead to efficient ownership (494–495). In practice, however, they conclude that territoriality, rather than worldwide residence-based taxation, is the best way to go from a CON standpoint. They note that, if some countries have worldwide systems while others are territorial, ownership distortions that violate CON will occur. Thus, suppose that the United States and Germany have similar corporate tax rates, but that the former imposes worldwide taxation while the latter has a territorial system. German firms may outbid U.S. firms for assets in low-tax countries even if the U.S. firms could use these assets more efficiently. Meanwhile, U.S. investment would be expected to shift toward assets in high-tax countries, even where the German firms would have been the preferred owners but for the residence-based tax differences.

Against this background, Desai and Hines argue that, in general, "[i]ndividual countries have the potential to improve global welfare [as measured by CON] by moving their taxation of foreign income into conformity with an average global norm" (495). Under current circumstances, with the United States increasingly standing almost alone in maintaining major elements of a worldwide approach, this suggests to them that a shift toward territoriality would likely reduce worldwide ownership distortions, increasing global welfare if CON is the most important benchmark. Desai and Hines agree, however, that CON's importance must be weighed against that of the rival efficiency benchmarks from the prior international tax policy literature. With CIN largely having been discredited on the ground that countries cannot pursue it unilaterally (493), this leaves CEN and CON as competing policy guides that generally will be in conflict, and that may require further empirical evaluation to resolve.

This is a worthwhile contribution to the literature, insofar as global welfare and alphabet soup are indeed the proper approaches. But what if they are not? Desai and Hines do not expressly defend the claim that this is how international tax policy analysis should be done. They also do not contest it, however. While they can reasonably say that they took the international tax policy literature as they found it, perhaps we can do better.

4. Where Does the Traditional Global Welfare Debate Leave Us?

The lessons that one can derive from fifty years of debate over global welfare norms for international tax policy include the following:

a. *Lack of consensus regarding the end*—There remains no consensus, among either policy makers or experts, regarding the end toward which countries should cooperate in international tax policy. Indeed, even when there was a relatively high level of expert consensus in favor of CEN, there was no general move to adopt it comprehensively in practice. For example, bilateral tax treaties regularly allowed the signatories to address double taxation through either foreign tax credits or exemption (and thus, in effect, to choose between CEN and CIN). Moreover, foreign tax credit limits, though inconsistent with CEN, have been universal and little criticized even by CEN proponents.

Even just within the scholarly literature, dissensus comes as little surprise, given the diversity of margins implicated by entity-level corporate income taxation—pertaining not just to location choice (as under CEN) but saving (CIN) and entities' place of residence (CON). As we will see in chapter 6, the intractability of international tax reform is closely linked to the radical imperfections of corporate income taxation, which make any tidy solution unattainable. Only through much broader and more fundamental tax reform, if feasible and otherwise desirable, could one slice through the set of Gordian knots that make the analysis of international tax policy so challenging (as well as dispiriting yet interesting).

b. *No sound basis for picking either CEN or CON as the outright "gold medal" winner*—In practice, each of the rival global welfare norms can be expected to matter in particular cases. For example, if U.S. companies would face the U.S. rate in any event, then surely in some instances they would shift investments to higher-tax locations, or else cease incurring the economic waste associated with income shifting, in either case advancing CEN. But at the same time, surely there are cases in which a territorial approach would forestall use of the wrong ownership arrangement, thereby advancing CON. And with home equity bias, even a CIN-inspired focus on the residence of the taxpayer, based on assuming that it is the same as the residence of the ultimate saver, may be accurate in particular cases.

In general, when multiple distortions arise, it would be surprising to learn that wholly eliminating one of them was preferable to abating each of them to some lesser degree. A public economics truism holds that, as people's incentives move further from the optimum, the rate of marginal increase in economic distortion steadily increases. For example, under standard assumptions, doubling a distortionary tax rate will quadruple the resulting deadweight loss, if all else remains the same (Rosen and Gayer 2009, 340). From this standpoint, if countries were coordinating their international tax policies in order to address CEN and/or CON, it is highly plausible that wholly eliminating one set of problems would be inferior to partly abating each. For example, if CON was being addressed first, shifting at some point to moderating CEN might be expected to have a higher marginal efficiency payoff than eliminating the very last vestiges of CON. A single-bullet approach to global welfare ignores this point.

c. *What happens when one or few countries try to advance global welfare through unilateral action*—As noted above, if we have globally integrated capital markets, then even so large a country as the United States has only a limited ability to promote global welfare through its own unilateral international tax policy decisions. For example, our pursuing global production efficiency through CEN would be undercut by clientele effects even if there were no cross-border shareholding, and is further undermined by investors' capacity to respond by using non-U.S companies to invest in low-tax jurisdictions. One could call these phenomena "leakage," by analogy to the setting in which a country seeks to address global warming by enacting a carbon tax, and producers to some extent respond by shifting their carbon-emitting activity to other countries, rather than actually reducing such activity. And even insofar as there is a net increase in global production efficiency, the benefit accrues to everyone, not distinctively to us. Meanwhile, we distinctively bear the welfare costs of departing from the set of policies that would have been unilaterally national optimal—for example, from "making a present of the revenue to other countries" through foreign tax credits (Graetz and O'Hear 1997, 1047).

An analogous story holds if we exempt U.S. companies' foreign source income, with an eye to increasing global output via CON, in circumstances where unilateral self-interest would have indicated taxing such income at a rate above zero. Once again, we would distinctively bear the cost of this at least assumed departure from doing what was best for us. (In chapter 5, I address what the national welfare costs might be.) Meanwhile, leakage in reverse—that is, the tax-motivated use of U.S. entities to invest abroad, or else to combine domestic with foreign operations in cases where this reduced output—would reduce the global efficiency gains with respect to ownership. And any remaining net global welfare gains would accrue to everyone in the world, rather than being enjoyed distinctively by U.S. individuals.

d. *Limited significance for the global welfare debate of the widespread policy shift toward territoriality*—Recent years have seen substantial movement around the world toward territoriality—albeit, subject to rising concern about profit shifting to tax havens. Does this mean we have an emerging consensus about how best to pursue global economic welfare through international tax policy?

It would certainly be comforting to interpret recent shifts toward territoriality in this way. But there is little reason to believe that countries are becoming more territorial for the sorts of cooperative reasons that we may discern when, say, they act in concert to lower trade barriers. To the contrary, the political impetus appears to be predominantly national welfare based, reflecting concern about tax competition with other countries, and having elements as well of domestic interest group politics (via the influence of powerful resident companies). In the United Kingdom, for example, the move toward territoriality was heavily influenced by resident companies' threats to expatriate for tax purposes, and by the government's frequently expressed desire, throughout the process, to win the companies' approval of the new regime.

The evidence that pressures of tax competition predominantly explain the shift toward territoriality does not, of course, refute the view that it has increased global welfare. As we will see in chapter 5, a basic point about competitive markets generally is that, under some conditions, they yield good outcomes via the operation of Adam Smith's invisible hand. However, one has to look at the particular market setting more carefully in order to assess this with respect to tax competition. But if the incentives are right, one has no need to invoke global welfare as a motivating standard, whereas, if they are wrong, that still leaves the question for particular countries of whether and when it makes sense for them to swim against the tide.

A final point about recent international tax policy shifts around the world is that, even before concern about profit shifting to tax havens took on its current prominence, there clearly was no consensus to go all the way toward territoriality and/or CIN/CON. For example, Japan limits exemption for resident companies' active business FSI to that which bears a source country effective tax rate of at least 20 percent. A number of other countries, such as France, Germany, and the United Kingdom, similarly limit exemption under specified circumstances.

D. Moving Beyond the Misguided Focus on Single-Bullet Global Welfare Norms

By now, it should be clear that the case for basing U.S. international tax policy, or that of any other country, on global welfare considerations—or, worse still, on the claimed counsel of single-bullet global welfare norms—is exceptionally weak. Why, then, has the appeal of this approach proven so enduring? I believe that there are two main explanations. The first is that global welfare arguments, while surely not consciously insincere, have been, to a large extent, if not entirely pretextual, then certainly all too convenient. They appeal to, and help to reassure, their proponents by offering high-minded grounds for following policies that would also serve more controversial goals. On the one side, if you want big companies to pay more tax, either as an end in itself or as a stand-in for directly taxing rich shareholders, the case for CEN may sound more anodyne and universal. And on the other side of the debate, once CEN has gained widespread attention, the ability to respond in kind with CIN and/or CON may be preferable to responding solely in terms of "competitiveness" or the interests of U.S. companies. We thus end up with a set of Kabuki rituals that no side has especial reason to disavow, since all are able to play.

The second reason for global welfare's continuing appeal has more intellectual substance. If you start from certain premises, international taxation poses a classic prisoner's dilemma, in which the only alternative to terrible outcomes is a general spirit of cooperation, exercised without demanding explicit quid pro quos, and yet potentially leaving everyone better off if good and bad behaviors are sufficiently contagious.

In the classic prisoner's dilemma setup, two partners in crime are being held and interrogated by the police in separate rooms. Each must decide whether to confess, and in so doing implicate the other, or to stonewall the police. If both hold out, the police will be unable to prove the crime but will convict each on some lesser charge, resulting in short jail terms. If only one prisoner confesses, he or she will get to turn state's witness and be set free after sending the other one to prison for a long time. If both confess, no testimony will be needed, and each will be sentenced to a medium-length jail term.

Each prisoner faces a choice between cooperating and defecting from the other prisoner's standpoint (that is, cooperating with the police constitutes "defecting"). What gives the prisoner's dilemma its bite is the fact that, while collectively the prisoners would be best off cooperating with each other and stonewalling the police, each of them, considered in isolation, is better off defecting no matter what the other does. By defecting you eliminate any jail term if the other prisoner cooperates with you by holding out, and you shorten your jail term if he defects by turning state's witness. Thus, if the prisoners cannot observe each other and coordinate their behavior, their pursuit of rational self-interest may have the pathological effect of leaving both worse off than if both had acted altruistically.

Prisoner's dilemmas are ubiquitous in public policy. Thomas Hobbes's state of nature, featuring the war of all against all, is an example, since all would be better off observing peace, but no lone individual has an incentive to do so. Another classic example is pollution, where each individual's contribution to the sum total is sufficiently trivial that he would be better off not having to comply with emissions standards. One way of solving prisoners' dilemmas is through centralized command, be it Hobbes's sovereign or a government enacting pollution laws. Obviously, this is not feasible in the international tax realm. However, a second possibility is that the parties will be able to achieve at least some measure of cooperation by following social norms, which can be defined as "informal social regularities that individuals feel obligated to follow because of an internalized sense of duty, because of a fear of external non legal sanctions, or both" (McAdams 1997, 340). Norms in this sense may serve partly as a self-disciplinary device, keeping one on the path to greater long-term benefit even if this means sacrificing occasional short-term gains.

Once we see it this way, a further argument seems to emerge in support of the conventional focus on global, rather than national, welfare. Suppose we assume that countries' lagged and imperfect monitoring of each other's behavior, along with their own internal political choice problems, effectively create prisoner's dilemmas in the international tax realm even though, in principle, they ought to be able to observe and respond to each other's degrees of cooperation. If countries have internal political predilections to cheat too much (leading through contagion to bad long-term outcomes for all), then their treating a cooperative norm as valuable for its own sake might conceivably tend, over the long run, to improve their political decisions from a purely self-interested standpoint.

For a good illustration, consider the question of whether the United States should enact a carbon tax (or alternatively an economically similar cap-and-trade system) in order to reduce global warming. If we were the only country so to act, we would bear the entire leakage cost of inducing carbon emitters to locate elsewhere, while all countries would get to share with us the global benefit from slowing down climate change. It is highly plausible that this would not be in our self-interest unless other countries responded by adopting their own carbon taxes or cap-and-trade systems. Yet, given the severity of the underlying problem, along with the difficulty of negotiating a global deal up front as well as the grounds for hoping that we would inspire reciprocal or imitative adoption elsewhere, I myself would support unilateral U.S. enactment of a carbon tax, followed by some degree of patience in waiting for others to follow suit—thereby effectively accepting a global welfare framework comparable to that which I propose rejecting in the international tax realm.

A key question, of course, is just what prisoner's dilemma in the international tax policy realm might require countries to cooperate at the expense of short-term and unilateral self-interest. As it happens, there are two opposing possibilities, one from pervasive overtaxation, and the other from pervasive under-taxation, of cross-border activity relative to that occurring in just one country. We therefore need to consider each in turn.

Avoiding pervasive overtaxation of cross-border activity—Suppose that countries were inclined, when considering just their unilateral self-interest, to tax in full all income within their reach on both a residence and a source basis. This, of course, would lead to unmitigated double taxation, and thus—of greater interest—to significant discouragement of cross-border economic activity unless tax planning could sufficiently neutralize the sting. Countries therefore ostensibly must recede from pursuing unilateral self-interest—for example, by offering foreign tax credits or exemption—if they are to avoid an unfortunate global outcome. In this scenario, both global welfare, and that of each country, ostensibly might decline over time if the countries, whenever they considered defecting, were too shortsightedly calculating about the prospects for immediate strategic responses by other countries.

There are two main problems with relying on this view to support basing one's international tax policy decisions on global welfare after all. First, as we will see in chapter 5, it appears fundamentally to misstate countries' unilateral incentives. Countries have compelling reasons, both of national self-interest and domestic politics, for *not* pushing either residence-based or source-based taxation to its maximum reach.

Second, recall that the global welfare debate in international tax policy has mainly been about choosing between an exemption system and a worldwide-with-foreign-tax-credits system. Its aim is to determine which of these two alternatives would lead to higher global welfare if adopted by everyone. This is not a "cooperate versus defect" choice. It is a "how best to cooperate" choice. In this setting, it is easy to lose sight of just how off-kilter it is to claim that the U.S. decision should depend on what would be best if everyone made the same choice. (This is what I called the "global convention fallacy" in chapter 1.) We are not in fact deciding for everyone—and we are not even providing a signal to other countries regarding how much cooperation, as compared to defection, they should expect. So the conventional focus on global welfare to guide this choice is strikingly misguided.

Avoiding pervasive under-taxation of cross-border activity—The opposite threat to global economic welfare, if countries decline to cooperate, involves systematic under-taxation. For example, as noted earlier, the pervasive difficulty of sourcing income accurately may create a globally inefficient tax preference for multinational activity—violating CON as correctly understood—if it means that multinationals have an advantage over other companies from their ability to shift reported taxable income to low-tax locations. In addition, if some income-producing activities are more mobile than others, whether in terms of where they occur or where the income is reported, such activities will be inefficiently tax favored. High-tech and pharmaceutical companies, for example, along with others that heavily rely on intellectual property or other intangibles, notoriously have special advantages over brick-and-mortar businesses, as well as over those that must operate face to face with consumers, such as in the course of offering services.

Such inefficiencies reduce global output by causing tax considerations to change the mix of economic activities that would result if only pre-tax profitability mattered. In theory, the global welfare gain from eliminating the inefficiency ought to make it possible for all countries to benefit from cooperating to address it. In practice, however, the effort to arrange such a deal would involve formidable, and perhaps even prohibitive, transaction costs. For example, countries might have varying incentives to hold out, in the hope of attracting business as a tax haven, and this prospect might require either bribing or coercing the would-be holdouts into cooperating.

In the absence of widespread cooperation, the pressures of tax competition give countries an incentive to respond by taxing mobile income at a lower rate than the rest. Should a given country refuse to do this, to its own direct cost and in the absence of strong grounds for believing that cooperation might gradually prevail? Here at least the logic is stronger than in the overtaxation setting, where the issue isn't even "cooperate versus defect" to begin with. (One should keep in mind, however, that selective national responses could lead to other global inefficiencies, such as those pertaining to locational or residence choice by businesses with mobile income.) But again, returning to the discussion at the start of this chapter regarding whether and when personal or national selfishness are defensible, it is asking a lot, and I would say too much, for countries to be quite this noble. And in any event, this is not the main issue raised by the global welfare debate, with its predominant focus on the battle of the acronyms.

E. Cooperative Possibilities

The discussion thus far may have sounded almost relentlessly skeptical about the feasibility of relying on multilateral cooperation to increase national as well as global welfare.

However, the fact that cooperation is difficult does not mean that it is generally impossible. In particular, its feasibility may vary with the substantive area.

Consider two ambitious multilateral efforts that (as of this writing) remain works in progress. The first pertains to information reporting, in particular to address tax evasion by individuals. In 2010, the U.S. Congress enacted the Foreign Account Tax Compliance Act (FATCA), a statute that aims to induce financial institutions all over the world to report to the U.S. Treasury about financial activity by U.S. account holders. While FATCA started out as a unilateral U.S. effort to enlist foreign financial institutions as foot soldiers in our enforcement efforts, it has given rise to much broader discussions regarding multilateral cooperation with respect to information reporting (see Grinberg 2012).

Second, the fact that many countries are struggling in parallel to address multinationals' profit shifting to tax havens has led to discussion of broader cooperative efforts. An example is the OECD's current project regarding base erosion and profit shifting or "BEPS" (see OECD 2013a). Thirty-nine countries plus the European Union recently endorsed the proposition that BEPS should be cooperatively addressed, such as through multilateral adoption of forthcoming OECD recommendations (see OECD 2013b).

Given countries' diverse motivations and the possible benefits from being a holdout, cooperative efforts such as those with regard to FATCA and BEPS face serious obstacles. This does not, however, doom out of hand the prospects for widespread positive payoffs from such efforts. Nor does it counsel against trying to arrange broad multilateral cooperation. Even if these efforts are highly successful, however, the scope of multilateral tax cooperation is likely to remain significantly limited. Moreover, no thoughtful or useful analysis of its potential can largely ignore (as did the international tax policy literature for many decades) the question of *how*, in a particular case, one is to bridge the gap between global and national welfare.

* * * * *

In sum, the international tax policy literature took a significant wrong turn by giving so much focus to global welfare considerations in general, and to the alphabet soup of CEN, CIN, and CON in particular. While global welfare considerations may be important when multilateral cooperation is sufficiently feasible, in the main countries must and will make international tax policy choices in a largely unilateral setting—at least, leaving aside very specific constraints such as those raised by particular treaties that they have signed. It is vital, therefore, to address the main determinants of their unilateral self-interest, which is the topic of chapter 5.

Endnotes

1. Global consumption efficiency is not directly implicated by the decision to impose an income tax, given that the tax base is production, rather than consumption. Obviously, however, in practice a given set of income tax rules can undermine consumption efficiency. Suppose, for

example, that the U.S. individual income tax offered a special deduction for owning or renting a U.S.-made, rather than a foreign-made, car.

2. Two considerations make the second-best argument for trade distortions that fortuitously offset other distortions all the easier to ignore. First, there may be no reason to expect that the tariffs or export subsidies that have the strongest domestic political support will be well-selected from this standpoint. Second, "[i]n such cases, it is generally better to eliminate the distortion than to counteract it with trade policy because trade intervention introduces new distortions even if it reduces others" (Slemrod 1995, 473), and hence has been compared to "acupuncture with a fork: no matter how carefully you insert one prong, the other is likely to do damage" (Deardorff and Stern 1987, 39).

3. Tax competition for individual residents can be affirmatively desirable, whether or not the same conclusion holds as to mobile capital. For example, in the Tiebout (1956) model of competition for residents by local governments within a given region, mobility gives local governments incentives to offer diverse and appealing tax-benefit packages (causing them to act like businesses in an efficient market that need to please customers).

4. On how to design a progressive consumption tax with graduated marginal rates, see, e.g., Bradford 2004; Weisbach 2003; Carroll and Viard 2012. On its capacity to achieve progressivity comparable to that of an income tax with graduated rates, see Shaviro 2004.

5. There may, for example, be inefficient diversion of trade away from parties that are outside of the limited free trade web.

6. An earlier article by Michael Devereux (1990) anticipated some of the analysis in Desai-Hines (2003), but was unpublished.

7. For lucid discussions of the problems with CON that overlap with my own critique, see Kane 2006 and Kane 2009.

8. Desai and Hines (2003, 494–495) state this more generally, as a requirement (for satisfying CON) that, if tax rates differ between investors, they do so in fixed proportions no matter where anyone invests.

9. This argument is very similar to that which I discussed above rebutting the claim that adherence to CIN is necessary on competitiveness grounds.

5   The Unilateral National Welfare Perspective

WITH GLOBAL WELFARE properly consigned (for the most part) to the background, we can now more productively turn to the questions of whether, to what extent, and if so how, countries should tax cross-border income from the standpoint of their own unilateral national self-interest. The discussion proceeds as follows. First, I review the traditional battle-of-the-acronyms literature, and show why it fails to offer adequate guidance. Next, I draw on two literatures that offer more useful analytical tools. One is the international trade literature, which shows how countries with the requisite market power can benefit from levying "optimal tariffs" on particular items. The other is the optimal commodity tax literature, which addresses efficient tax rate setting for different consumer goods, and finds that varying rather than uniform rates may be optimal. I then discuss how these tools may apply to source-based and residence-based income taxation, given the treatment of corporations as separate taxpayers.

In the traditional international tax policy literature, it is invariably assumed that the statutory tax rate on FSI should either be zero or the same as the tax rate on domestic source income—but nothing in between—depending on which neutrality argument one favors. However, while the concept of neutrality often plays an important role in tax policy analysis—especially when there is just one margin to consider, rather than several—the optimal tariff and optimal commodity tax literatures help to show that a neutrality-based approach is inappropriate here. Rather, from a unilateral national welfare standpoint, the optimal average and marginal tax rates on FSI—at least for a country that, like the United States, retains some market power with respect to corporate residence—is likely to lie somewhere between zero and the full domestic rate.

Regarding how best to tax FSI, this chapter will suggest that the concept of neutrality has a larger (though still incomplete) role to play there than it does with respect to setting the rate. If we think of FSI as a distinct tax base on which imposing a given level of tax burden—neither too low nor too high—is unilaterally optimal, the classic tax reform idea of lowering the rate and broadening the base has a clear implication. It suggests that both deferral and foreign tax credits be eliminated, and that the tax rate for FSI be set in light of the consequent base broadening. This conclusion reflects that, as discussed in chapter 3, deferral has no good efficiency rationale, foreign taxes are just an expense like any other from a unilateral national welfare standpoint, and eliminating just one of these two rules would worsen the distortions caused by the other. For foreign taxes, however, the analysis is more complicated, given that their being very low can serve as a "tag" that tends to be associated with profit shifting that is at least potentially undesirable from a unilateral national welfare standpoint. While the optimal approach to foreign taxes therefore cannot be determined in the abstract, focusing directly on the set of effective MRRs that result from any particular regime can help enormously in rule design.

A. The Battle of the National Welfare Acronyms

In chapter 4, we saw that, even if one ignored the implausibility of basing national-level policy choices on global welfare considerations, the contest between single-bullet global welfare norms would be flawed because it misconceives how one should analyze efficiency when there are distortions at multiple margins. Eliminating one set of distortions is likely to be inferior to mitigating several or all. This point remains relevant when we turn to the traditional national welfare debate's battle of the acronyms.

This debate features just two welfare norms. The first, national neutrality or NN, was introduced by Peggy Musgrave in her 1960s work. The second, national ownership neutrality or NON, was introduced by Mihir Desai and James R. Hines in conjunction with their work describing CON. As we will see, the two norms differ not just with regard to which margins one should address, but also in how they define neutrality. NON uses the concept of neutrality in a fundamentally different way than the rest of the international tax policy literature (not to mention several decades of voluminous literature discussing fundamental tax reform). While there is nothing inherently wrong with this—both usages of neutrality are semantically defensible, even if one disagrees with Humpty Dumpty's contention (in *Alice Through the Looking Glass*) that one can use words however one likes—neither proves satisfying, in the end, as a guide to good international tax policy.

1. National Neutrality

Under NN, as first set forth by Peggy Musgrave (in Richman 1963), residents would be taxed on all of their worldwide income at the full domestic rate, and foreign taxes would merely be deductible, like all other business expenses, rather than being creditable. The result, of course, would be double taxation as it typically is defined in the international tax policy literature. But whether one adopts this terminology or not (given that foreign taxes are being deducted), and whether one cares about double taxation as such or not, Musgrave clearly was correct that this would significantly discourage cross-border economic activity.

Again, suppose that both Assyria and Babylonia have income taxes with a 40 percent rate, applying on both a residence and a source basis. A taxpayer from either country would get to keep $60 out of every $100 earned at home. However, if an Assyrian earned $100 in Babylonia (or vice versa), the $60 that remained after paying the source tax would be further reduced to $36, by the residence tax. Thus, cross-border activity would be taxed at an aggregate 64 percent rate, as compared to the 40 percent rate on activity in one country only.

Globally suboptimal though this end result may be, NN's underlying logic from each country's unilateral standpoint is clear. The approach that it endorses has two separate elements: mere deductibility for foreign taxes, and applying the same tax rate to residents' FSI as to their domestic source income. Each of these two elements has a clear rationale. For foreign taxes, the point is that they are purely a cost from the domestic standpoint, because foreign individuals end up with the revenues. Thus, when Assyrians earn $100 in Babylonia and pay $40 of tax, the end result is that Assyrians end up with $60, no less than if they had earned this net amount (pre-tax) at home.

The rationale for applying the same tax rate to residents' FSI as to their domestic source income is likewise clear. Suppose we take Assyria's source-based tax as given—although, as I discuss later in this chapter, it is a closely related part of the same puzzle. Given that *someone* in Assyria will presumably get the money whenever tax is paid into the national treasury, imposing the source-based tax creates an incentive problem with respect to prospective taxpayers (both Assyrian and Babylonian), who will regard it purely as a cost to themselves, without regard to the Treasury's gain. One way to address this incentive problem is to make the tax unavoidable via locational choice, by imposing it at the same rate no matter where one earns income. The tax would then cease to discourage investing in Assyria, relative to investing anywhere else.

If Assyria could apply the 40 percent tax to everyone in the world, no matter where they lived or invested, the incentive problem resulting from the source-based character of the tax would indeed be wholly eliminated (reflecting, of course, that it would no longer be a source-based tax). However, this option is unavailable with respect to foreigners, such as Babylonians, whom Assyria cannot charge any tax unless they actually invest in Assyria.[1] Since the same-rate worldwide option *is* available with respect to Assyrians who invest abroad, however, NN supports thus applying it.[2]

So far as it goes, the logic behind NN is compelling. Indeed, even the fact that it discourages cross-border activity does not rebut its unilateral optimality. To be sure, by following NN, Assyria would adversely affect Babylonia, relative to the case where Assyria just levied a source-based tax. Likewise, Babylonia's following NN would adversely affect Assyria. Both countries might therefore gain from reciprocal forbearance. But if Assyria is setting its tax policy unilaterally, then Babylonia's choices are not a relevant policy variable, and NN already takes full account of the benefit to Assyrians from earning profits in Babylonia. That is, it encourages them to do so whenever the return, after paying local taxes, is higher than that available at home.[3]

Nonetheless, an initial ground for caution about NN's seemingly self-evident correctness arises from the fact that we do not generally observe attempts around the world to implement it. As a general matter, countries frequently adopt unilaterally self-interested policies, without regard to the costs imposed on others. An example is tax competition, whether exemplified in the income tax setting or by countries' preferring a zero carbon tax to a positive rate. Where, then, is the evidence that countries feel the pull of NN, and decline to follow it only due to concern about retaliation?

In trying to explain the apparent lack of appeal of domestic political appeal of NN-based policies, widespread intuitive dislike for "double taxation" might count for something. Interest group politics and the gut appeal of helping "our" companies to compete successfully abroad against their foreign rivals might matter as well. Even so, however, there is a strong "dog that didn't bark" quality to the lack of evidence that countries are inclined to "cheat" as much as they can get away with, by imposing full double taxation on outbound investment, as one might expect if NN's account of unilateral self-interest were correct.

Several years ago, when I was still (as I now see it) unduly influenced by the traditional international tax policy framework, I attempted to discern evidence of the subtle cheating that one might expect if countries liked NN but feared retaliation. Thus, I noted that U.S. international tax law, in some settings, applies asymmetric source rules that tend to over-measure domestic source income relative to FSI, potentially triggering double taxation. For example, dividends "paid by a U.S. company remain U.S. source even if the company has extensive foreign operations, but those paid by a foreign company are subject to pro rata classification as U.S. source" if the company has sufficiently U.S.-centered operations (Shaviro 2007, 169). Likewise, the U.S. rules for sourcing interest deductions could be viewed as manifesting much greater eagerness to treat a multinational group's U.S. borrowing as reducing foreign source income, than its foreign subsidiaries' borrowing as reducing U.S. source income. Nonetheless, it is plausible that there would be much more to the story if NN had as much domestic unilateral appeal as the traditional analysis posits.

What, then, could the case for NN be missing? An initial clue arises from its being analytically very similar to CEN, apart from its placing foreign taxes outside the charmed circle. By reason of this overlap, the issues that triggered the decline of CEN have left NN bleeding as well. In particular, the fact that a country can only apply worldwide taxation to its own residents undermines NN for the same reasons that it undermines the prospects for unilateral advancement of CEN. Clientele effects and corporate residence electivity can greatly reduce or even eliminate the benefits that a country might have hoped to generate by adopting international tax rules based on NN.

Thus, suppose the United States follows NN, by making all FSI currently includable and foreign taxes merely deductible, in the hope that this will boost domestic investment and tax revenues. The new policy would eliminate any U.S. tax benefit to U.S. taxpayers both from holding foreign rather than U.S. assets, and from treating any of their income as FSI. However, one likely consequence would be portfolio swaps, with foreign assets migrating from U.S. to foreign investors while U.S. assets moved the other way (i.e., the clientele effect). A second would be inducing U.S. and foreign individuals alike to use foreign companies, rather than U.S. companies, when investing abroad. If, by reason of these effects, there ended up being no net effect either on U.S. investment or on U.S. tax revenues, then none of the intended national welfare benefit from following NN would have been realized. Meanwhile, there would also have been deadweight loss to U.S. individuals, such as from instances in which they accepted lower pre-tax profitability, from the use of foreign rather than U.S. companies, in order to avoid the domestic tax hit.

Unfortunately, as an empirical matter it is hard to tell what steady-state net effects on domestic investment and tax revenues an NN-based system would have, relative to such alternatives as U.S. present law, a pure worldwide system, or a territorial system. Researchers have, however, devoted significant resources to studying a question that has some bearing on that of net investment effects. Specifically, a number of studies have examined the question of how foreign direct investment (FDI) by resident multinationals relates to the amounts that they invest at home. In particular, is resident companies' FDI a substitute for home country investments that they would otherwise make, or is it unrelated or even a complement to additional home country investment?

To illustrate, suppose we observe that a given U.S. multinational invests $100 million abroad. Substitution holds if this money would otherwise have been invested at home, with all else remaining the same. This might reflect the company's having exactly that amount to invest in one place or another (and no further access to world capital markets), or its needing to build a single factory for its global production activities that would be located either at home. or abroad. By contrast, unrelatedness holds if the firm scours the world looking for investment opportunities, each operating independently of all the rest, and secures financing on global capital markets for all of the good ones that it finds. Finally, complementarity holds if the company's overseas investments create new opportunities to engage in profitable U.S. operations. Thus, suppose that, by opening a cheap motorcycle assembly plant in Bangalore, a U.S. multinational becomes newly able to profit from engine manufacture at home.

A finding that net substitution occurs when U.S. companies engage in FDI would appear to be necessary, although not sufficient, to support the view that following NN would increase net U.S. investment. As to the "necessary" point, it is hard to see how overall U.S. investment could decline, by reason of outbound investment by U.S. companies, if the companies themselves do not invest any less overall at home by reason of their investing abroad. However, even if one definitively proved company-level substitution, this would not establish that NN was increasing overall U.S. investment. Thus, suppose that, as U.S. companies shifted their domestic operations abroad, thereby increasing the availability here of productive resources (such as factory sites and capable workers), foreign companies responded by moving in to fill all of the gaps. Indeed, some response of this sort is plausible, whether or not it reaches the 100 percent replacement level, given that U.S. productive resources (such as suitable production sites and workers) are finite, and hence subject to congestion.

What does the empirical literature suggest? In general, firm-level studies range from finding outright complementarity of outbound and domestic activity to finding very small downward domestic effects from increased FDI.[4] These mixed results are generally consistent with contemporaneous work finding that the firm-level effect should depend on the motive for investing abroad and on underlying firm characteristics. For example, Hejazi and Pauly (2003, 284) suggest that outbound investment motivated by seeking access to foreign markets should be expected to increase complementary domestic activity, whereas seeking cheaper productive inputs could go either way, as it implies substitution but also may open new opportunities for globally integrated production.[5] Likewise, Harrison and McMillan (2008) find complementarity among firms with vertically integrated global production networks and thus affiliates in different countries performing distinctive tasks, but substitution among firms that do the same thing in parallel in multiple places.[6] Simpson (2008) finds a similar divide between companies in high-skill and low-skill industries.

While the firm-level evidence is thus mixed, several studies that look at economy-wide or industry-level data support complementarity.[7] Overall, Desai (2009b, 68) has reasonable grounds for arguing that "it is hard to find systematic evidence of significant negative effects of the overseas activities of firms on domestic investment or employment," and perhaps even that "the emerging consensus is that the average effect is positive, although it may mask some underlying heterogeneity." This in turn surely weakens the case for treating an NN-based international tax policy as unilaterally optimal.

One should not, however, regard the case for NN as turning solely on the hope that it would increase net U.S. investment. Even with no net effect at that margin, following NN would still prevent profit shifting by U.S. companies from having any effect on their domestic tax liability. This would eliminate the companies' incentive to waste resources on profit shifting, although it would encourage using foreign rather than U.S. multinationals even to invest at home. Following NN also would avoid creating incentives for U.S. firms to integrate domestic with foreign production in circumstances where this would fail to pay off before-tax but would create profit-shifting opportunities.

Where does this leave us overall with regard to NN? Recall that it supports two distinct conclusions: that foreign taxes should merely be deductible, and that FSI should be taxed at the full domestic rate. The former conclusion is wholly unaffected by evidence rebutting the view that FDI is a substitute for domestic investment. Such evidence has no bearing on the point that foreign tax revenues do not benefit U.S. individuals, and that the United States is better off, all else equal, if companies owned by U.S. individuals are willing to spend up to a dollar in order to avoid a dollar of foreign tax liability—for example, by investing in low-tax rather than high-tax countries.

By contrast, NN's second claim, which is that resident companies' FSI should be taxed at the same rate as their domestic source income, is indeed significantly weakened by evidence against substitution. In a substitution scenario, the case for making the two tax rates the same is straightforward, as in the example where an Assyrian firm's decision whether to invest in Assyria or Babylonia depends on which offers a higher after-tax return. However, if companies' domestic and foreign investments are instead determined entirely separately, this scenario does not arise. Instead, one needs a more complicated analysis (discussed later in this chapter), in which the key efficiency question is what pair of rates for the two types of income would minimize the overall deadweight loss associated with raising a given amount of revenue, taking into account that decisions at the two distinct margins (i.e., investing at home and abroad) may differ in their tax elasticity.

Even if substitution had no application whatsoever with respect to where companies invest, it clearly would (and does) apply with respect to where companies report their global income as arising. Not only may a variety of tax return reporting positions be at least minimally legally defensible—for example, concerning a given claimed transfer price—but careful planning may end up yielding a pro-taxpayer legal answer as to source based on considerations that have little or no economic significance. Only by taxing all of a U.S. company's global income at the same rate can the United States eliminate the company's incentive to devote resources to providing legal support for the FSI characterization.

For these reasons, even very powerful evidence against substitution with respect to where U.S. companies invest would fall far short of establishing that the optimal U.S. tax rate on U.S. companies' FSI is zero. Desai and Hines, along with a coauthor, assert only that nonsubstitution makes it "more attractive [than it would otherwise be] to exempt active foreign business income from domestic taxation" (Desai, Foley, and Hines 2009).

Despite the difficulty of determining what U.S. tax rate on U.S. companies' FSI would be optimal, there is widespread consensus that NN would set it too high. This conclusion is evidently shared by proponents both of territoriality, who would impose a zero tax rate on FSI; and of a worldwide system with foreign tax credits, who can count on the credits to reduce the outbound effective rate. As we will see later in this chapter, the core problem with NN is that its notion of neutrality falls short of being unilaterally optimal. Even given substitution between domestic and foreign investment or reported income—causing NN's imposition of tax neutrality as between them, for U.S. taxpayers, to have desirable properties—there are reasons why the optimal tax rates on the two types of income might nonetheless, in the end, be different.

Before addressing these optimal tax rate issues, however, there is one further entry to consider in the battle-of-the-acronyms competition. Desai and Hines (2003), in response to the weakening of NN by the evidence against viewing home investment and FDI as substitutes, argue for the relevance and importance of what they call national ownership neutrality (NON).

2. National Ownership Neutrality

NON is almost the last entry in the international tax policy literature's battle of the acronyms. (Later in this chapter, I discuss global portfolio neutrality or GPN, which pertains to taxing passive or portfolio income.) Desai and Hines (2003, 496) tell us that NON supports exempting from domestic tax the foreign earnings of domestic companies, wholly without regard to what other countries do.

An initial problem in understanding NON is its use of the term "neutrality" to describe a scenario in which resident companies simultaneously face a positive tax rate on their domestic source income and a zero tax rate on their FSI. Whether good or bad from a unilateral national welfare standpoint, how can this possibly be described as "neutral"? The answer is that Desai and Hines give the term "neutrality" a fundamentally different meaning than it has under any of the other global and national welfare norms in the international tax policy literature.

To show the difference, let's start with how neutrality is deployed elsewhere. For example, recall NN, which promotes neutrality (from a U.S. national welfare standpoint) as to U.S. companies' investment and income-reporting choices, by *equally* discouraging them from earning both U.S. source and foreign source income.[8] Thus, suppose the United States had a 30 percent corporate tax rate that applied to all income earned by U.S. companies, whether at home or abroad. Every time such a company that was wholly owned by U.S. individuals earned $100 (net of any foreign taxes), whether this was domestic source income or FSI, Americans as a whole would be $100 richer, but the company's owners would be only $70 richer. Since they would not value the $30 that they paid in U.S. taxes, their incentive to earn income either at home or abroad would be, in a sense, too weak, but at least it would be equally diminished no matter where they earned the income. With equal diminution of incentives for all of the choices (such as foreign versus domestic investment), whatever is most profitable before considering U.S. taxes will remain so afterward. The tax system remains concededly non-neutral, however, with regard to earning taxable income of any kind as opposed to, say, enjoying leisure.

In the global welfare debate, CEN, CIN and CON all define neutrality similarly, apart from their counting all taxes, rather than just domestic taxes. Thus, CEN is the same as NN except for its treating foreign and domestic taxes as relevantly the same. CIN requires equalizing the global tax discouragement of saving with regard to a particular investment, so that taxes will not alter who ends up funding it. CON requires that global taxes, even if they generally discourage profitable economic activity, be uniform in such a way as to avoid reducing global output by altering ownership patterns.

This way of defining neutrality also is commonplace outside of the international tax realm. Thus, consider the standard case for income tax base broadening, premised on the idea that one should tax all income equally, thereby equalizing across taxpayer choices the same level of discouragement of work and saving. The same holds for the prominent argument that consumption taxes are more efficient than income taxes, because only the former are neutral as between present and future consumption (see, e.g., Bankman and Weisbach 2006, 1418–1419). Efficiency-promoting neutrality is defined as equal tax discouragement of all consumption, even though not discouraging it at all (such as through the use of a lump sum tax) would be more efficient still.

NON uses the term "neutrality" entirely differently. What exemption of foreign source income from home country taxation creates is *no tax discouragement* of earning FSI. An overseas activity that would have earned the company $100 before considering the home country tax will also earn $100 after tax, and the company's incentive to earn FSI will therefore be socially optimal. This is "neutrality" in the same sense that a lump sum tax, such as a uniform head tax, is neutral with respect to choices such as how much income one earns.

Desai and Hines (2003, 496) rationalize the approach as follows:

The reason [for exemption] is that additional outbound foreign investment does not reduce domestic tax revenue, since any reduction in home-country investment by domestic firms is offset by greater investment by foreign firms. With unchanging domestic tax revenue, home-country welfare increases in the after-tax profitability of domestic companies, which is maximized if foreign profits are exempt from taxation.... Hence it is possible to understand why so many countries exempt foreign income from taxation.

The main assumptions here are as follows. Not only does "additional outbound foreign investment...not reduce domestic tax revenue," but the mechanism for this outcome is that "any reduction in home-country investment by domestic firms is offset by greater investment by foreign firms." In effect, under this assumption, global investment is simply a giant game of musical chairs, in which not only is the "seating" around the world fixed, but so is the number of seats per player. Thus, the only open question is who will sit where.[9]

Under the assumed mechanism, Desai and Hines show that taxing U.S. companies' FSI would create deadweight loss that could be eliminated by having an exemption system, while possibly failing to raise any more revenue than exemption. Obviously, increasing deadweight loss without raising any more revenue is never desirable from an efficiency standpoint. If we change the operating assumption, however, the conclusion becomes considerably more tenuous.

To further explain their argument (more fully elaborated in Hines 2009, 278), suppose that a U.S. company, owned entirely by U.S. individuals, is choosing between a U.S. asset that would earn $100 before U.S. tax and $70 afterward, and a foreign asset. Given the assumed musical chairs scenario, a decision by the U.S. company to hold the foreign asset would simply mean that a foreign company held the U.S. asset. Suppose further that, under the source-based U.S. tax, this foreign company would pay the same $30 of tax on the U.S. asset that the U.S. firm would have owed. This means that, prior to considering the U.S. company's return on the foreign asset, U.S. individuals are out $70 by reason of the shift (i.e., the after-tax return that they would have retained if they owned the U.S. investment).

Now let's consider the foreign asset. If it nets more than $70 after foreign taxes, U.S. individuals as a whole come out ahead. However, while the effect on U.S. welfare depends on the foreign asset's *before*-U.S. tax economic return (since any U.S. taxes collected are merely an intra-U.S. transfer), the U.S. company is presumably going to base its decision on the *after*-U.S. tax return. Thus, unless FSI is exempted from U.S. tax, the company will have distorted incentives, and will wrongly (from a U.S. national welfare standpoint) choose the U.S. asset in cases where the U.S. tax on FSI drives the foreign return below $70. In such cases, the U.S. tax on FSI not only creates deadweight loss, but fails to raise any revenue.

This, of course, is hardly unusual in the income tax setting. Thus, suppose the parents of young children are willing to pay a teenager up to $10 for an hour of babysitting, and that the teenager (who will not otherwise work) is willing to do it so long as he or she will end up clearing close to $10 after tax. A tax on babysitting income will mean, in some cases, that the transaction does not take place—leading in those cases to deadweight loss in exchange for zero tax revenue. We might nonetheless conclude that babysitting income, like other income, should be taxed—even if some prospective babysitters will respond by not working at all—given that this will not be the result in *all* cases, and thus that the tax on babysitters (like the income tax generally) will raise some revenue in addition to generating some deadweight loss. Thus, if one has a fixed overall revenue target, one can use the revenue that is raised here to finance reducing deadweight loss that would otherwise be incurred in the course of using other tax instruments.

A similar point applies to U.S. companies' foreign source income, even assuming the full musical chairs scenario. After all, in some cases U.S. firms may earn enough from their foreign assets to hold them despite the U.S. tax on FSI. Thus, in the above example, even if the U.S. rules taxed FSI at the same 30 percent rate that it hypothetically was applying to U.S. source income (and without offering foreign tax credits), the U.S. firm would still prefer any foreign asset on which it could earn at least $100 before U.S. tax. Accordingly, even in the pure musical chairs scenario, it is plausible that the tax on FSI would not just increase deadweight loss, but also raise revenue. Needless to say, we generally expect deadweight loss to accompany revenue-raising under an income tax. The question of interest, from an efficiency standpoint, is *how much* deadweight loss one is creating per dollar of revenue raised—an issue that NON does not and cannot address.

Now let's turn to the scenario in which U.S. companies can access world capital markets to finance all good projects, causing their domestic and foreign investments to be unrelated. Once again, taxing FSI, and thereby discouraging investment abroad by U.S. companies, may lead to U.S. deadweight loss, such as in cases where U.S. individuals respond by investing through foreign entities that earn less before tax. However, taxing FSI will also increase overall U.S. tax revenues (treating the source-based U.S. tax as fixed) in cases where U.S. investors go forward despite the tax.[10] Once again, therefore, we fail to observe the straightforward, unambiguous case of higher deadweight loss without revenue gain.

Finally, consider the fact that exempting FSI may reduce U.S revenues from the source-based tax, even if domestic investment remains the same, because it gives U.S. companies an incentive to characterize income as foreign source—and indeed, to be willing to incur deadweight loss in the cause of supporting this characterization. Hines (2009, 278–279) concedes that his analysis of NON omits this consideration, but nonetheless argues that the problem is "best addressed directly with enforcement of existing and potentially new rules rather than by modifying the taxation of foreign income to accommodate income shifting behavior on the part of taxpayers."

This is a questionable stance, given that it is not as if one can get the source rules "right" with just a bit more effort, when the source concept itself so often lacks clear meaning. So long as U.S. taxpayers have any discretion to reduce U.S. source-based tax revenues by characterizing ambiguous income as foreign source (whether through mere reporting discretion or actual tax planning on the ground), a positive tax rate on FSI reduces their incentive to do this, and in particular instances may not only raise overall U.S. revenue but reduce wasteful behavior. To be sure, taxing FSI also creates instances of deadweight loss that Hines's preferred direct approach might avoid. For example, it only affects profit shifting by *U.S.* companies, as distinct from foreign ones, and thus distorts ownership incentives. This, however, means that we are in the realm of tradeoffs, and should compare the overall relationship between deadweight loss and revenue under various alternative approaches might involve. It does not support treating NON as a single-bullet national welfare optimum.

Once we understand that there are tradeoffs and multiple margins, it becomes clear that NON—just like NN and all the global welfare norms—does not offer an appropriate benchmark for analyzing international tax policy. An approach that treats eliminating deadweight loss at one particular margin as a national welfare optimum cannot be viewed as persuasive. What about all the other margins? Desai and Hines have made a valuable contribution to the literature by pointing out that inducing deadweight loss with respect to ownership matters in a national welfare analysis, and that the optimal domestic tax rate on FSI is likely to be lower—perhaps even a lot lower—in light of clientele effects and corporate residence electivity than it would have been if NN's underlying assumptions were more accurate. But in the end a proper efficiency analysis must rest on comparing the relationship between revenue raised and deadweight loss under alternative sets of tax regimes.

For example, it is unclear why one should start by taking the U.S. source-based tax as given, when it creates huge distortions such as discouraging inbound investment, and then simply ask what tax rate on FSI would lead to zero deadweight loss at the ownership margin. The source-based corporate income tax and the corporate income tax on FSI are closely linked with each other logically, practically, and politically. Thus, a better approach than urging adherence to NON would recognize the practical importance of tradeoffs between getting revenue from the source-based tax and from the tax on FSI.

Suppose we started with source-based taxation at some positive rate—say, 15 percent, 25 percent, or 35 percent—along with a 0 percent tax rate on FSI under exemption. A revenue-neutral change that lowered the source-based tax rate—thus likely increasing domestic investment—while raising the latter rate would have an excellent chance of reducing overall deadweight loss. Recall that, as discussed in chapter 4, the deadweight loss from a distortionary tax generally rises much faster than the tax rate (for example, quadrupling if the tax rate doubles). Thus, reducing a significant positive rate on domestic source income, while increasing a 0 percent rate on FSI, has a good chance of reducing overall deadweight loss, even if the former rate ought to be significantly the higher of the two. Thus, instead of perpetuating the battle of the acronyms, we ought to shift to an approach that sheds light on how one might think about the optimal rate relationship between the two, given overall revenue goals, and taking into account any relevant distributional objectives in addition to efficiency.

3. National Welfare-Based Arguments for Exempting Foreign Source Income That Are Based on "Competitiveness"

Before turning to a mode of national welfare analysis that is more promising than the battle of the acronyms, it is worth briefly discussing the argument from national self-interest that is most prominent politically, albeit not academically, in support of territoriality. This is the claim that the United States should not tax its firms' foreign source income because this would handicap them in competing abroad with rival firms from other countries. Ostensibly, U.S. national welfare is advanced if our firms win the battles over access to particular foreign markets.

As Michael Knoll (2010, 773) notes, competitiveness "lacks a clear and specific meaning," and "can mean different things to different people and at different times," helping to explain economists' frequent reluctance to use it even though "the public dialogue about taxes is filled with talk about competitiveness" (772). For example, it can readily be interpreted to include the concern about ownership distortions that underlies CON and NON, and that clearly is relevant to an overall efficiency analysis even once one rejects reasoning by acronym. However, the common public sense of competitiveness may have more to do with rooting for the success of particular U.S. firms and industries as against their foreign rivals (773–774).

An elementary point in response to this concern is that U.S. individuals, not firms, are the proper focus of national welfare-based concern. Political actors may be prone to believe, as the old adage put it in happier times for the domestic auto industry, that "what's good for General Motors is good for the country," but one needs a specific link to the welfare of U.S. individuals for this rooting interest to matter as more than an entertainment item. With home equity bias, however, it is plausible that U.S. individuals would be the main winners if U.S. firms did especially well. So it is worth considering the claim that higher tax burdens on U.S. firms than foreign firms, by reason of U.S. taxation of FSI, would tend to reduce U.S. national welfare via its effect on the wealth of U.S. individuals who are shareholders in U.S. companies.

In evaluating this claim, it is important to distinguish between two types of return that U.S. firms might earn from their overseas investments. The first are normal returns, or those that merely replicate the general available rate of return to capital in the world economy (adjusted for risk). The second are extra-normal returns, or rents, reflecting special opportunities to earn pure profits—for example, by reason of valuable intellectual property (such as the Coca Cola trademark or the iPhone design) that the owner has unique opportunities to exploit.

In the case of normal returns, U.S. shareholders would not directly lose anything if, by reason of the U.S. tax burden on FSI, foreign rather than U.S. companies became the ones to invest overseas. The U.S. shareholders would merely be losing the normal returns on these investments that they could get in any event by making other investments instead. It is true that discouraging the U.S. companies from investing abroad could reduce desirable economic diversification, at either the shareholder or the entity level. However, such diversification can be achieved by other means, such as holding stock in foreign companies, or any financial instruments that, in effect, "short" the U.S. economy or currency relative to those of other countries. Exempting U.S. companies' FSI, if not otherwise desirable, would be an odd and ill-targeted way of addressing under-diversification.

For extra-normal foreign returns, the issue is different. U.S. individuals really would be poorer if, by reason of U.S. taxation of FSI, foreign firms owned by foreign individuals ended up being the ones to earn these returns. Nonetheless, it is difficult to credit the claim that this concern supports exempting FSI. For one thing, if U.S. and foreign firms are actually competing in foreign markets to be the ones to earn extra-normal returns, one might expect this competition to drive the returns down to merely normal levels. For another, if U.S. firms actually have the opportunity to earn rents overseas, the prospect of having to pay U.S. tax ought not to deter them. Pure profits are worth claiming even when reduced by a tax bill, and for this reason it is a standard economic truism that taxing them is efficient (Shaviro 2009a, 22).

A second argument would be that it is good for U.S. workers if U.S. firms do well abroad. This might, for example, be due to complementarity between U.S. and low-cost foreign production. To the extent that such complementarity exists, however, it is unclear why U.S. incorporation, the defining legal element for a resident U.S. company, would be needed to motivate taking advantage of it. And even if the recent complementarity research throws cold water on the view that U.S. firms' overseas "runaway factories" are reducing domestic investment and employment, there is little evidence supporting the opposite view that a well-designed domestic jobs or wages program would prioritize treating FSI favorably.

B. Tariffs and Inbound Capital

For the unilateral national welfare analysis of international tax policy, as for that which is global welfare based, it is useful to start by looking at the international trade literature, which both involves a simpler set of problems and has been thoroughly developed. As we will see, this literature helps to show that the optimal tax rate at a particular margin varies with the taxing authority's degree of market power, and thus is not necessarily either zero or the same across all commodities. This literature applies most directly to source-based taxation, but also has potential implications for worldwide residence-based corporate taxation.

1. Standard Tariffs and Optimal Tariffs

As we saw in chapter 4, the international trade literature holds that tariffs, in the standard case, reduce both global and unilateral national welfare. Thus, only domestic political choice problems relating to the power of interest groups create a need for free trade agreements in which countries reciprocally agree to do what it is in their unilateral self-interest to do any way.

The resulting consistency in the standard case between national and global welfare, while initially it might seem extraordinarily fortuitous, in fact merely reflects Adam Smith's notion of the invisible hand, in which an efficient optimum results from all actors' separate pursuit of their own interests. In a competitive market, individual sellers who tried to extract wealth from buyers by demanding more than the market price, as well as buyers who tried to pay less, would find themselves unable to accomplish this. Thus, all they can effectively do is consult their own self-interest regarding whether (and how much) to buy or sell at the market price. The result is efficient, because all transactions are consummated in which the buyer is willing to pay more than the minimum that the seller would accept.

This convenient overlap between the individual pursuit of self-interest and overall efficiency breaks down if either buyers or sellers have market power and thus can influence the price. On the seller side, a monopolist or a sellers' cartel can profit from restricting output and thereby raising the prevailing price. Likewise, a monopsonist or a buyers' cartel can benefit from restricting expressed demand so that the price falls. In either case, there is deadweight loss, from the nonoccurrence of mutually beneficial transactions that would have been consummated at a "true" market price. Nonetheless, the side with market power to affect the price has no reason to recede if transaction costs impede simply compensating it for the wealth transfer that it has the power to extract by changing the market price.

This analysis applies straightforwardly to import tariffs. To illustrate, suppose that French champagne sells for $30 a bottle, and that the United States is considering charging French producers an import tariff of $5 per bottle—not as a device for inefficiently aiding domestic champagne producers at the expense of domestic consumers, but rather with the aim of transferring money from French individuals to U.S. individuals. This would work as intended if the French firms still charged $30 to their U.S. counterparties, but now only got to keep $25. But if $30 is the world price for champagne, and if the United States is too small a player in the champagne market to affect the world price, the firms will start demanding $30 after tax, or $35 before, and the tariff will actually be borne by U.S. consumers. Hence there is no well-founded U.S. national welfare motivation, under these circumstances, to impose an import tariff on French champagne.

Now, however, suppose that U.S. consumers' demand for French champagne is significant enough as a component of global demand, and sufficiently price sensitive at around the $30 level, for the tariff actually to result in lowering the equilibrium world price for champagne—say, to $28 per bottle ($33 after tax in the United States). If this happens, then the U.S. tariff, by changing the terms of trade for champagne, actually has succeeded in extracting wealth from French individuals, in the amount of $2 per bottle imported under the tariff regime. In this regard, the tariff creates a U.S. national welfare benefit, albeit at the efficiency cost of distorting U.S. consumers' choices (and eliminating the surplus from enjoying any champagne that U.S. consumers would have valued at between $30 and $33).

In sum, if the United States can affect the world price for French champagne, this drives a wedge between the trade policies that would promote, respectively, its unilateral national welfare and global welfare. In theory, one could have the best of both worlds if France sufficiently compensated the United States for not imposing the tariff, potentially leaving both sides better off, given that the accompanying deadweight loss could thereby be eliminated. However, transaction costs may make this unlikely or even impossible (at least, leaving aside the issue of retaliation, such as through a trade war).[11]

Given this possibility, the international trade literature recognizes that countries may benefit from unilaterally imposing what are called optimal tariffs. The optimal level for such a tariff, with respect to a particular commodity, depends in part on how much market power one has to affect the world price. If not for the domestic deadweight loss created by the tariff, the aim would simply be to generate the largest possible transfer from foreign producers (which depends on the impact of the price change, rather than on the tax revenues collected from foreign sellers). This benefit, however, must be netted against the domestic distortionary costs, which can be expected to increase with the tariff level.

For a country that lacks any such market power across the board—sometimes called a "small" country in the trade literature, although it is important to keep in mind that *all* countries may turn out to be small in this sense—the optimal tariff for all items is zero. However, for countries that are "big" in the relevant sense as to particular import commodities, the optimal tariff rate may vary for each such item. Tax neutrality between items—including those that are produced domestically or as to which one lacks the requisite market power—does indeed have value, since adhering to it would reduce the domestic distortionary costs that one must weigh against the available transfers from foreign producers. But the bottom-line optimal tariff result is *not* one of taxing everything the same.

2. Source Taxation in the Absence of Entity-Level Taxes

The optimal tariff literature's implications for international income taxation are of two kinds. First and more generally, when a national government is attempting to exercise taxing authority in the setting of a global marketplace that it cannot cordon off at the geographic border, its degree of market power at particular margins is crucial to what it can hope to accomplish through various tax instruments. Second and more particularly, the tariff analysis is directly applicable to one of the main issues raised by source-based taxation.

Suppose that all income earned through corporations was easy to measure, even from afar, and was taxed directly to the individuals, such as shareholders, who were the ultimate owners. For example, Apple's shareholders and other economic owners (such as option holders), rather than Apple itself, would include its annual profits in their taxable incomes, in proportions based on the true economic split given their financial interests in the company. With worldwide residence-based taxation of individuals, both U.S. and foreign companies' income would be taxable under U.S. law to the extent that it accrued to U.S. individuals who were the ultimate owners. By contrast, foreign owners of interests in U.S. companies would not be taxable under U.S. law by reason of the companies' place of incorporation. Thus, they would not pay U.S. income tax unless U.S. law, in addition to imposing worldwide residence-based taxation of individuals, also imposed a source-based tax on foreign individuals (again, without regard to the use of a corporate entity or to corporate residence).

Under these circumstances, the source-based component of the U.S. income tax—applying just to foreigners, since U.S. individuals would be taxable on all of their worldwide income, no matter where and through what entity (if any) they invested—truly would fall on inbound capital investment, along with any labor income that visiting foreigners earned while in the United States. With respect to capital income, the source-based tax would therefore not merely look like a tariff—it would actually be one, albeit levied on imports of capital, rather than of specific commodities such as champagne, steel, or sugar.

In this scenario, suppose we agree that inbound capital, far from imposing negative externalities, is if anything affirmatively desirable (for example, because it increases U.S. workers' productivity and wages). Then the only plausible reason for imposing a source-based tax on it would be to transfer wealth from foreigners to domestic residents. This, however, may be difficult to accomplish. Suppose further that the taxing country is too small to affect the global rate of return to capital. Then foreigners who hold globally mobile capital, with respect to which they can earn the normal return to capital in multiple places, and who will not get their source-based taxes rebated via home country foreign tax credits, will respond to source-based taxes by investing less, such that they wholly avoid the economic incidence of the tax.

A simple chart (repeated from Shaviro 2009a) may help to depict this scenario. In Figure 5.1, capital is assumed to flow freely around the world in pursuit of the prevailing rate of return, which is 6.5 percent. Thus, in a small open economy such as Country X, all investments that earn at least 6.5 percent, but only those investments, are made. Moreover, since the reach of Country X's tax system is "small" relative to the size of worldwide capital markets, nothing that X does can affect the prevailing rate of return. Local resource owners, who control either their labor or the use of land and natural resources, cannot move out of the country in response to after-tax price changes, but they capture any return to a given investment opportunity that exceeds the required 6.5 percent rate. For simplicity, suppose that only foreigners have capital to invest.

Absent any tax on capital, the amount invested is that shown at B. The entire triangle (to the left axis) above the 6.5 percent line to the left of B represents profits

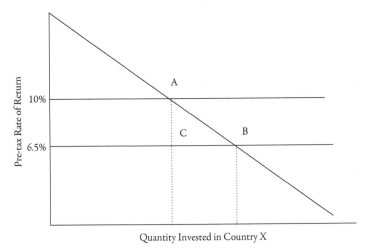

Quantity Invested in Country X

FIGURE 5.1 Effect of capital income tax in a small open economy.

accruing to local resource owners after paying the 6.5 percent rate to those furnishing the capital. Suppose, however, that Country X imposes a 35 percent source-based tax on foreign furnishers of capital. As a result, a 10 percent pre-tax return is now necessary for them to get the 6.5 percent after-tax rate that they can readily procure by investing elsewhere.

The consequence of this tax is that investment declines from the amount shown at B to that at line AC. The incidence of the tax falls entirely on the local resource owners, who now earn only the amount shown by the triangle over the 10 percent line to the left of A. They lose the profits represented by the rectangle (extending to the left axis) between the 6.5 percent and 10 percent lines, due to the higher interest rate that they now need to pay, while the profits represented by the triangle ABC simply go unrealized (representing the deadweight loss of the tax).

The foreign furnishers of the capital, although they are actually sending tax payment checks to the treasury of Country X for 35 percent of their pre-tax profits, bear none of the incidence of the tax. After all, they still earn the same 6.5 percent after tax that would have accrued to them if it did not exist. The assumed perfect supply elasticity of capital, which can freely go wherever a 6.5 percent return is available, is what permits complete shifting of the incidence of the tax to local resource owners, who are assumed to be sitting on a fixed set of differentially profitable investment opportunities.

This is the same analysis as that applying to commodity tariffs where the importing country has no market power. The result in Figure 5.1, where the interest rate earned by furnishers of capital jumps from 6.5 percent to 10 percent by reason of the tax, is just like that in the earlier champagne example, where a $5 tariff increased the price charged by French firms from $30 to $35. Thus, if source-based taxation served no purpose other than trying to burden foreigners—which, as noted above, might be the case if all corporate income was taxed directly to individuals and was easy to measure, even from afar— then any observed positive source-based taxes, other than in a country that was large enough to affect the global return to capital, would surely reflect either (1) domestic political failure; or (2) successful exploitation, by the source country's tax system, of the foreign capital importers' opportunity to earn location-specific extra-normal returns in that country.

As we will see, the other issues raised by source-based taxation in practice—in particular, due to the entity-level corporate tax—prevent the issues from being this simple, and cause the widespread use of source-based taxation to be verging on inevitable. Even if one wants to impose a zero tax rate on truly inbound capital, such capital cannot be separately identified once one has an entity-level corporate income tax that applies based on determinations of corporate residence. However, the question of how market power affects the optimal rate at particular margins remains important, and will turn out to be relevant to evaluating residence-based as well as source-based corporate income taxation.

C. The Marginal Efficiency Cost of Funds (MECF) and Optimal Commodity Tax Literatures

Neutrality's limited purchase in resolving complex and multifaceted international tax issues should come as no surprise. Important tax policy questions that lack simple or straightforward answers—such as those that neutrality can at least purport to provide—are regrettably, but unavoidably, pervasive. Suppose, for example, that one is asking what tax rates should apply to high-income individuals, or how frequently the IRS should audit people's tax returns, or how rigorously one should apply economic substance requirements to tax-motivated transactions. None of these questions can be given a precise answer, or one that would receive consensus expert support. Fortunately, however, a useful general framework that was first offered by the economists Joel Slemrod and Shlomo Yitzhaki (1996) helps to describe how the relevant considerations can be placed in a consistent framework, and what information would be needed (under a given normative approach) to provide definitive answers.

Slemrod and Yitzhaki start by exclusively considering efficiency, although they then address incorporating distributional considerations. Again, the issue here is minimizing deadweight loss, or cases where someone loses and no one gains. Deadweight loss most obviously arises when a tax, by affecting people's incentives, causes them to choose outcomes that they consider suboptimal on a pre-tax basis, and thus to lose utility from more than just paying taxes to the government. Taxpayers' costs also exceed the government's fiscal gain when they devote resources to tax planning and compliance. In addition, the government's net fiscal gain from a given tax is less than the gross revenue that it collects, insofar as it must devote resources to administration, enforcement, and collection (178–182).

The greater taxpayers' overall cost relative to the government's net fiscal gain, the more social waste is being incurred per dollar of revenue collected. To focus on this issue, Slemrod and Yitzhaki describe a measure that they call the marginal efficiency cost of funds (MECF)—that is, the ratio of waste to net fiscal gain that would result from using a given tax instrument (a term that can be defined as broadly as one likes) to increase tax revenues by a given dollar amount (185).

To illustrate, suppose the government imposed a uniform head tax, which has no effect on taxpayers' incentives given that they will pay the same amount no matter what. In addition, suppose not only that everyone had enough cash to pay it, but that paying and collecting it cost zero. Under these fanciful assumptions, a head tax of, say, $10,000 would cost each taxpayer just $10,000 and not a penny more, and would net the government the full amount paid. Thus, its MECF would be $10,000 divided by $10,000 (in each case, multiplied by the number of taxpayers), or exactly 1.0.

The lower the MECF, the better, at least from an efficiency standpoint. Of course, real-world taxes are rarely if ever so delightfully efficient as the hypothetical head tax described above, both because the world is not frictionless and because, in tax design, we trade off efficiency against distributional considerations. This is the main reason why we use instruments such as income taxes instead of uniform head taxes. Thus, suppose a real world income tax raises, on average, $10,000 per taxpayer. In addition to raising this revenue, it will affect people's incentives. Even if it were perfect in the sense of taxing all income equally, it would discourage work and saving. In practice, moreover, it is likely to favor some types of income relative to others, thus distorting people's work, saving, and investment decisions. Moreover, any real-world income tax is likely to involve significant tax planning, compliance, and administrative costs.

Thus, in a real world income tax under which I pay $10,000, the numerator may be significantly higher than in a hypothetical lump sum tax, while the denominator is somewhat lower. Suppose that, per each $10,000 of income tax revenues collected, deadweight loss was $3,000, and the government's administrative costs were $100. Then the income tax's MECF would be $13,000/$9,900, or about 1.31.

In principle, with full information, one could compute the MECF for any marginal change in the tax system—for example, for "a proposed change in IRS audit practices, or in the items that are included in the income tax base" (Shaviro 2000b). However, one problem with MECF as described so far is that, by looking purely at the taxpayer and the government, it ignores externalities, or the effects on other individuals of tax-induced changes in a given taxpayer's behavior. Thus, consider a pollution tax that charges industrial producers for the disvalue to others of emitting noxious chemicals into the air and water. Insofar as the producers responded by polluting less, rather than by using tax planning to avoid the tax without a change in emissions, others would benefit. To reflect this in MECF, one would need to subtract this benefit to others from the cost to the taxpayers in the numerator. For this reason, a well-functioning pollution tax might end up having an MECF of less than 1.0, reflecting its efficiency advantage over a uniform head tax in that it would actually improve people's incentives, rather than merely not worsening them.

One could also, in principle, add distributional considerations to the analysis (Slemrod and Yitzhaki 1996, 190–192), although in practice this would be extremely challenging. Thus, suppose one favors progressive redistribution on the view that money has higher marginal utility to poorer people than to richer ones. Then, when evaluating the enactment of a revenue-neutral tax change that would increase such redistribution at an efficiency cost, one would want to account in the numerator for the utility consequences of the change's shifting after-tax wealth to people who one believed would derive greater utility from it. The measure might then be relabeled the marginal efficiency and equity cost of funds (MEECF?). However, if one is convinced that this is hopelessly impractical but that MECF comes closer to being at least conceptually useful, the measure can remain one of efficiency only, and distributional considerations kept in mind merely as something that one realizes must be integrated (even if just informally) with the efficiency analysis.

Slemrod and Yitzhaki do not address international considerations in their discussion. However, it is easy to specify what adjustments are needed if a tax potentially affects foreign individuals, but their welfare is excluded from the calculus because one has accepted a national welfare framework. First, neither foreigners' tax payments nor their deadweight loss counts in the numerator. Only the effects on domestic individuals of imposing taxes on the foreigners would be relevant. This could be important, for example, where foreigners nominally are taxed but the incidence shifts to domestic individuals through the price effects of the tax on cross-border transactions. Second, the taxes that foreign individuals pay do indeed count fully, subject to the administrative costs of collection, in the denominator. This helps to illustrate why taxing foreigners, if they actually bear the incidence of the tax, is so appealing from a unilateral national welfare standpoint. It gives the taxing country free money, with an MECF of zero, to the extent that only foreigners are affected.

The idea that MECF could be used to evaluate real-world policy proposals would be merely a pipe dream if it required actually measuring people's utilities under alternative circumstances. In fact, however, its use, at least as a general conceptual guide, can be surprisingly practical. Suppose that, for simplicity, we ignore tax planning and compliance costs, externalities, and administrative costs, along with the distinctive features of the international tax setting, and assume that "taxpayers can sufficiently fine-tune their tax avoidance behavior such that, at the margin, they sacrifice exactly a dollar to reduce tax liability by a dollar" (Shaviro 2000b). Then, as David Weisbach (1999, 1666–1667) explains, MECF is "simply the ratio of the revenue that would be raised from a tax absent any behavioral distortions to the actual revenue raised. The revenue actually raised and the revenue raised without behavioral changes are the 'dynamic' and 'static' revenue estimates routinely computed for tax law changes. Thus, policymakers can learn, in real time, the efficiency costs or benefits of a tax law change."

The relative MECFs for different instruments have strong implications for how to balance the tax burdens that are imposed at different margins. If multiple instruments are available, then something like what economists call the Ramsey rule should apply. That is, "[t]o minimize *overall* excess burden, the *marginal* excess burden of the last dollar of revenue raised from each [instrument] must be the same. Otherwise, it would be possible to lower overall excess burden by raising the rate on the [instrument] with the smaller marginal excess burden or by lowering the rate on the commodity with the larger marginal excess burden" (Rosen and Gayer 2009, 354).

The Ramsey rule arose in a particular setting that is worth comparing to that of corporate income taxation. The specific issue that economist Frank Ramsey (1927) and subsequent writers addressed was the following. Suppose the government is trying to raise revenue through taxes on specific consumer items or commodities. What is more, suppose that commodity taxation's sole purpose is to raise revenue for the government at the lowest possible efficiency cost—rather than, say, either to address externalities like a pollution tax, or to address distributional goals. Finally, suppose that lump sum taxes, such as uniform head taxes, are assumed to be unavailable, as are comprehensive income or consumption taxes.

Against this background, one might initially suppose that it would be most efficient for all of the taxable commodities to face the same tax rate. Ramsey showed, however, that the goal of minimizing overall deadweight loss, by equalizing each particular commodity tax's marginal deadweight loss, had instead a very different implication. In particular, suppose that some commodities are more tax elastic than others, meaning that there would be more substitution away from them if all were taxed at the same rate. Recall, moreover, that, as noted above, the deadweight loss per dollar of revenue raised generally rises with the tax rate (Rosen and Gayer 2009, 340). Thus, each commodity tax would be expected to feature rising MECF as one raises its rate.

With this in mind, the way to equalize different commodity taxes' MECF while keeping overall revenue constant, starting from the scenario where all of the tax rates are the same, is to raise the rate on relatively inelastic commodities while lowering it for those that are relatively tax elastic. Thus, the Ramsey rule is an inverse elasticity rule (Rosen and Gayer 2009, 357), holding that optimal commodity tax rates and the particular items' tax elasticity generally are inversely related.

How does the Ramsey/inverse elasticity rule fare in a modern income tax setting? One could think of a comprehensive income tax as equivalent to a uniform commodity tax on all consumer goods—at least, leaving aside the point that income taxation effectively applies a higher rate to items that are consumed later, rather than sooner, since it taxes the interim return to waiting (Bankman and Weisbach 2006). Is the desirability of using such a tax rebutted by the logic behind the inverse elasticity rule? Louis Kaplow (2008, 122–148) has shown that, when one adds distributional considerations to the analysis and assumes, unlike Ramsey, that one *can* uniformly tax all consumer goods, uniformity may generally be best after all. The key underlying idea here is that one needs to embed commodity choice in a broader framework, in which people are deciding how much to work and earn. After all, without earnings one cannot pay for consumer goods. In this framework, it turns out that the only reason to tax particular commodities at different rates, assuming full flexibility to set the applicable personal tax rates however one likes, relates to the underlying choice between work and leisure that the income tax (along with any more limited commodity tax) distorts by discouraging work. Given this efficiency problem, it might be desirable, relative to the uniform commodity tax baseline, to raise the tax rate on leisure complements (i.e., goods that tend to be consumed jointly with leisure) while lowering it for leisure substitutes (i.e., those that tend to be consumed more when leisure declines) (Corlett and Hague 1953).[12] Otherwise, however, Kaplow (2008, 148) demonstrates that "results derived in the original Ramsey framework, in which no income tax is available, fail to provide proper guidance in a world with an income tax."

Kaplow's conclusion implies that if, instead of taxing corporate income at the entity level, we were taxing U.S. individuals directly on their earnings whether derived through a corporation or not, there would be no place for differential commodity taxation, leaving aside the labor versus leisure issue, as well as the possible optimal tariff grounds for taxing inbound capital. Presumably, in this scenario, the commodities that people purchased using foreign source income would face the same tax rate as those that they purchased using domestic source income. But as soon as we change the factual premises to include entity-level taxation of corporate income, with residence determinations being made at the entity level, we are no longer in an "income tax world" as Kaplow uses the term, but rather are in one where, at least to a degree, "no income tax [on certain activities of the relevant individuals] is available." Thus, Ramsey-style reasoning is relevant to the choice of tax rates both for inbound and outbound corporate income taxation, as defined by our residence rules, and helps defeat the assumption that any particular pair of tax rates necessarily should be the same.

D. Source-Based Entity-Level Income Taxation

From this general conceptual background, what do we learn regarding source-based, entity-level income taxation? As noted above, the fact that we do not, and probably cannot, look through corporations and tax their income directly to the owners makes a source-based corporate income tax almost inevitable. Otherwise, U.S. individuals who operate U.S. businesses might be able to shelter their labor income by incorporating abroad, serving as owner-employees, and underpaying themselves. Unfortunately, taxing U.S. source income at the entity level results in our applying the same tax regime to multiple types of income that, from an optimal tax standpoint, might each be handled distinctively. In particular, a source-based, entity-level income tax amalgamates within its reach both labor income and capital income of both U.S. and foreign individuals.

For labor income that U.S. individuals earn through corporations, if it can be distinguished from all other income that arises in corporate solution, a plausible approach would be to tax it exactly like labor income that such individuals earn directly. This would both serve the distributional aims underlying the individual income tax, and avoid distorting the choice whether to use a corporate entity. Moreover, while corporate income potentially faces a second level of tax when distributed to shareholders, owner-employees generally can prevent this from happening with respect to labor income by paying themselves arm's-length salaries.

Under present U.S. law, however, it is extremely difficult to distinguish the labor income of under-compensated owner-employees from corporate returns generally. This might change if the United States followed the lead of several Scandinavian countries that enacted so-called dual income taxes, under which amounts presumptively constituting the labor income of owner-employees were deducted at the entity level and included at the owner level. The basic methodology involved automatically treating extra-normal corporate returns as attributable to such under-compensation, thus permitting an adjustment to be made (relative to stated salaries) without requiring case-by-case factual inquiry into the ostensible value of the services provided by a given owner-employee (see Kleinbard 2010). Absent U.S. enactment of a well-functioning dual income tax, however, the problem of identifying and taxing labor income that U.S. individuals earn through corporations remains quite serious.

The analysis is different for U.S.-source labor income that foreign individuals may earn here, presumably during short-term visits, either directly or as undercompensated owner-employees. Since such individuals' well-being does not directly matter from a unilateral national welfare standpoint, the aim might be to maximize the transfer from them (i.e., the U.S. tax liabilities that they actually bear as a matter of economic incidence), subject to taking into account any distortionary costs that taxing them would impose on U.S. individuals.[13] If the labor market equivalent of the small open economy scenario applied, the bottom line might nonetheless be taxing foreign individuals less than residents, and perhaps even exempting them. However, since opportunities to earn labor income may often be location specific, it is plausible that the United States has sufficient market power for some level of domestic source-based taxation of foreigners' labor income to be nationally optimal.

Standing alone, the grounds for wanting to distinguish between domestic and foreign individuals' domestic source labor income may not be of great practical importance. However, the complications become more serious when we extend the analysis to capital income that is earned through a corporate entity. In particular, the distinction between domestic and foreign individuals becomes especially important, given that the latter may can wholly avoid the source-based U.S. tax on capital income simply by investing elsewhere.

There is a vast literature on how much we should want to tax domestic individuals' capital income. For example, consumption tax proponents favor exempting the "return to waiting" that is among its integral components (see, e.g., Shaviro 2004; Bankman and Weisbach 2006). However, taking as given current U.S. law's treatment of capital income when U.S. individuals earn it directly, there probably is little to gain by having this treatment change when they invest through U.S. companies.[14] At the most, one might want to address the fact that such income is potentially subject to double taxation if fully taxed at the corporate level and then distributed to shareholders.

U.S. individuals have some ability to avoid current U.S. taxation of their capital income if earned abroad, rather than at home, but subject to significant burdens and limitations.[15] Obviously, one can hold stock in U.S. companies that earn FSI benefiting from deferral, but subpart F, at least in principle, makes such companies' passive FSI currently includable. Alternatively, a U.S. individual can hold stock in foreign companies, which generally face no U.S. taxation of their FSI, thus entirely eliminating U.S. taxation prior to shareholder-level realization. However, a U.S. individual who invests abroad through a passive foreign investment company (PFIC), or one that holds mainly passive assets and/ or earns mainly passive income, generally is currently taxable under U.S. law on his share of the PFIC's income.[16] In sum, however, even insofar as there is a case for lowering the tax that U.S. individuals face on domestic capital income due to their ability (even if limited) to avoid this tax by investing abroad, it is at best debatable to what extent lowering the domestic corporate rate is a good way to go about this.[17]

When we turn to foreign individuals' capital income, however, the case for a significantly lower source-based U.S. tax rate becomes considerably stronger. Such individuals can wholly avoid any U.S. tax by investing entirely abroad and through foreign companies. Accordingly, their capital income is potentially subject to the small open economy scenario, as depicted above in Figure 5.1. This suggests that, from a unilateral U.S. national welfare standpoint, their U.S. source capital income should face a zero U.S. rate if the U.S. cannot affect global rates of return and the foreign investors are not earning rents in the United States. Moreover, even if these conditions do not entirely hold and the optimal U.S. rate on their U.S. source capital income is therefore positive, that rate may be significantly lower than it is for the other three categories of income that fall within the reach of a source-based, entity-level U.S. income tax.

This brings to mind one of the main rationales for lowering the statutory U.S. corporate tax rate, in response to its being significantly higher than most peer countries' rates. The problem of tax competition, causing concern that the U.S. loses mobile capital investment to peer countries by reason of the tax rate differential, pertains most forcefully to investment by foreign individuals. It is in the nature of the dilemma, however, that the instrument of choice (i.e., the source-based U.S. corporate tax) pertains to several other types of income as well, the optimal tax rate for which is likely to be higher. If the best one can do, in setting the source-based U.S. corporate tax rate, is effectively to compromise as between the rates that would be best for the various distinct components, then it is plausible that this rate should be lower than that for U.S. individuals, and higher than the rate that we would like to apply just to foreign individuals' U.S.-source capital income.

E. Residence-Based Entity-Level Taxation of Foreign Source Income

This brings us to the question of how to tax resident companies' FSI from a unilateral national welfare standpoint. The question has two parts: (a) how heavily or lightly should it be taxed, which is a question about the average or effective tax rate; and (b) exactly how should it be taxed, which is a question about the base and rate design, involving such features as deferral versus immediate inclusion, and MRRs for foreign taxes paid.

1. How Much to Tax Resident Companies' Foreign Source Income

U.S. companies' reported FSI, like domestic source corporate income, can be either labor or capital income of either U.S. or foreign individuals. In principle, U.S. individuals' labor income should generally be treated as U.S. source, even when earned by an under-compensated owner-employee of a U.S. multinational. Yet consider the case of Apple. As Martin Sullivan (2012, 777) notes: "Apple does most of its research in the United States. Most of its key employees are in the United States. Fifty-four percent of its long-lived assets, 69 percent of its retail stores, and 39 percent of its sales are in the United States. . . . Apple continues to keep most of its product design, software development, product management, marketing and other high-wage functions in the U.S. . . . Yet the company reports only 30 percent of its profits as being from the United States." Accordingly, the source-based U.S. corporate tax is substantially failing to achieve entity-level proxy taxation of Apple's under-compensated owner-employees, such as the late Steve Jobs with his famous $1 per year salary.

In assessing whether, and if so to what degree, the United States should tax resident companies' FSI, two things should be clear. First, so long as we have (or can have) significant market power with respect to U.S. corporate residence, the optimal rate is likely to be greater than zero. Taxing FSI can serve multiple purposes, such as indirectly taxing U.S. individuals' labor income, deterring U.S. companies from playing costly profit-shifting games, and imposing tax burdens on foreign individuals if they value and will pay for the attributes that trigger U.S. corporate resident status. And while the tax comes at a distortionary cost, such as by reason of its deterring the use of U.S. companies to generate FSI, the distortion is likely to be initially small as the effective U.S. tax rate on FSI rises from zero. Again, if we start from a zero tax rate on FSI and a significant positive tax rate on domestic source corporate income (such as 2013's 35 percent), and start raising the former rate while lowering the latter one, it appears likely that the overall MECF effects will initially be desirable.

Second, the optimal average U.S. tax rate for FSI appears likely to be lower than that for domestic source income. With respect to the source-based tax, the United States has a huge internal market. Location-specific opportunities to earn rents, as well as labor income that remains inside a corporate entity, are widespread. A tax that falls on the use of U.S. companies to earn FSI relies on something that seems unlikely to be quite so substantial or resilient. Thus, while empirical specification would be needed to support firm conclusions, it is unsurprising that nearly everyone today—including pro-worldwide proponents in the current U.S. debate, if they favor foreign tax credits—seems to accept that U.S. law should place lower tax burdens on FSI than on domestic source income.

2. Tax Base and Rate Issues in Structuring the Tax on Resident Companies' Foreign Source Income

With respect to how a residence-based U.S. corporate tax on FSI should be structured, this book has already discussed the main issues. Present law achieves a much lower average tax rate for U.S. companies' FSI than for domestic source corporate income through two main mechanisms: deferral and the foreign tax credit. Alternatively, however, one can steer to the same aggregate endpoint by broadening the base and lowering the rate—that is, by accompanying a statutory rate cut for FSI with (a) narrowing or eliminating deferral; and (b) reducing the MRR for foreign taxes, such as by moving towards their mere deductibility.

Broadening the base and lowering the rate is, of course, the classic prescription for revenue-neutral, efficiency-enhancing fundamental tax reform. It should therefore have been an obvious move to make (or at least consider) in the case of international tax policy, whether or not one ultimately endorsed it. Only the severe blinders under which international tax policy scholarship has operated for so many decades—in particular, the assumption that one can only have a territorial system or a worldwide/foreign tax credit system, reflecting the literature's conflation of multiple margins, failure to consider the possibility of intermediate statutory rates, and failure to grasp the problems associated with foreign tax creditability—could have prevented it from even being considered.

How should one evaluate a package that consisted of reducing or eliminating deferral, reducing the MRR for foreign taxes, and enacting a lower statutory tax rate for FSI than for domestic source income? To avoid conflating distinct issues, this analysis is best begun by assuming (subject to reconsideration later on) that one will in any event get to the same overall place so far as the average or effective tax rate for U.S. companies' FSI is concerned.

Deferral—For good reason, almost no one likes or defends deferral as such. It arose historically for formalistic reasons, relating to the legal fiction that even wholly owned subsidiaries are distinct from their corporate parents. Proponents of territoriality may prefer deferral to raising the average tax rate on FSI by going to a pure worldwide system, while proponents of worldwide taxation may prefer it to eliminating altogether the domestic tax on resident companies' FSI. But otherwise each group rightly condemns it, in the course of noting that enacting their preferred systems would make it a thing of the past. U.S. companies would no longer be tax deterred from repatriating their overseas earnings if the repatriations were tax free, either under dividend exemption or because the earnings had already been taxed here.

There are only two things that one might reasonably like about deferral—but in each case, only if we assume that the U.S. international tax rules are otherwise fixed. First, it reduces the effective U.S. tax rate on FSI, which conceivably might otherwise be too high. Second, as noted in chapter 3, despite new view-type scenarios in which deferral would fail to reduce the otherwise 100 percent MRR for creditable foreign taxes, in practice it probably does reduce substantially the MRR that U.S. companies anticipate when they are making overseas tax planning choices. For this reason, eliminating deferral, but otherwise keeping the U.S. rules the same, is hard to evaluate confidently, given the iron box. It would increase the effective tax rate on U.S. companies' FSI (the desirability or not of which depends on wholly separate considerations) and it would cause U.S. companies to be genuinely and completely indifferent to whether their creditable foreign taxes were low or high, other than in cases where foreign tax credit limits would potentially apply.

These points, however, offer no defense against the proposition that one could improve the U.S. rules by accompanying the repeal of deferral with suitable changes to the treatment of foreign taxes and/or the applicable statutory tax rate for FSI. A bad rule that creates wasteful tax planning and needless economic distortion does not become a good one just because it can help to mitigate the bad consequences of other mistakes.

Foreign tax creditability—From a unilateral national welfare standpoint, it is simply impossible directly to rationalize offering foreign tax credits, with their 100 percent MRR for foreign taxes paid. A dollar that someone else gets is not the same as a dollar that we get. Try asking a creditor to whom you owe money if you can satisfy the debt by paying some third party instead.

It is true that reciprocal foreign tax credits, provided by peer countries that are otherwise similar, may be defensible from a national welfare standpoint. Even in that scenario, one's own taxpayers and the peer countries that are levying creditable taxes face marginal incentives that are adverse to one's best interests, but at least the overall end result may be tolerable. However, in a world where territorial systems, featuring implicit foreign tax deductibility, are increasingly widespread, the multilateral perspective that offers a potential defense of foreign tax credits is close to irrelevant.

The fact that deferral makes foreign tax credits more tolerable, by often causing the MRR that companies anticipate to be considerably less than 100 percent, also falls far short of offering an adequate defense. Again, a system featuring both deferral and foreign tax credits inevitably has a distressingly bad ratio of tax planning, compliance, and administrative costs to revenue actually raised. Moreover, the frequently offsetting character of these two bad rules does not prevent foreign taxes from actually offering a 100 percent MRR whenever an "excess-limit" U.S. taxpayer faces a potential repatriation of FSI that would trigger U.S. tax liability. The array of economic substance-inflected rules and standards that address foreign tax credit "abuses" (discussed in chapter 2) are testament to the ongoing problems that this scenario guarantees. And, as discussed in chapter 3, the apparently galling fact that taxpayers who are engaged in foreign tax credit "abuse" deliberately throw away their own money, because they are counting on the U.S. government to reimburse them for foreign tax payments, holds equally for any situation in which one accepts a subpar after-foreign tax return because the taxes will be reimbursed anyway.

From the standpoint of resident taxpayers' incentives to minimize their foreign tax liabilities, the obviously correct rule, from a unilateral national welfare standpoint, is foreign tax deductibility, which can also be defined as setting the MRR equal to the applicable marginal tax rate (MTR) for FSI. (Again, this is why an exemption system offers implicit foreign tax deductibility.) Foreign tax deductibility causes the taxpayer to be indifferent between paying a dollar of foreign taxes and otherwise incurring a one-dollar expense (or forgone gain). It thus creates exactly the right marginal incentive from the standpoint of the residence country, absent any positive or negative externalities that are associated with the choice.

However, the otherwise straightforward unilateral national welfare case for simple foreign tax deductibility is complicated by the fact that, when one observes tax haven income that bears an extremely low (if any) rate of source-based tax, it is likely that the income was earned someplace else, such as in one's own country. For example, under the technology for creating stateless income that Edward Kleinbard (2011a) discusses, even profits that appear to have been shifted to a tax haven from another high-tax country may actually be domestic source income. This in turn may motivate imposing higher domestic taxes on FSI when tax haven income is observed. Territorial countries frequently limit the applicability of exemption for foreign source income in a manner suggesting that they take this concern very seriously.

Thus, consider Japan's recently enacted international tax regime, which generally provides 95 percent exemption for Japanese companies' receipt of dividends from their foreign subsidiaries, so long as the foreign jurisdiction where the income was earned has an effective tax rate of at least 20 percent. The Japanese surely would not be pleased if this rule's sole effect were to induce particular tax havens to specialize in charging 20 percent effective rates, so that Japanese companies could invest there and avoid the higher Japanese rate. Rather, the aim presumably is to protect the Japanese domestic tax base by limiting the global tax reduction that Japanese companies can achieve by re-labeling domestic source income as FSI.

I will further discuss relevant design considerations in chapter 6. For now, however, it is worth mentioning the basic design challenge that is posed by worse-than-deductibility rules for foreign taxes. The approach inherently involves a tradeoff between (a) the desirability of giving resident taxpayers the optimal incentive with regard to foreign taxes paid (holding FSI constant), and (b) the desirability of reducing incentives to re-label domestic source income as FSI. It thus ought to be designed thoughtfully in terms of the MRR pattern that it actually creates. For example, a 100 percent MRR seems unlikely to be nationally optimal, even in light of the tagging point, given that, where applicable, it wholly eliminates foreign tax cost-consciousness. If not well-designed, antitax haven rules that respond to the tagging concern can easily create MRRs in excess of 100 percent.

In illustration, suppose a Japanese company earns $100 abroad, pays zero in foreign taxes, and thereby incurs a Japanese tax liability of $38. If the company had instead invested in a country where it would pay foreign taxes of $20 rather than zero, it would have wholly eliminated this domestic tax liability. Thus, under these assumed facts, its MRR with respect to this choice is actually 190 percent.

Statutory tax rate differential between domestic source income and FSI—Eliminating deferral and making foreign taxes merely deductible (antitax haven rules aside), if unaccompanied by any other changes, would greatly increase the U.S. tax burden on resident companies' FSI—very likely to an excessive level, given the tax elasticity of U.S. corporate residence. Thus, an accompanying tax cut for FSI might be needed if such changes were adopted, and this presumably should involve lowering the statutory tax rate, rather than enacting some other kind of targeted special benefit that undermines the incentive to maximize one's after-foreign tax economic return from overseas economic activity.

A logical way to lower the tax rate on FSI, applying symmetrically to gains and losses, would be to provide that a fixed percentage of each item of foreign source income, deduction, gain or loss, is disregarded for U.S. federal income tax purposes. Thus, suppose that the tax rate for domestic source income is 35 percent, and that one wants to apply a 20 percent rate to FSI. Providing that each foreign-denominated item is 3/7 (or roughly 42.9 percent) disregarded would result in a 20 percent tax rate for FSI that effectively applied to net losses as well as net income.

Obviously, creating a tax rate differential between domestic source income and FSI is not an ideal solution, given that it retains some incentive for resident companies to engage in profit shifting. To put the same point another way, NN is optimal, and the approach I am suggesting is worse, when the only relevant margin is where a resident company will locate a given dollar of profits. In that scenario, just as foreign tax deductibility creates the socially optimal incentive (from a national welfare standpoint) regarding foreign tax cost consciousness, so charging a uniform rate for domestic source income and FSI has this same effect regarding the location of reported profits. However, with multiple relevant margins, including that pertaining to corporate residence, one enters the realm of tradeoffs rather than of seeking particular neutralities. Once one accepts that the average tax rate for resident companies' FSI should be lower than that for their domestic source income, only the use of the tax rate variable can avoid creating further distortions within the category of foreign business and investment choices that would need their own specific justifications (such as that for a "tagging" approach).

E. Special Issues Raised by Passive or Portfolio Income

The discussion so far has focused on multinational companies' active business income, which typically reflects observable activity in particular locations. Thus, a final topic worth addressing here is whether the analysis changes significantly with respect to passive or portfolio income. Here, three key differences from active business income could potentially matter.

First, the location of passive income for tax purposes is highly formalistic and manipulable, causing such income to be highly mobile in practice. For example, a foreign passive investor's profits from betting on the success of a company that has U.S. business operations may escape being treated as U.S. source income in either of two ways. The company may be incorporated abroad, causing dividends it pays to be non-U.S. source, and/or the investor may use alternative financial arrangements, such as swaps, in lieu of direct stock ownership.

Second, in evaluating the efficiency effects of a given set of tax rules, passive assets' ownership generally does not affect business productivity. Passive investors do not control or even greatly influence the issuers' business operations, such as by deciding where capital should be used (Graetz and Grinberg 2003, 555). One thing that potentially *does* matter is the investor's capacity to achieve global economic diversification (Desai and Dharmapala 2009). However, the formalistic character of source rules for passive income weakens the relationship between source for tax purposes and actual economic diversification.

Third, foreign portfolio investments (FPI) are predominantly held by individuals, whereas foreign direct investment (FDI) is predominantly made by corporations (Graetz and Grinberg 2003, 547). Taxpayer residence electivity is a much smaller issue when the taxpayer is an individual who actually lives somewhere, rather than being a corporation. Thus, residence-based worldwide taxation stands on stronger ground for FPI than FDI, at least when individuals are the taxpayers.

For inbound taxation of passive income, a big U.S. international tax policy issue for many years (as noted in chapter 3) was the use of swaps to avoid withholding taxes. With respect to outbound taxation of passive income earned by U.S. residents abroad, Michael Graetz and Itai Grinberg (2003) argue that U.S. law should follow a national neutrality (NN) approach, and generally treat foreign taxes on passive income as merely deductible, rather than creditable. Mihir Desai and Dhammika Dharmapala (2009) respond by arguing that residence-based worldwide taxation with foreign tax credits is optimal, based on a principle called global portfolio neutrality (GPN) that they assert applies equally from the perspectives of global and national welfare.

Inbound—Should the United States actually regret foreigners' use of swaps to avoid withholding taxes on dividends paid by U.S. companies? If the small open economy scenario fully applied, this might actually be a good thing, as it would avoid discouraging inbound investment through taxes that U.S. individuals would bear anyway. However, the scenario may not fully apply here.

There are two reasons why foreign individuals may bear some of the withholding taxes that U.S. law levies on dividends. First, the tax depends in the main on U.S. incorporation of the dividend-paying company, an attribute that foreign investors may in some circumstances value and be willing to pay for. Second, any U.S. withholding taxes that are creditable by the investor's country of residence will in effect lead to cash transfers from the foreign treasury to the U.S. Treasury. Given these points, it is plausible that the optimal U.S. withholding tax on dividends is greater than zero.

There also is a possible rationale for, on the one hand, generally permitting foreign investors to use equity swaps to avoid the U.S. withholding tax, but, on the other hand, requiring these swaps to have some economic substance, rather than being equivalent to direct ownership, if they are to be tax effective. The idea would be to ensure that using them is not so easy as to become the universal default approach. Equity swaps that are at least mildly burdensome to use in lieu of direct stockholding may give rise to efficient price discrimination by the United States with respect to withholding taxes. Suppose, for example, that a meaningful economic substance requirement caused equity swaps to be used, in lieu of direct stockholding, exclusively by tax-adverse foreign investors, while those whose home countries reimbursed their U.S. withholding taxes via foreign tax credits chose direct ownership of stock in U.S. companies.

Outbound—Readers may not be surprised that I agree with Graetz and Grinberg (2003) that U.S. individuals' foreign taxes should generally be deductible, rather than creditable. While Graetz and Grinberg support charging the full U.S. source domestic tax rate on foreign source portfolio income, rather than a lower rate as I suggest with regard to U.S. companies' active business FSI, this reflects an important difference between the two settings. U.S. individuals face more NN-like circumstances than U.S. companies that are deciding whether to invest abroad, because the individuals cannot do the equivalent of raising new equity on world capital markets to fund all portfolio investments that they find appealing. Rather, they are better viewed as having a fixed amount to invest in either domestic or foreign assets, making the main relationship between the two types of investments one of substitution, rather than unrelatedness or complementarity. Thus, charging the full domestic rate appears to make sense.

U.S. companies that hold foreign portfolio assets admittedly pose a closer case. On the one hand, if they do not generally raise equity in world capital markets in order to fund particular portfolio investments, then they, too, are largely in a substitution world with respect to FPI. Thus, exempting passive FSI might simply induce them to hold foreign in lieu of domestic portfolio assets. On the other hand, U.S. and foreign individuals who are deciding whether to invest in a U.S. or foreign company that was expected to hold portfolio assets, in addition to making active business investments, may take into account the U.S. tax treatment of passive income, as one input into the choice.

The alternative analysis proposed by Desai and Dharmapala (2009) rests on several assumptions that appear questionable. The main point underlying GPN, in both its global and national welfare manifestations, is that investors benefit economically from diversification. Thus, a CEN-like result, in which one faces the same tax rate (i.e., the domestic rate) no matter where one invests, with foreign tax credits eliminating the impact of foreign withholding taxes, ostensibly is desirable, so that one will optimally diversify one's global holdings.

Unfortunately, this claim rests on under-appreciating the distinction between which countries' unique economic risks are associated with a given investment, and what is the source for tax purposes of a given item of portfolio income. A U.S. individual can diversify globally without having to hold the stock of companies located in countries that charge withholding taxes. For example, she can hold the stock of U.S. companies that are active abroad, while also using equity swaps and other diversification tools such as foreign currency swaps, in order to diversify economically without incurring foreign tax liabilities.

Things get worse when Desai and Dharmapala explain why foreign tax credits ostensibly cost the United States zero, and thus are defensible under a unilateral national welfare analysis. They rightly note that the United States does not actually lose money from the foreign tax reimbursement itself, since the payment goes from the Treasury to the U.S. individuals who paid the foreign taxes. However, that is not the issue. Rather, the problem with a 100 percent MRR is that it eliminates the reimbursed individuals' incentive to try to minimize their foreign tax liabilities.

In their model, this simply is not a problem, for two reasons. First, foreign tax credits are assumed to be fully reciprocal between countries. By offering them to foreign investors, we assure that foreign countries will offer them to our investors. The relevant countries are assumed to have the same tax rates, so that the amount credited per dollar of dividends is the same in each direction (Desai and Dharmapala 2009, 24). Second, the authors assume that cross-border capital flows are –exactly the same in each direction. For example, if U.S. individuals invest more abroad and less at home because foreign withholding taxes are creditable, then foreign individuals will respond by investing more in the United States and less at home. So there will simply be portfolio asset swaps, leaving the United States with the same overall tax revenues no matter what.

These are questionable assumptions to make in evaluating the actual effects of foreign withholding tax creditability. We operate in a multilateral setting in which reciprocity in offering foreign tax credits is incomplete, and countries' withholding tax rates may differ. In addition, the formalistic character of source determinations under international tax rules rebuts expecting the sort of zero net capital flows that Desai and Dharmapala assume. For example, there is no reason to expect the amounts of "U.S. stock" and "French stock" to be fixed, so that, if U.S. individuals hold more of the latter, French individuals will hold more of the former, when individuals in both countries have considerable flexibility to manipulate the source of portfolio income for tax purposes, independently of what actual economic investments they are making.

No realistic model of global portfolio capital flows, based on actual international tax rules, could make unilateral foreign tax creditability nationally optimal. Foreign withholding tax creditability inevitably affects resident investors' sensitivity to foreign withholding taxes that frequently can be avoided through simple tax planning. Thus, the only good case for such creditability pertains to cases where it actually is reciprocal, such as in the bilateral treaty context. As it happens, however, bilateral tax treaties between peer countries with similar tax rates often involve reciprocal reductions in withholding taxes on portfolio assets, in lieu of or in addition to reciprocal withholding tax creditability.

Endnotes

1. The actual Assyria might have responded to this problem by sending its war chariots storming over the border, and incorporating Babylonia into its empire. Even the United States, however, cannot respond similarly today.

2. Indeed, if investment at home has positive externalities, such as from the fact that a higher capital stock may increase domestic workers' productivity, one could even argue for taxing residents' (and if feasible everyone's) FSI at a *higher* rate than domestic source income.

3. This simple pro-NN story does not take account of the possible benefit to Assyrians of diversifying their home country economic risk through investment in Babylonia. But in principle there are other ways of achieving such diversification—for example, through the Assyrian government's taking a financial position that in effect shorted the Assyrian economy and went long on the performance of the Babylonian economy.

4. See, e.g., Buch, Kleinert, Lipponer, and Toubal (2005) (finding evidence suggestive of complementarity, using German data); Harrison and McMillan (2008) (finding offsetting effects but a small overall employment decline, using U.S. data); Simpson 2008 (finding mixed results, with high-skill industries showing more complementarity than low-skill industries, using U.K. data); Desai, Foley, and Hines 2009 (finding complementarity, using U.S. data); and Kleinert and Toubal (2009) (finding no significant net effect, using German data).

5. In this regard, firm-level complementarity arguably is more broadly supported by evidence in Buch, Kleinert, Lipponer, and Toubal (2005) that outbound investment by the firms studied was more motivated by seeking access to foreign markets than by seeking cheaper inputs.

6. Although Harrison and McMillan find a small aggregate firm-level decline in U.S. employment from U.S. multinationals' outbound investment, one could perhaps count their work as supporting the complementarity story over the long run if one believes that rising vertical integration is the wave of the future.

7. See Desai, Foley, and Hines 2005 (finding time-series evidence that foreign and domestic investment are positively correlated in the United States); and Faeth 2006 (finding that foreign domestic investment increases domestic economic activity, using Australian data). Recent industry-level studies of the effect of outbound investment by resident multinationals on domestic activity include Hejazi and Pauly 2003 (finding support for complementarity in Canadian data) and Arndt, Buch, and Schnitzer 2007 (similar, using German data).

8. As noted above, NN leads to tax discouragement of cross-border activity if one takes a global perspective and thus counts everyone's taxes. However, from a domestic national welfare standpoint, in which foreign taxes are merely a cost since domestic individuals do not get the money, a "neutral" system in the standard sense is one in which *domestic* taxes are relevantly equalized as between choices.

9. Oddly, the assumed mechanism here is *not* that domestic firms' outbound investments are unrelated or complements to domestic investment. To be sure, Desai and Hines (2003) pre-dates the above-cited empirical studies that assess firm-level substitution versus unrelatedness or complementarity. However, Hines (2009, 278) continues to emphasize the musical chairs scenario, after much of the firm-level research had come out.

10. In the case of foreign-to-domestic investment complementarity, there may be a case for subsidizing U.S. companies' outbound investment, on the ground that the added U.S. source-based tax revenues from their added U.S. investment is a positive externality that they ignore. However, the firm-level empirical literature does not suggest significant overall complementarity. In addition, one would have to consider whether any other externalities—for example, from domestic investment being made by U.S. firms—are relevant to the overall analysis.

11. This example relies on U.S. monopsony power that creates potential national benefit from imposing an import tariff. For producers with monopoly power, a similar analysis can apply to export duties, as well as to cartels such as the Organization of Petroleum Exporting Countries (OPEC), which succeeded in significantly raising world energy prices in the 1970s.

12. For example, suppose that restaurant and take-out meals are leisure substitutes, due to their appeal to people who are working long hours, while groceries are a leisure complement because one needs free time to prepare meals at home. Then it may be efficient to tax groceries and subsidize restaurant meals, as a way of lowering the labor-leisure distortion (Kaplow 2008, 138 n. 16).

13. In a reciprocal framework, the United States might benefit from deals with other countries in which each side agrees to mitigate taxing labor income earned within its borders by the other's citizens.

14. Thus, it comes as no surprise that several existing U.S. income tax rules attempt to impede U.S. individuals' opportunities to lower taxes on their capital income by placing it in corporate solution. Examples include the accumulated earnings tax (Code section 531), the personal holding company rules (Code section 541), and the passive foreign investment company rules (Code section 1297).

15. This is partly an enforcement issue, and the United States has made strides, in recent years, through information-sharing agreements with other countries, towards addressing individuals' illegal non-reporting of taxable foreign source income.

16. The price of deferring one's share of the PFIC's income, rather than including it currently, is an interest charge on the deferral, along with the potential loss of certain tax benefits such as the low rate for long-term capital gains.

17. One argument for lowering the domestic corporate rate, even if one remains committed to an income tax approach and is not responding to the avoidability of the source-based tax by investing abroad, is that this would reduce the pro-debt, anti-equity bias of the existing corporate income tax. This, however, reflects the point, noted above, that neutrality between corporate and noncorporate income may potentially be advanced by a rate differential, given double taxation of equity-financed corporate earnings.

6   What Is to Be Done?

WHEN ONE FACES a hard problem, the proper solution depends on the available tools. Even Alexander the Great could not have undone the Gordian knot without a sword. In international tax policy, a key question is how sharp a tool we have available in addressing current law's myriad dilemmas. Should we assume that continued reliance on entity-level income taxation is inevitable? If not, the rules' character could fundamentally change. But if so, some knots will not untie, and the best one can do is to identify approaches that, even if superior to present law, would still be untidy and unedifying at best.

This chapter therefore proceeds in two stages. First, I show how and why dispensing with entity-level income taxation, if possible and appropriate, would ease or even eliminate most of the problems that this book has discussed. Second, I turn to the question of how U.S. international tax policy might be more marginally improved if entity-level corporate income taxation remains our system's lodestar (or millstone).

A. Slicing through the Gordian Knot of Entity-Level Corporate Income Taxation

From the standpoint of elegance and simplicity, it is almost "game over" for the U.S. international tax system once we accept that the basic instrument for taxing multinational business will be entity-level income taxation. A core problem is the inherent administrative difficulty of measuring income, in light of a realization requirement that responds to the difficulty of contemporaneously measuring value fluctuations. A further problem is the difficulty of telling apart domestic from foreign individuals, whom we have good reason to treat differently, once we are determining tax residence at the entity level. As noted in chapter 5, the existence of an income tax on individuals that does not directly reach corporate income strongly motivates taxing such income directly at the entity level. This, however, necessitates relying on corporate residence and/or source rules to establish tax jurisdiction, leading in turn to what we have seen is a long-standing and distressingly feeble "race between two very slow participants," in which there can be "few cheers for the winner" (Auerbach 2012, 20).

In principle, there are three ways of escaping this dilemma. First, one could tax corporate income directly to the individuals to whom it accrued economically, rather than at the entity level. Second, one could forgo levying any current tax on corporate profits until the occurrence of shareholder-level realization. Third, one could convert the corporate income tax into something else, such as a levy on net cash flows that follows consumption tax principles. As we will see, each of these approaches could eliminate the very slow race. Yet the first is unfeasible; the second is probably undesirable so long as we retain income taxation of individuals; and the third, while probably feasible and perhaps even desirable, shows no current sign of being likely to happen.

1. *Taxing corporate income directly to individuals*—It is easy to see how much simpler things would be if one could reliably look through corporate entities and attribute all of their income to the ultimate owners (whether shareholders or those holding other financial interests). Then the United States, for example, would have no difficulty in taxing all U.S. individuals on their worldwide income. The only even remotely hard issues, in this scenario, would be twofold. First, if other countries levied source-based taxes on our people—notwithstanding pressures of tax competition, which might conceivably induce them to back off—we would have reason to consider the use of coordinating devices to arrange reciprocal forbearance. And again, it is not impossible that this might take the form of reciprocal tax creditability, perhaps even with foreign tax credit limits (requiring source determinations) to limit the bad marginal incentives that this creates, although mutual exemption for each other's nationals would be more straightforward.

Second, even though source-based taxation would no longer be needed to prevent one's own residents from escaping taxation on income earned at home through the use of foreign entities, there would still be the question of whether to impose source-based taxes on foreigners. Clearly, one might want to regulate their domestic economic activity, although this need not be done through the income tax. In addition, as we saw in chapter 5, there is good reason to tax them insofar as they would actually bear the economic incidence of the tax.[1] However, a well-designed source-based tax on foreign individuals would not necessarily be based on their domestic source income. For example, it might instead focus on distinctive types of activity, or on extra-normal rates of return that might conceivably tip off the presence of location-specific rents. It also would not necessarily use the domestic income tax rate for U.S. individuals. Withholding taxes on foreigners' U.S. passive income can be viewed as an example of this rate differentiation approach.

Even with a source-based income tax on foreign individuals, however, the source concept would be doing far less work than it does at present. Its irrelevance to the taxation of U.S. individuals other than in the case of foreign tax credit limits, along with the complete elimination of corporate residence as a legally relevant concept, would mean that the very slow race had finally, and mercifully, been ended.

Unfortunately, however, there is little chance of our getting to this world. U.S. partnership taxation, which does indeed contemporaneously tax entity income at the owner level, is notoriously inaccurate and manipulable. The main problems that make it so pertain to the difficulty of discerning both true owners and the true economics of people's deals. Even if one could handle all that, however, a further problem arises when the tax system fails to measure entity-level economic income accurately. If one is mismeasuring such income, whether due to administrative issues or deliberate tax preferences, the question of how to allocate taxable income to the entity's various owners really has no correct answer to begin with. When taxable income is just a number on a piece of paper, rather than something that has actually accrued economically, the question of *whose* income it is lacks any well-defined economic answer (see Shaviro 1989).

2. *No tax on corporate income before owner-level realization*—If one wants to tax U.S. individuals on income that they earn through corporate entities but this cannot be done contemporaneously on a flow-through model, there is a standard solution. The tax system could simply await owner-level realization, such as from selling stock or receiving a dividend, and impose the tax at that point. This option thus is the same as option (1) above, except that it permits deferral of any tax that U.S. individuals earn through corporations until they personally realize the income. This approach would therefore similarly make corporate residence wholly irrelevant, and the source of income largely irrelevant.[2]

In practice under the existing U.S. income tax, waiting to tax corporate income until it is realized at the individual level would all too often mean *never* taxing it. Under Internal Revenue Code section 1014, appreciated assets enjoy a tax-free step-up in basis at death, thus permanently eliminating taxation of any unrealized appreciation. Suppose, however, that, at least for corporate stock, this provision was repealed, and death (along, perhaps with the transfer of an asset by inter vivos gift) was treated as a realization event.[3] Would this make it reasonably tolerable to defer any tax on U.S. individuals, with respect to the income that they earn through corporate entities, until they personally realized their shares of corporate profits?

If not for the mismatch with how the individual income tax treats noncorporate income, this result might be defensible. Roughly speaking, if realization was defined broadly enough, the approach might lead to something resembling consumption tax treatment of the income that U.S. individuals earn through corporate entities. Suppose we converted the existing income tax into an individual-level consumption tax, by providing unlimited savings deductions and not taxing people on accretion to their savings until they withdrew the funds for use in consumption. Corporations need not be taxpayers under such a system, as they are in effect savings vehicles for the owners. Such a system is typically called cash flow or consumed income taxation.[4] Unlike a business-level consumption tax, such as a retail sales tax or VAT, it can apply graduated rates that depend on one's overall consumption for the year. It thus may be able to achieve similar progressivity to that under the existing income tax (Shaviro 2004). Switching from income taxation to progressive consumption taxation has many supporters (see id., Bankman and Weisbach 2006; Carroll and Viard 2012)—although, as we will see shortly, the consumed income tax is merely one of two main methodologies that have been widely discussed.

Now let's return to the existing income tax, but as hypothetically modified to exempt corporations, thus eliminating any tax on corporate income until it is realized at the individual level. Two key results would be exempting savings that are invested in corporate entities, and permitting corporate owner-employees to eliminate any current taxation of their labor income by underpaying themselves. While both of these planning opportunities involve tax avoidance if one is applying an income tax baseline, under a consumed income tax they would be the results that everyone gets, without regard to using a corporate entity. For example, in the owner-employee case, paying oneself one's true salary would make no tax difference if one could then deduct it again by reinvesting it in the company.

Does this mean that, even under the existing income tax but without section 1014, we should consider these results not so bad? There are two reasons for saying no. The first involves the distortions that would result from limiting consumption tax-equivalent treatment to corporate investment on the savings side, and to corporate owner-employees on the labor income side. The second is that the existing income tax, minus section 1014 and the corporate income tax, might end up giving better than consumption tax-equivalent treatment to owner-employees.

A consumed income tax works best if it treats consumer borrowing as current "income"—which is what a retail sales tax effectively does, by virtue of reaching expenditures that are made out of consumer borrowing.[5] Absent this feature, or in the alternative an adequate mechanism for collecting the deferred liability later with interest, there would be a gap in the reach of the consumed income tax that would especially benefit people who are rich enough to borrow easily. For example, absent a rule treating (or long-term equivalent to treating) consumer borrowing as currently taxable, people such as Bill Gates, Steve Jobs, or Mark Zuckerberg might find it easy to avoid tax liability indefinitely. However, while well-designed consumed income taxes therefore typically treat consumer borrowing as "income," this might be hard to do under the current system, as modified to lack an entity-level corporate income tax.

In sum, it is difficult to see elimination of the corporate income tax as an appealing option so long as we still apply an income tax, rather than a well-designed progressive consumption tax, to individuals. And if one drops the assumption that bequest (and perhaps gift) transfers of corporate stock could be treated as taxable realizations, contrary to their status under present law, the approach becomes wholly untenable.

3. *Convert the corporate income tax into a cash-flow consumption tax*—A third option for eliminating the very slow race between residence-based and source-based corporate income taxation would involve adopting a version of the other leading approach to progressive consumption taxation, which is commonly known as the X-tax.[6] However, before explaining why and how this would help, some background is needed.

As we saw in chapter 2, the source concept can be defined on either an origin basis or a destination basis. When a business in one jurisdiction sells goods or services to consumers in another jurisdiction, the origin basis asks where production occurred, while the destination basis asks where consumption occurred. Thus, in the earlier example of the New York architect who designs a luxury apartment in Italy without leaving home, the fee is U.S. source under the origin basis, and Italian source under the destination basis. Over the long run, if the amount a country's people get to consume is equal to what they produce, the two methods work out similarly as ways of dividing the global tax base between trading partners.

The great advantage of using the destination basis is that it makes source a much clearer and easier concept to apply. Consider sales of iPhones to consumers. Rather than having to ask where, within the global chain of Apple affiliates, value was actually created in the production process, all we need to do is locate the consumer. Thus, the proceeds from selling an iPhone would be U.S. source, under the destination basis, if the consumer was a Chicagoan, and Russian source if she lived in Moscow. This does not solve all of the problems—for example, suppose that an American tourist buys an iPhone in Moscow—but it gets rid of transfer pricing and the associated intractable dilemmas.

There also are arguments in favor of using the origin basis, rather than the destination basis. For example, newly enacting a destination basis tax might, for complicated reasons that Carroll and Viard (2012, 110) explain, result in a one-time wealth transfer from Americans to foreigners amounting to several trillion dollars. So the point is not that a shift to the destination basis would necessarily be better policy, all things considered, but that it would indeed permit greatly simplifying the international tax rules (which is my main focus here).

Why would one need to shift from an income tax to a consumption tax, just in order to get rid of the origin basis (and thus transfer pricing)? The answer is that, while a consumption tax can use either the origin basis or the destination basis, under an income tax one is pretty much stuck with the origin basis (Shaviro 2004, 110). Conceptually, the core reason for this difference is that the origin basis actually offers a measure of national production (i.e., income), rather than of national consumption. So it starts in the right place from an income tax standpoint, whereas the destination basis starts in the wrong place.

To be sure, it is equally true that the origin basis starts in the wrong place from a consumption tax standpoint. The reason a consumption tax can nonetheless use either method is that, if national production and consumption are the same in present value over the long run, then so will be the taxes levied under both methods—at least, if tax rates are the same for all years. So why is an income tax less administratively flexible? The problem is that here "the long-term equivalence of national consumption and national production is insufficient, given that the burden of an income tax depends on the [relative] sequence of consumption expenditures (that is, to what extent it is deferred through saving or accelerated through dissaving)" (Shaviro 2004, 110). Taxable income should be higher over time when saving precedes consumption than when it does not.

To make this more concrete through an illustration, suppose that a given firm has two cross-border transactions in a given year. The first is an export sale of labor services for $1 million, while the second is its payment of $1 million to a foreign supplier for inventory goods that it holds for later domestic sale. Under a consumption tax, it makes no difference whether we take account of both under the origin basis, or ignore both under the destination basis. The net tax base effect is zero either way.[7] Under an income tax, however, use of the origin basis yields $1 million of taxable income in Year 1, since the outlay for inventory must be capitalized until the goods are sold, rather than being immediately deductible. This is the correct income tax result, given that the firm has earned $1 million and then merely converted its sales proceeds into a valuable asset that it retains. One cannot easily get to the same place by using the destination basis, however, given that it ignores both imports and exports.

Suppose, therefore, that we want to shift from the existing origin-basis income tax to a destination-basis consumption tax, while still having rate progressivity. How might one do this? The answer offered by the X-tax is as follows. First, one turns the corporate income tax (and that for businesses generally) into a cash-flow consumption tax, by permitting current deductions for items that an income tax treats as capital outlays. This tax would have a single flat rate. Second, in the most common versions of the X-tax, one modifies the corporate/business tax base to ignore all financial flows, such as interest payments and receipts.[8] Third, the existing income tax on individuals, other than when their economic activity fell under the rubric of the new business tax regime, would be eliminated with one exception. Wage payments that one received from a business, in addition to being deductible at the business level, would be includable under a wage tax on individuals with a graduated rate structure. Thus, suppose the business rate is a flat 35 percent, which also is the top individual rate. Having a graduated rate structure in the wage tax instrument—say, with a zero bracket followed by several intermediate rates before it topped off at 35 percent—would cause wage payments to generate net refunds for taxpayers. In effect, it would result in offering workers progressive rebates with respect to the consumption tax that (as described above) was being collected at the business level.

Whether one should replace the existing individual and corporate income taxes with an X-tax is a huge topic that falls outside my present scope, as it properly could occupy an entire book, or perhaps a library full of books (as indeed it has over the years). In this debate, the fact that the X-tax, if done on the destination basis,[9] would vastly improve the U.S. international tax regime seems unlikely to be decisive all by itself. For now, it is enough to note both making this change would indeed solve the "very slow race" problem in international tax, and that surely this counts in its favor.

Before leaving this topic, however, one further variant of this proposed approach merits attention. In the above discussion, the only reason for assuming adoption of an X-tax, rather than simply replacement of the corporate income tax with a destination-basis consumption tax, was to show the connection between the contemporary debate over fundamental tax reform and the prospects for eliminating the very slow race. However, one can get the same effect on international tax policy just by changing the corporate income tax into a destination-basis consumption tax. Obviously, doing so would have the disadvantage of combining an entity-level consumption tax with an individual-level income tax, which is not ideal. Given, however, that the U.S. tax system as it stands is far from ideal, this is not dispositive against it.

Alan Auerbach (2010) recently proposed such a corporate-level change that would not be conditioned on eliminating income taxation of individuals. He argues that the existing U.S. corporate income tax has the following main defects. Domestically, it discourages productive investment and encourages the excessive use of debt. Internationally, it faces the pressure of global tax competition and has trouble taxing multinational firms due to such difficulties as that of defining source. The solution he proposes is conversion of the corporate income tax into something that resembles the business-level portion of a destination-basis X-tax.

In the purely domestic realm, the Auerbach proposal would be a pure cash-flow tax on all corporate receipts and disbursements other than the proceeds from issuing equity. Thus, all capital outlays would be immediately deductible, making the system a consumption tax. However, unlike in X-tax variants that ignore financial transactions, all financial inflows other than for issuing equity would be included, while all financial outflows would be deducted. Thus, a company that borrowed $100 for a year at 10 percent interest, repaying $110 the following year, would include $100 upfront and deduct $110 on the back end, creating a net tax burden on the loan of zero.[10] Of course, the $100 inclusion would typically be offset by a $100 deduction from using the money to fund a business outlay (Auerbach 2010, 7–10).

Again, the shift to consumption taxation would just be for corporations, along with any other business entities that were sufficiently similar to be brought within the scope of the change (13–14).[11] The existing income tax for individuals generally would, or at least could, remain the same. While savings and investment would thus be treated differently inside as opposed to outside the scope of the new tax, this would not create huge tax planning opportunities for owner-employees who underpaid their own salaries. Paying oneself a lower, as opposed to a higher, salary would have no net tax effect if the applicable corporate and individual rates were the same.

Internationally, the use of the destination basis would mean that all cross-border transactions were ignored in computing a company's tax base. Thus, in sales transactions with foreign firms, proceeds received would not be includable, and those paid out would not be deductible. The same would hold for financial flows between U.S. firms and foreign firms, including when the two were corporate affiliates (10). The system would therefore effectively be territorial, except that it would be taxing domestic consumption, rather than domestic production, and thereby eliminating transfer pricing issues (10–11).

While the Auerbach proposal clearly has large potential advantages, there may be avoidance concerns, such as from its placing corporations on a different tax regime than other taxable businesses. For example, Noel Cunningham and Mitchell Engler (2012, 32-33) argue that exporters might generally incorporate so they could use the destination basis and ignore receipts from abroad, while importers generally avoided incorporation so they could stay on the origin basis and deduct amounts paid to foreigners.

However one evaluates such concerns, the sheer significance of the changes that the proposal would make—for example, by reason of its making debt principal flows includable and deductible—seems likely to induce caution about adopting it. And absent its adoption, or that of some other alternative discussed in this section (such as an X-tax that uses the destination basis), the main international tax policy dilemmas that this book discusses will remain in force. I therefore next ask how they might be addressed if entity-level corporate income taxation remains an unshakable feature of U.S. tax law.

B. Marginally Improving the Existing U.S. International Tax System

In evaluating the available policy options if we are stuck with entity-level corporate income taxation, an initial step is revisiting the "very slow race" metaphor. Unsatisfying and ill-functioning though the source and corporate residence concepts may both be, they are not actually engaged in a race unless we are trying to pick just one of them as the "winner." However, current international tax law, not just in the United States but also abroad, commonly uses both. Even predominantly territorial countries, such as the United Kingdom and Japan, apply various rules limiting the exemption of resident companies'FSI. The analysis in chapter 5 provides support for this practice, as it suggests that the optimal domestic tax rate on both the domestic source income of foreign companies and the FSI of resident companies is likely to exceed zero if entity-based taxation prevents our distinguishing between investment by resident and foreign individuals.

Accordingly, the dilemma we face in international tax policy is less one of adjudicating a very slow race than of trying to perform a set of tasks with two very dull tools. Perhaps this makes unsurprising the conclusion that neither tool should be wholly discarded so long as it retains even minimal utility, given the other tool's limitations.

With respect to taxing resident companies' FSI, chapter 5's unilateral national welfare analysis (based on assuming that what we did would have no effect on other countries' rules) reached the following main conclusions. Resident companies' FSI should be taxed at a significantly lower rate than domestic source income, albeit at a higher rate than zero. Both deferral and foreign tax credits should be repealed. The fact that very low foreign taxes may be a tag indicating domestic profit shifting may support applying anti-tax haven rules, although such rules would create a tradeoff by making higher foreign tax payments (i.e., those to non-haven countries) effectively better than deductible.

This chapter will add two main elements to the analysis. First, I ask whether other countries' possible responses to our rule choices might affect the conclusions reached. Second, without offering a specific proposal—which would require, not just making this book far longer than it already is, but greater certainty than I have regarding exactly what would be best—I offer additional detail regarding how to think about the design choices that are presented. This includes following up briefly on the suggestion in chapter 3 that the U.S. rules regarding both residence and source could likely be improved.

1. What's in a Name? "Exemption" After All?

Suppose one were to determine (or at least believe) that, for the United States today, the optimal tax rate for resident companies' FSI, enacted to accompany the repeal of deferral and foreign tax creditability, was as high as, say, 20 percent. Enacting this package would violate dozens of bilateral tax treaties with other countries, under which the signatories agree to avoid double taxation via either foreign tax creditability or exemption. Some, including policy makers in other countries, might even view it as offensive, given the widespread belief (contrary to the arguments in this book) that avoiding double taxation is indeed an important principle. What is more, our treaty partners would actually lose something of value, by reason of our ceasing to reimburse U.S. companies that pay their taxes, although it is true that we could have ended the reimbursement, without offering them grounds for complaint, by adopting implicit foreign tax deductibility via exemption.

Such concerns clearly reduce the desirability of this approach, relative to how it looks in a purely unilateral analysis. Suppose, for example, that other countries expressly retaliated in some fashion that we found undesirable.[12] Even absent specific and direct responses, any lasting harm to our reputation as a reliable treaty partner might conceivably have adverse consequences down the road.

Insofar as this actually is a binding dilemma, we face an unfortunate tradeoff. Its ineluctability might create a scenario in which the price of eliminating deferral and foreign tax creditability—rules which, as discussed earlier, create pointlessly bad incentives and guarantee that the overall system will have a very poor ratio of tax planning and compliance costs to revenue raised—is adopting too low a tax rate for U.S. companies' FSI.

While this dilemma, insofar as it exists, is cause for regret, this would do nothing to undermine the correctness (and continuing relevance) of this book's unilateral analysis of deferral, foreign tax creditability, and the optimal domestic tax rate for resident companies' FSI. Sometimes in life we face dilemmas that we wish were avoidable, and it remains desirable to understand and know about them. However, one should not too readily assume that the dilemma is in fact posed quite so sharply. In particular, one should consider just how low the tax rate on FSI must be in order for a country to have an "exemption" system, both optically and for treaty purposes.

A literalist would say that "exemption" requires that the domestic tax rate on FSI actually be zero. However, existing exemption systems do not always follow this approach. Japan, for example, exempts from tax only 95 percent of the qualifying foreign dividends paid from foreign subsidiaries to resident companies. A prominent recent U.S. proposal to establish a territorial system, released in a 2011 "Discussion Draft" by House Ways and Means Chairman Dave Camp, would likewise have provided only a 95 percent exemption. According to the Camp bill's published Technical Explanation, imposing tax on the remaining 5 percent of FSI at the generally applicable domestic rate would be "intended to be a substitute for the disallowance of deductions for expenses incurred to generate exempt foreign income" (House Ways and Means Committee 2011, 18).

There are two different ways in which one could look at these instances of nonexemption exemption. One would involve emphasizing that both Japan's approach and that in the Camp bill result in taxing FSI at less than a 2 percent rate, given their 95 percent exclusions and corporate tax rates below 40 percent. Hence, neither provides direct support for more than a de minimis departure from literal exemption.

The other perspective would start by asking whether there is room here for employing a slippery slope argument. Could the tax rate on FSI, rather than just the inclusion percentage, be 5 percent? Could it even be as high as 8 or 10 percent? The ground for pushing in this direction is not just that, once we agree that "exemption" permits a non-zero tax rate for FSI, arguably all that remains is haggling over the price. Rather, consider the broader implications of the statement in the Camp bill's Technical Explanation that a non-zero tax rate on FSI merely takes the place of disallowing domestic deductions that related to incurring it.

From an income measurement standpoint, if one allows domestic deductions that, in some cases, are generating FSI, one effectively is permitting understatement of the taxpayer's domestic source income, accompanied by overstatement of its FSI. The ground for allowing such deductions, presumably, is the administrative difficulty of telling them apart from those that are incurred to generate domestic source income. If one can respond to this problem by taxing FSI at a low rate, one arguably has established a broader principle that, under exemption generally, it is permissible to respond to presumed profit shifting via the reported FSI, rather than just through the source rules. In effect, imposing a low-tax rate on FSI is merely an indirect way of permissibly taxing domestic source income, adopted for administrative convenience or even necessity, and limited only by the requirement that it be done reasonably and in good faith.

There are, to be sure, objections to pushing this argument too far, even with entire good faith and in the absence of either retaliation or significant harm to the United States' reputation as a reliable treaty partner. For example, a regime of applying a low but non-zero tax rate to resident corporations' FSI might prove less politically stable than either the current regime or outright exemption, leading to overly frequent rate changes for FSI. In addition, the political temptation to over-tax FSI might be greater if the tax rate, rather than deferral and foreign tax creditability, were doing the work of keeping it in check.

The treaty concerns that are posed by my proposed approach are not, however, limited to the question of whether one can really take a deep breath and assert that, say, a 10 percent tax rate on FSI is actually "exemption" plus an indirect tax on misreported domestic source income. Important as well is the question of how vehemently treaty partners would object. This might affect, for example, the concessions that they would demand in the course of treaty renegotiation, the retaliations (if any) that they would undertake in the interim, and the degree of global ill-will that a unilateral U.S. initiative would end up generating.

There are reasons for hoping—although admittedly without certainty—that many treaty partners' level of objection would be low, rather than high. Again, the detriment that they would suffer from our eliminating foreign tax creditability is one that we could impose today without creating grounds for complaint, by switching to a pure exemption system. In addition, our simultaneously strengthening anti-tax haven rules (as discussed below) might actually benefit them, by reducing the extent to which U.S. companies would shift profits to tax havens at their (as well as our) expense. Finally, suppose they "retaliated" by themselves adopting similar international tax regimes, thus reciprocally violating their treaty obligations to us with regard to double taxation. This would do little or no harm to U.S. fiscal interests, especially given the already limited creditability abroad of our source-based taxes. So the blowback that we encountered might end up being quite low.

On the other hand, perhaps this rosy scenario overrates the rationality and flexibility that one realistically can expect in real-world politics. Moreover, given the prevalence of the belief that "double taxation" matters for its own sake, it is hard to rule out the possibility that U.S. unilateral action might be viewed very negatively, even (or perhaps especially) by close allies. So the question of how we should evaluate the costs of actual or apparent tax treaty violation concededly is an open one.

In any event, the higher the tax rate on FSI that is permissible under "exemption," the weaker the dilemma that is posed if we cannot otherwise eliminate deferral and foreign tax creditability. Suppose, for example, that one would like to tax FSI at a 12 percent rate while eliminating foreign tax credits and deferral, but that one is indeed restricted to a maximum 5 percent rate. Lowering the price of tax base improvement, by not requiring that the tax rate on FSI drop all the way to zero, increases the likelihood that the price is worth paying. And indeed the dilemma disappears altogether if 5 percent should turn out to be the optimal tax rate for FSI.

In sum, while recognizing that further analysis would be needed to resolve the empirical issues that chapter 5 suggests are crucial to the assessment of international tax policy, I would tentatively propose changing the U.S. international tax system as follows (as well as in other respects that are further discussed below). Deferral and the allowance of foreign tax credits would be repealed. U.S. companies' active business FSI would generally be taxed at a rate of at least 5 percent, and possibly higher (such as 8 or 10 percent). Their passive income would be currently taxable at the full U.S. rate, as under present law, although likewise accompanied by the repeal of foreign tax credits, as proposed by Graetz and Grinberg (2003), in the hope that U.S. companies would respond by ramping up their efforts to avoid foreign taxation of such income. This still, however, leaves the question of how to tax FSI that is reported as arising in tax havens—to which Japan, for example, does not apply exemption.

2. Tax Havens, Foreign Taxes, and the Tagging Issue

As noted in earlier chapters, even in a purely unilateral framework the optimal treatment of foreign taxes is complicated by the fact that, when they are very low, this may correlate with profit shifting at the expense of the domestic tax base. Thus, suppose a U.S. company has millions of dollars of global profits that are reported as income of a Bermuda or Caymans subsidiary. We can probably be confident that these profits do not actually reflect economic activity that occurred in the putative source country. Rather, given the lack of substantial productive resources in many tax haven countries, along with our understanding of tax planning incentives, we have good reason to believe that the economic activity that produced these profits probably occurred someplace else.

Insofar as this activity occurred at home, and especially if it involved activity by U.S. individuals such as under-compensated owner-employees, we may want to subject the profits to the full source-based U.S. tax. On the other hand, if the activity occurred abroad, we may be glad that the U.S. company was able to avoid foreign taxes, presumably to the economic benefit of its U.S. (among other) shareholders.

In either case, further information might reverse the conclusion. For example, if we have reason to want to tax U.S. multinationals' domestic source income at a low rate, on the view that it is unusually mobile, tolerating profit shifting may be one way to implement the preference. On the other hand, in cases where outbound investment by U.S. companies is a substitute for domestic investment, rather than being unrelated or a complement, permitting the companies to benefit from foreign profit shifting out of high-tax peer countries may worsen the tax competition problem that we face.

On balance, I consider it plausible that the tagging rationale supports imposing a higher tax rate on FSI when the source country tax is extremely low. Given, however, that this is in tension with inducing U.S. companies to equate a dollar of foreign taxes paid with any other dollar of foreign expenses or forgone revenue, one needs to do it thoughtfully, and with an eye to the incentives that are created. This, in turn, requires considering how a given rule would affect the resident companies' foreign tax MRRs.

Two illustrations may be in order. First, consider Japan's international tax rules, which generally deny exemption (as well as deferral) to FSI that Japanese companies earn through foreign subsidiaries that are headquartered in tax haven countries. As we saw in chapter 5, the discontinuous character of this rule—in that it goes from "on" to "off" at one precise point—can lead in practice to MRRs that exceed 100 percent. It might even, especially if adopted by more countries, lead to the emergence of tax havens that specialize in levying just enough tax to ensure that home country exemption is available.

Second, the Obama administration has recently discussed imposing an overall global minimum tax rate on U.S. companies' FSI, which would be computed without regard to deferral. To illustrate how this might work, suppose that Acme Products, a U.S. multinational, has $50 million of FSI in a given year through its foreign subsidiaries, none of which it repatriates. If the mandated minimum rate was, say, 20 percent, Acme might owe U.S. tax on this income equal to $10 million minus whatever foreign income taxes it paid. (Amounts repatriated for U.S. tax purposes, and thus taxable without regard to the minimum tax rule, presumably would count toward the overall $10 million floor.)

Before evaluating this rule more fully, a technical clarification is in order. In the case where Acme paid no foreign taxes and thus owed a full $10 million of U.S. tax on its FSI, it could have triggered the same $10 million of U.S. tax (at a 35 percent U.S. rate) by repatriating $28.57 million of FSI. Thus, a sensible rule design might treat what happened in the zero-repatriation case as a deemed $28.57 million repatriation, followed by deemed reinvestment of this money in the same CFCs. Imposition of the tax would therefore be accompanied by reducing the CFCs' earnings and profits (E&P), thereby avoiding duplicative taxation of the same FSI if they actually repatriate funds later on.

This detail helps to show that enacting the minimum tax would be tantamount to scaling back deferral, by effectively denying it in circumstances where Acme's global tax benefit would otherwise have been too great. This interrelationship between the minimum tax rule and deferral helps to illuminate the rule's likely broader incentive effects on U.S. companies.

From an MRR standpoint, one evident virtue of the minimum tax approach is that it avoids discontinuous cliff effects. U.S. companies' foreign tax MRRs would never exceed 100 percent. On the other hand, they would actually equal 100 percent for all foreign taxes up to the threshold, since, until that point, the taxes would indeed reduce taxpayers' U.S. liability dollar for dollar.

At first glance, a 100 percent MRR, even if it is too high, might appear to be nothing new. After all, we have lived with the foreign tax credit for almost a century. What such a conclusion would miss, however, is the fact that the minimum tax would in effect partly repeal deferral. The "iron box" would therefore apply to the analysis. To the extent that the minimum tax resulted in immediate U.S. residence-based worldwide taxation— as it would, in the above Acme illustration, until the taxpayer's net foreign tax liability, as a percent of FSI, rose from 0 to 20 percent, or to \$10 million—U.S. companies now actually would have zero cost consciousness with respect to their foreign tax liabilities in this range.

Thus, suppose Acme has foreign subsidiaries in Germany and the Cayman Islands, and that, but for the minimum tax, it would locate the great preponderance of its FSI in the Caymans, and therefore pay foreign taxes of only \$1 million on its \$50 million of FSI. A natural response to U.S. enactment of a 20 percent global minimum tax on FSI would be to undo enough of this profit shifting to raise its German tax bill back to \$10 million. While this is only a breakeven move relative to paying the extra \$9 million of U.S. tax, it might reduce the tax planning and compliance costs that were associated with the profit shifting. The end result, if Acme was owned entirely by U.S. individuals, would simply be to transfer \$9 million from U.S. individuals to the German Treasury, in exchange for reducing tax planning and compliance costs by a much smaller amount.

This is not to deny that a minimum tax rule would also reduce the tax benefit to be derived both from shifting profits from the United States to the Caymans, and from deferral generally. The point is not that profit shifting to tax havens should remain unaddressed, but rather that one should be mindful of the foreign tax MRRs that one is creating, and that setting them as high as 100 percent is likely to be unwise.

Unfortunately, so long as the U.S. international tax system offers foreign tax credits, a 100 percent MRR is hard to avoid, other than where it is reduced by deferral, which of course has its own serious drawbacks. Suppose, however, that U.S. law shifted to foreign tax deductibility, accompanied by the repeal of deferral and reduction of the U.S. tax rate for FSI (whether or not through a system that we called "exemption"). Then, with proper design, the U.S. tax rate on FSI could rise as the foreign tax rate declined, without the creation of foreign tax MRRs as high as 100 percent.

Just by way of illustration, suppose that U.S. law adopted the following variant of the minimum tax approach for resident multinationals' FSI. So long as the taxpayer's overall foreign taxes equaled at least 20 percent of its FSI for the year, such FSI would be taxed under U.S. law at only a 5 percent rate, with foreign taxes being deductible for this purpose. At the other end of the spectrum, if the U.S. company paid no foreign income taxes, it would face a 15 percent rate on its FSI. In between those two endpoints, the U.S. tax rate on the FSI would rise ratably as the overall foreign tax rate declined. For example, at a 10 percent overall foreign tax rate, the applicable U.S. tax rate would be 10 percent (i.e., halfway between 5 percent and 15 percent). The MRR for this range as a whole, reflecting both foreign tax deductibility and the gradual rate change, would be 80 percent.[13]

Again, this example is merely meant to illustrate the feasibility of combining a tagging approach to low-taxed foreign income with keeping effective MRRs below 100 percent. Many different kinds of approaches could be used toward this end. For example, one might instead adopt a version of the Japanese approach, under which one focused purely on the FSI that is reported in particular low-tax foreign jurisdictions, rather than on one's overall foreign tax rate. Such an approach could likewise be designed to respond gradually to marginal changes in the relevant foreign tax rates.

3. The Transition Issue If We Shift to Exemption or a Current Accrual System for Foreign Source Income

Suppose the United States repealed deferral, such as by shifting to an exemption system or one with a low positive rate for U.S. companies' subsequently earned FSI. This would raise the question of what should be done with pre-enactment FSI that had not yet been repatriated. The amount at issue might be about $2 trillion (Morse 2013, 102).

At a 35 percent corporate rate, under new view assumptions and in the absence of any foreign tax credits, the deferred tax on these foreign earnings would have a present value of $700 billion. Obviously, this amount might be significantly lowered by the prospect of claiming foreign tax credits upon repatriation (albeit not for earnings situated in tax havens). In addition, whether or not a given company has taken the accounting position that its foreign earnings are permanently reinvested abroad, it may genuinely anticipate never taxably repatriating them. However, even in that scenario, the company may anticipate that avoiding repatriation would generate ongoing tax planning costs while the current system remained in place.

The bottom line is that eliminating the deferred tax on earnings that U.S. companies have already accumulated abroad would be a hugely consequential retroactive change in their favor. Indeed, this may be a key reason for the strong political pressure that has been exerted in recent years in favor of adopting exemption and/or repeated repatriation tax holidays. Even if profit-shifting technologies have been steadily improving, making it ever easier and cheaper to classify income as FSI and keep it abroad indefinitely, the costliness to U.S. companies of avoiding repatriation may be increasing as the percentage of their assets that are held abroad keeps rising (see Grubert 2009a).

How should we evaluate the retroactive gain that U.S. companies would reap if the repatriation tax were simply eliminated? To the extent that the capital markets, in pricing U.S. multinationals' stock, had not fully anticipated the repeal of deferral, the companies' shareholders would reap a huge windfall gain that would serve no evident policy objective. At least in substantial part, it would represent a transfer from other investors and from U.S. taxpayers generally, rather than net social gain.

Suppose, however, that the prospect of our adopting exemption without eliminating the transition gain was to a degree anticipated, at least probabilistically as something that might happen, and perhaps with rising odds as adoption nears. The main incentive effects on investors and U.S. companies would be twofold. First, the possible disappearance of the repatriation tax (and of the need to plan around it) would reduce the U.S. tax system's discouragement of U.S. incorporation—a desirable effect from the standpoint of tax neutrality. Second, and undesirably, pre-enactment repatriations of U.S. companies' foreign earnings would be additionally discouraged, and profit shifting encouraged. I have argued elsewhere that the bad incentive effects are likely to be the more significant ones, on the ground that profit shifting and internal corporate fund flows appear to be more tax elastic than investors' incorporation choices (Shaviro 2011b, 424).

Thus, there is a powerful case for imposing a transition tax to eliminate the "windfall" gain. To be sure, this would pose a number of design issues. However, both Susan Morse (2013) and I in earlier work (Shaviro 2011b) have concluded that the challenges are not insuperable. Both of these studies propose eliminating unclaimed foreign tax credits, but roughly compensating taxpayers for this loss through the adoption of a transition tax rate that is below the existing statutory rate—say, from 5 to 20 percent depending on one's assumptions and aims (Morse 2013, 152; Shaviro 2011b, 427). Both of us propose defining the tax base as the E&P of U.S. companies' foreign subsidiaries, which are supposed to be computed on an ongoing basis (Morse 2013, 140), although Morse notes that one could also consider using financial accounting measures of unremitted earnings (146).[14] Thus, if the transition tax rate was 10 percent and a given U.S. company's foreign subsidiaries had $500 million of E&P, it would owe a transition tax of $50 million. Concerns about the effect of the transition tax on companies' liquidity, if they had to pay it immediately, could be addressed by allowing them to pay it over several years, perhaps with an interest charge for the deferral.

4. Revising the Corporate Residence and Source Rules

If the "very slow race" between residence-based and source-based taxation is destined to continue, with each of the contestants stumbling forward indefinitely in the absence of any reason to pick a single winner, it is important to ask how each of them might be at least marginally improved. Rather than seeking to develop or fully evaluate detailed proposals regarding either concept, I will settle for briefly exploring what we should be looking for with respect to each.

The current legal standard for U.S. corporate residence, which relies on U.S. incorporation, sounds easy to avoid at least on a prospective basis, but (as we saw in chapter 3) has proven surprisingly resilient in practice. Evidently, at least for now, the United States retains significant market power at this margin. Both U.S. individuals, and those from outside who want to be economically active here or to access our capital markets, still frequently choose U.S. incorporation due to nontax advantages that they associate with it. Once here, they may find exit difficult or unduly costly (especially in light of the anti-inversion rules), even if they would now choose to expatriate if it were purely an election.

This line of reasoning, in addition to supporting a tax rate above zero on U.S.-incorporated companies' FSI, also has possible implications for modifying the definition of a U.S. company. In particular, it can potentially motivate expanding the definition so that it also includes companies that incorporated abroad but have U.S. headquarters (as in Senator Levin's Stop Tax Haven Abuse Act, which would reach such companies if they had at least $50 million in gross assets or were publicly traded).[15] The key empirical issues here include how the expanded definition would affect the tax elasticity of U.S. corporate residence, and how U.S. individuals' welfare would be affected by tax-discouraging foreign-incorporated companies from having U.S. headquarters. Without attempting to resolve these issues here, I believe it is plausible that this would be a good change overall.

A further expansion might involve attaching U.S. resident status to any company issuing equity that was registered and/or actively traded on U.S. capital markets. Again without purporting to resolve the issues definitively, I would tend to consider this a more dubious reform, both because other countries might view it as overly aggressive (and therefore as inviting retaliation) and due to the impact it might have on the functioning of U.S. capital markets.

The other of the two stumbling contestants in the very slow race is, of course, the source rules. However, the broader issue that these rules raise goes beyond merely defining domestic source and FSI. The more general issue of normative interest is how various particular types of income ought to be taxed, given not only the source determination but any other pertinent information about them. Thus, while subpart F does not recharacterize FSI as domestic source income, its end result (i.e., current U.S. taxation) is the same, leaving aside the application of foreign tax credit limits. Likewise, when a country with a generally territorial system imposes a tax on resident companies' FSI that is passive or was reported as arising in a tax haven, it effectively treats such income more like domestic source income than like other FSI.

While chapters 2 and 3 contain fuller discussions of source problems than I will offer here, the following is an overview of how one might think about some of the main issues—in particular, though not exclusively, if a shift toward territoriality increased the tax benefits associated with profit shifting by U.S. companies.

Passive FSI of U.S. companies—Countries with territorial systems commonly tax resident companies' passive FSI, even though the standard arguments for exempting active business income could be deployed here. For example, given that active businesses may anticipate holding working capital in the form of portfolio assets, taxing resident companies' foreign passive income may encourage investing through foreign firms, in lieu of domestic ones, even in the active business setting.

Nonetheless, the rationale for taxing resident companies' FSI is sufficiently clear to have won widespread acceptance. Given that resident companies would be taxable on the income from domestic portfolio assets, and can easily move portfolio income (as determined under the source rules) wherever they like, territoriality would have a clear adverse impact on the domestic tax base. Nor would this necessarily be fully offset by foreign companies holding U.S. financial assets instead. There is no inherent reason why the dollar amounts on pieces of paper denominating U.S. financial assets must remain constant.

As I noted in chapter 5, the argument in Graetz and Grinberg (2003), to the effect that foreign taxes on passive income should merely be deductible, would have the advantage of making U.S. taxpayers properly foreign tax cost conscious. And there is even a case for combining this with application of full domestic rates to passive FSI, if one believes that the choice between foreign and domestic passive assets is far more tax elastic, and thus relevant here, than that between using U.S. and foreign entities to invest abroad.

Active business FSI (such as that of "base companies") that appears to reflect profit shifting—The motivation for the foreign base company rules in subpart F resembles that for denying deferral to passive FSI. While active business operations may face practical constraints that impede placing them in tax havens with only limited productive capacity, no such constraint applies to empty-shell affiliates that are placed in tax havens and then used to siphon off taxable income from their U.S. or high-tax foreign affiliates via transfer pricing and debt placement.

The problem here, however, is that the effect of this tax planning on U.S. welfare appears to be more ambiguous than that pertaining to passive assets. Insofar as the strategy reduces the taxes that U.S. companies would otherwise pay abroad, without affecting U.S. domestic tax revenues or the amount invested domestically, it would appear to be a good thing from our standpoint. In addition, even insofar as the U.S. domestic tax base is at issue, the effectiveness of a crackdown via subpart F is reduced to the extent that taxpayers respond by using foreign, rather than U.S, corporations to make paired U.S./foreign investments. It is difficult to assess the relative importance of these considerations without greater empirical information, including about the long-term revenue effects.

This issue is relevant not only because the base company rules could be repealed, either in connection with a shift toward territoriality or under the current system, but also because taxpayer self-help has in recent years achieved a near equivalent of repeal. As we saw in chapter 3, the use of the check-the-box rules to create hybrid entities, such as a Caymans affiliate that U.S. tax law wholly disregards, has made the base company rules easily avoidable by well-advised U.S. multinationals.[16] This prompted a 2009 Obama administration budget proposal to address the use of such hybrid entities in global tax planning, although the administration did not renew the proposal in 2010, apparently due in part to the concern that the revenue yield would be disappointing. Whether the reduced U.S. revenue estimates that apparently helped prompt the administration's retreat were right or wrong, they clearly identified a crucial issue in analyzing the proposal's merits.

Royalties—As noted in chapter 3, the tax treatment of royalties from abroad provides a good illustration of how the current U.S. system can actually be more generous in practice than a well-designed territorial system. Thus, suppose a U.S. parent develops valuable intangibles that it licenses to foreign subsidiaries, in exchange for their making royalty payments. The royalties generally are treated as active business FSI. If their amount is predictable in advance, the U.S. parent may find it easy to use specially acquired foreign tax credits in order to limit the U.S. tax liability that otherwise would be triggered by their receipt. Meanwhile, even if the subsidiaries are in high-tax countries, the royalties that they pay generally are deductible abroad (and often do not face withholding taxes). Royalty income may therefore end up being taxed nowhere—a tax haven-like result that does not require actually using a tax haven.

Territorial countries, in contrast to the United States, typically treat inbound royalties as yielding domestic source income that is fully taxable to the resident company. A number of U.S. commentators have proposed changing the U.S. tax treatment of royalties to be similar, whether in the context of shifting to exemption or under the existing system. What makes their argument convincing is less the point that royalty income is being taxed nowhere if it generates foreign deductions (since we may be glad if U.S. companies can minimize their foreign taxes), than the fact that inbound royalties presumably reflect U.S. economic activity in creating valuable intangibles.

Interest expense of U.S. and foreign multinationals—The use of interest deductions is matched only by transfer pricing as a crown jewel of profit-shifting activity by multinationals. What makes this tool so potent and attractive is its resting on the legal fiction that the affiliates in a multinational group are meaningfully separate. Thus, *which* member of the group is the one to borrow from a third lender may affect source determinations (as well as the scope of U.S. deferral for the group's worldwide income) despite its likely economic triviality. Better still, intra-group loans can generate interest deductions for affiliates in high-tax countries, in exchange for interest income in low-tax (or no-tax) countries, even if the underlying loan principal is merely traveling in a circle—as in the case where a high-tax parent borrows back funds that it has just inserted as equity into a tax haven subsidiary.

This is cheap electivity with a vengeance. The U.S. rules combat it to a degree, but only for U.S. companies. One important tool, unavoidably limited to U.S. companies, is treating foreign subsidiaries' interest income from intra-group loans as subpart F income. This can eliminate U.S.-to-foreign profit shifting through the use of intra-group loans, unless one can use foreign tax credits to shelter the currently taxable FSI (which is harder to arrange for passive than active business income). For foreign-to-foreign profit shifting, however, subpart F's effectiveness has been greatly weakened by the use of hybrid entities.[17]

A second tool, also limited to U.S. companies but not as inevitably so, is the use of the interest allocation rules to address disproportionately U.S. borrowing within a multinational group. The rules' only effect, however, is to require that the affected deductions reduce FSI rather than domestic source income, thereby potentially affecting the application of the foreign tax credit limit. This makes the interest allocation rules effectively irrelevant to companies that do not need to worry about becoming excess-credit. The rules would matter more generally under a system in which the global group's FSI, while not benefiting from deferral, was taxed at a lower rate (including zero) than U.S. source income. In such a guise, interest allocation could apply to foreign as well as U.S. multinationals, so long as IRS auditors could look through U.S. subsidiaries to their foreign parents, and examine the entire global groups' financial structures and interest flows.

An alternative approach, aimed at making electivity costlier, would be to ignore all intra-group interest flows, as well as the question of who within the group was the borrower. Instead, at least as a general rule, interest paid to third parties would in effect be allocated on some formulary basis between the production of U.S. source income and FSI. (One might also consider netting interest expense against passive income, so that borrowing to hold such assets, or in lieu of selling them, would not have large net effects.) In effect, this would involve applying a worldwide consolidated or unitary business approach to both U.S. and foreign-headed multinationals, at least with respect to interest expense.

The rationale would be that, since accurate tracing of loan proceeds to their true marginal uses is impossible (Graetz 2008), sourcing error is inevitable no matter what approach one uses. In the average case, however, a well-designed formulary approach might prove less manipulable and inaccurate than present law. Obviously, further inquiry would be needed to establish that such a formulary approach to net third-party interest expense was actually preferable to the leading alternatives. But if it succeeded in making profit shifting out of the U.S. costlier, that would likely be a point in its favor.

Michael Graetz (2008) proposes that something like this be done through a process of multilateral agreement between residence and source countries around the world, leading to the adoption of a uniform formula. However, while multilateral agreement is surely worth exploring, that does not mean that U.S. policy makers should wait for it to occur before adopting a wholly formulary approach. Indeed, proceeding unilaterally could have advantages that created affirmative pressure on other countries to follow suit.

Thus, suppose that the United States stood alone in disregarding the question of whether borrowing by a multinational group had occurred domestically. This would give both U.S. and foreign multinationals an incentive to generate interest deductions outside the United States, since this would improve the foreign tax result without worsening that which was achieved here. In effect, multinationals would be encouraged to strip income out of foreign high-tax jurisdictions, rather than out of the United States. Yet even if peer countries "retaliated" by adopting similar rules (i.e., by moving toward the equivalent of a multilateral agreement), we (and they) might still be better off than in the world of cheaper taxpayer electivity that we inhabit today.

Transfer pricing versus formulary apportionment—Here once again, the argument for a formulary approach cannot plausibly rest on the view that it will get things right—in terms either of the marginal effects of particular taxpayer choices or overall income allocation. Rather, the pro-formulary case rests on the hope that it will indirectly lead to better marginal and overall results than highly imperfect transfer pricing, by reason of its making profit shifting suitably costlier.

If formulary apportionment (or a more formulary approach to what was still called transfer pricing) were adopted, it would be important to think about the proper choice of factors. As noted in chapter 3, Avi-Yonah, Clausing, and Durst (2008, 15) advocate emphasizing the sales factor, rather than property or payroll, on the ground that it is less manipulable. Companies generally want to increase their sales everywhere, whereas they may flexibly decide where to locate (or purport to locate) property and payroll. Altshuler and Grubert (2010, 1172) respond, however, that so sanguine a view of relying on the sales factor fails to do adequate justice to taxpayers' ability to manipulate where they report (or even actually have) sales—for example, by purchasing high-volume, low-margin businesses in low-tax countries.

In assessing this debate, it is worth considering the point that, the more practically distinct factors one uses under formulary apportionment, the lower the marginal payoff to manipulating any one of them. Thus, at the risk of being too Solomonic, one possible approach that merits further evaluation is to use all three of the traditional factors, but giving the sales factor extra weight in the apportionment formula. This is what twenty-two U.S. states currently do, out of the forty-six that have corporate income taxes (Lohman 2012).[18]

C. A Final Word

Almost no one likes the existing U.S. international tax system, and no one should like it. It is at once too burdensome and too flexible, and it raises too little revenue relative to its tax planning, compliance, and administrative costs. It not only compromises between very different visions, but does so in a singularly convoluted and illogical way.

The obstacles to enacting a satisfying reform of the U.S. international tax system are not just political, although partly that. The lack of expert consensus, not just about desired outcomes but also concerning how to think about the system's core objectives and challenges, has contributed negatively as well. Expert consensus most definitely would not suffice to bring about the enactment of a better system. If it existed, however, it surely could serve as an important emollient, improving the chances that something good eventually will happen.

One reason for the lack of expert consensus about U.S. international taxation is the complexity of the subject, and the variety of different margins that any reform proposal would affect. Any change will involve tradeoffs, and it is unsurprising that experts disagree about how to evaluate the importance of competing objectives, or about how well a given set of reforms would work out in practice. To quote Yogi Berra once again, it is hard to make predictions, especially about the future.

However, a further problem has been deep-seated conceptual confusion, even among experts with high levels of insight and knowledge concerning international tax theory and practice. The fact that we have had decades of arid debate about single-bullet global welfare norms helps to exemplify the underlying problem, although not constitutive of it. Beyond that, there has too often been a failure to think clearly and coherently about one margin at a time. Consider, for example, the distinction between deciding on (1) the optimal domestic tax rate on resident companies' FSI, and (2) the optimal MRR for foreign taxes paid on this FSI. The commonly posited choice between worldwide and territorial systems typically conflates these two distinct margins, to the detriment of clear thinking about either of them.

I have never been sufficiently optimistic, or perhaps I should say deluded, to imagine that a single book—or, certainly, any of mine—would ever, at least all by itself, make a truly substantial difference in U.S. tax policy outcomes, or even in the dominant tenor of academic debate. The best one can generally hope for is to advance the discussion a bit. And even this happy outcome depends almost wholly on one's readers—who, even if they do not always entirely agree with what they read, can respond by pushing their own fresh thinking in new directions. I will close, therefore, with the hope that you, at least—the current reader—have found new ideas here that will stimulate further reflection.

Endnotes

1. There might also be domestic political support for taxing foreign individuals on their inbound investment even if this rested on mistaking the nominal incidence of the source-based tax with its true economic incidence. After all, the foreigners would observably be writing checks to the domestic Treasury, even if they were shifting the entire cost to domestic counterparties. In addition, even if imposing the tax was not ultimately desirable due to incidence shifting, the threat of imposing it might serve a useful function, by giving the domestic Treasury something to negotiate away in deals with peer countries.

2. As under option (1), source determinations might still matter with respect to reciprocal foreign tax credit deals with other countries, and/or efforts to impose source-based taxation on foreign individuals.

3. The rationale for treating inter vivos gifts of stock as realization events would be to prevent avoidance of the tax on appreciation through pre-death transfers. The case for doing this would be stronger than under present law if the entity-level corporate tax was being entirely eliminated. The main argument against taxing the appreciation upon a gift of corporate stock is that the existing gift tax sufficiently deters employing it as a device to avoid income taxation.

4. The classic full discussion of how to implement a cash flow or consumed income tax on individuals is in Bradford and the U.S. Treasury Tax Policy Staff 1984.

5. A consumed income tax need not expressly distinguish between consumer and other borrowing in order to reach only the former, as loan proceeds will generate an offsetting deduction if they are saved and invested.

6. For leading discussions of the X-tax, see Bradford (2004) and Carroll and Viard (2012). The Hall-Rabushka flat tax (see Hall and Rabushka 1995), although it was promulgated before the X-tax, could be seen as an example of it in which there are merely two rates, one of which is zero.

7. Obviously, the choice of method will make a difference in particular years when exports and imports are not equal. However, in a well-functioning consumption tax, it still ends up making no present value difference. Thus, suppose that the interest rate is 5 percent, and that a given company has a $100 import in Year 1, which it converts into a $105 export in Year 2. Thus, before tax it is earning exactly the market interest rate of 5 percent. If it gets a deduction for the import and is

required to include the export, it gets a $20 refund in Year 1 and pays $21 of tax in Year 2. These amounts are equivalent in present value at a 5 percent interest rate. The effect of the tax on its rate of return is also zero, since it ends up $80 out-of-pocket in Year 1 and has $84 after-tax in Year 2.

8. An alternative approach to X-tax design would involve including and deducting all financial flows—in the case of loans, not limited to interest payments, but also loan principal, which would be taxable when received and deductible when repaid.

9. Both Bradford (2004) and Carroll and Viard (2012) support enacting an X-tax that uses the origin basis, rather than the destination basis, despite the conceded superiority of the latter approach with respect to handling source issues in the international realm.

10. For example, at a 30 percent tax rate, the company would pay $30 of tax in Year 1 and receive a $33 refund in Year 2. The combined present value of the company's tax payments and refunds would be zero at a 10 percent interest rate.

11. For individuals, the only change that Auerbach (2010, 13) contemplates as part of the plan, reflecting that dividend payouts would be deductible at the entity level, is eliminating the special tax rates for dividends and capital gains on selling corporate stock.

12. If our treaty partners generally still operated worldwide systems with foreign tax credits, this concern might mainly take the form of their ceasing to credit our taxes when paid on U.S. source income by their resident firms. This concern is reduced, however, by the fact that so many countries have already ceased to credit our taxes, by reason of their adopting territorial systems.

13. Thus, suppose that Acme had $100 of FSI. If it paid foreign taxes of zero, its FSI would face a U.S. tax of $15. If its foreign tax liability was $20, its $80 of after-foreign-tax FSI would face a 5 percent U.S. rate, leading to a U.S. tax liability of $4. Therefore, a $20 increase in Acme's foreign taxes would reduce its U.S. taxes by $16.

14. Morse (2013, 140) observes that U.S. companies may in practice sometimes lack good records for pre-1987 earnings and profits, which are less likely to have ongoing tax relevance, by reason of changes made in the Tax Reform Act of 1986. She suggests that the financial accounting measure of unremitted earnings could serve as a backstop if the tax measure appears to be unreliable (146).

15. As noted in chapter 3, the Levin proposal would define a company as having U.S. headquarters if "substantially all of the executive officers and senior management... who exercise day-to-day responsibility for making decisions involving strategic, financial, and operational policies of the corporation are located primarily in the United States."

16. In addition, as discussed in chapter 3, Code section 954(c)(6), while it remains in force, permits one to shift income from high-tax to low-tax countries, without concern about the application of subpart F, even if one does not use hybrid entities.

17. In addition, if Internal Revenue Code section 954(c)(6) remains on the books, U.S. companies have carte blanche to shift active business income from high-tax to low-tax countries. As noted in chapter 3, this provision sets forth a "look-thru" rule, under which certain payments between related party CFCs will not give rise to subpart F income if they relate sufficiently to active business income of the payer. However, as of this writing, the provision, which has several times been extended, is scheduled to expire at the end of 2013.

18. Lohman (2012) further reports that twelve U.S. states equally weight property, payroll, and sales in their apportionment formula, while eighteen rely solely on sales, at least in some circumstances.

Bibliography

Allen, Eric, and Susan Morse. 2011. Firm Incorporation Outside the U.S.: No Exodus Yet. Available at: http://works.bepress.com/susanmorse/10.

Altshuler, Rosanne, and Harry Grubert. 2003. Repatriation Taxes, Repatriation Strategies, and Multinational Financial Policy. 87 Journal of Public Economics 73–107.

Altshuler, Rosanne, and Harry Grubert. 2010. Formula Apportionment: Is It Better Than the Current System and Are There Better Alternatives? 63 National Tax Journal 1145–1184.

Arndt, Christian, Claudia M. Buch, and Monika Schnitzer. 2007. FDI and Domestic Investment: An Industry-Level View. Center for Economic and Policy Research Discussion Paper DP6464.

Auerbach, Alan J. 2010. A Modern Corporate Tax. Washington, DC: Center for American Progress/Hamilton Foundation.

Auerbach, Alan J. 2012. The Mirrlees Review: A U.S. Perspective. 65 National Tax Journal 685–708.

Ault, Hugh J., and Brian J. Arnold. 2004. Comparative Income Taxation: A Structural Analysis (Second Edition). New York: Aspen Publishers.

Ault, Hugh J., and David F. Bradford. 1990. Taxing International Income: An Analysis of the U.S. System and Its Economic Premises. In Assaf Razin and Joel Slemrod (eds.), Taxation in the Global Economy. Chicago: University of Chicago Press, 1–46.

Avi-Yonah, Reuven S. 1996. The Structure of International Taxation: A Proposal for Simplification. 74 Texas Law Review 1301–1359.

Avi-Yonah, Reuven S. 2000. Globalization, Tax Competition, and the Fiscal Crisis of the Welfare State. 113 Harvard Law Review 1573–1676.

Avi-Yonah, Reuven S. 2008. The OECD Harmful Tax Competition Report: A 10th Anniversary Retrospective. University of Michigan Law School, Public Law and Legal Theory Working Paper Series, Working Paper No. 115.

Avi-Yonah, Reuven S., Kimberly A. Clausing, and Michael C. Durst. 2008. Allocating Business Profits for Tax Purposes: A Proposal to Adopt a Formulary Profit Split. University of Michigan Law School, Public Law and Legal Theory Working Paper Series, Working Paper No. 138.

Bankman, Joseph. 1994. The Structure of Silicon Valley Start-Ups. 41 UCLA Law Review 1737.

Bankman, Joseph, and David A. Weisbach. 2006. The Superiority of an Ideal Consumption Tax Over an Ideal Income Tax. 58 Stanford Law Review 1413–1456.

Bittker, Boris I. 1979. Equity, Efficiency, and Income Tax Theory: Do Misallocations Drive Out Inequities? 16 San Diego Law Review 735–748.

Blumenthal, Marsha, and Joel Slemrod. 1996. The Compliance Cost of Taxing Foreign-Source Income: Its Magnitude, Determinants, and Policy Implications. In Slemrod, Joel (ed.), The Taxation of Multinational Corporations. Boston: Kluwer Academic Publishers, 33–49.

Bradford, David F. 2004. The X-Tax in the World Economy: Going Global with a Simple, Progressive Tax. Washington, DC: AEI Press.

Bradford, David F., and the U.S. Treasury Tax Policy Staff. 1984. Blueprints for Basic Tax Reform (2nd edition). Arlington, VA: Tax Analysts.

Brauner, Yariv. 2008. Value in the Eyes of the Beholder: The Valuation of Intangibles for Transfer Pricing Purposes. 28 Virginia Tax Review 79–164.

Brennan, Thomas J. 2010. What Happens After a Holiday? Long-Term Effects of the Repatriation Provision of the AJCA. 5 Northwestern Journal of Law and Social Policy 1–18.

Brooks, Kim. Forthcoming. Inter-Nation Equity: The Development of an Important but Underappreciated International Tax Value. In Richard Krever and John Head (eds.), Tax Reform In The 21st Century. Frederick, MD: Kluwer Law International.

Brooks, Kim. 2009. Tax Sparing: A Needed Incentive for Foreign Investment in Low-Income Countries or an Unnecessary Revenue Sacrifice? 34 Queen's Law Journal 505–564.

Buch, Claudia M., Jorn Kleinert, Alexander Lipponer, and Farid Toubal. 2005. Determinants and Effects of Foreign Direct Investment: Evidence from German Firm-Level Data. 20 Economic Policy 51–110.

Carr, John L., and Michael C. Moetell. 2007. Indirect Foreign Tax Credits (Tax Management Portfolio 902-2nd). Washington, DC: Tax Management, Inc.

Carroll, Robert, and Alan D. Viard. 2012. Progressive Consumption Taxation: The X Tax Revisited. Washington, DC: AEI Press.

Chuhan, Punam. 2006. Poverty and Inequality. In Vina Bhargava (ed.), Global Issues for Global Citizens. Washington, DC: The World Bank.

Clausing, Kimberly A. 2011. The Revenue Effects of Multinational Firm Income Shifting. 130 Tax Notes 1580–1586.

Clausing, Kimberly A. 2012. A Challenging Time for International Tax Policy. 136 Tax Notes 281–283.

Clausing, Kimberly A., and Daniel Shaviro. 2011. A Burden-Neutral Shift from Foreign Tax Creditability to Deductibility? 64 Tax Law Review 431–452.

Clemens, Roy. 2009. U.S. International Tax Policy: Is Significant Reform on the Way? 124 Tax Notes 445.

Coase, Ronald. 1937. The Nature of the Firm. 4 Economica 386–405.

Corlett, W. J., and D. C. Hague. 1953. Complementarity and the Excess Burden of Taxation. 21 Review of Economic Studies 21–30.

Coval, Joshua D., and Tobias J. Moskowitz. 1999. Home Bias at Home: Local Equity Preference in Domestic Portfolios. 54 Journal of Finance 2045.

Cunningham, Noel B., and Mitchell L. Engler. 2012. Prescription for Corporate Income Tax Reform: A Corporate Consumption Tax. Available on-line at http://www.law.nyu.edu/sites/default/files/ECM_PRO_073858.pdf.

Deardorff, Alan V., and Robert M. Stern. 1987. Current Issues in Trade Policy: An Overview. In R. Stern (ed.), U.S. Trade Policies in a Changing World Economy. Cambridge, MA: MIT Press, 15–68

Desai, Mihir A. 2009a. The Decentering of the Global Firm. 32 World Economy 1271–1290.

Desai, Mihir A. 2009b. Taxing Multinationals: Securing Jobs or the New Protectionism? 55 Tax Notes International 61–75.

Desai, Mihir A., and Dhammika Dharmapala. 2009. Investor Taxation in Open Economies. Available on-line at http://www.law.northwestern.edu/colloquium/tax/documents/Dharmapala.pdf.

Desai, Mihir A., and Dhammika Dharmapala. 2010. Do Strong Fences Make Strong Neighbors?, 63 National Tax Journal 723–740.

Desai, Mihir A., and Dhammika Dharmapala. 2011. An Alternative Transfer Pricing Norm. Available on-line at http://www.sbs.ox.ac.uk/centres/tax/symposia/Documents/Dharmapala%20final.pdf

Desai, Mihir A., C. Fritz Foley, and James R. Hines. 2005. Foreign Direct Investment and the Domestic Capital Stock. 95(2) American Economic Review 33–38.

Desai, Mihir A., C. Fritz Foley, and James R. Hines 2009. Domestic Effects of the Foreign Activities of U.S. Multinationals. 1 American Economic Journal: Economic Policy 181–203.

Desai, Mihir A., and James R. Hines, Jr. 2002. Expectations and Expatriations: Tracing the Causes and Consequences of Corporate Inversions. 55 National Tax Journal 409–440.

Desai, Mihir A., and James R. Hines. 2003. Evaluating International Tax Reform. 56 National Tax Journal 487–502.

Desai, Mihir A., and James R. Hines. 2004. Old Rules and New Realities: Corporate Tax Policy in a Global Setting. 57 National Tax Journal 937–960.

Devereux, Michael P. 1990. Capital Export Neutrality, Capital Import Neutrality, Capital Ownership Neutrality, and All That. Institute for Fiscal Studies, unpublished.

Devereux, Michael P. 2008. Taxation of Outbound Direct Investment: Economic Principles and Tax Policy Considerations. Working Paper 08/24, Oxford University Centre for Business Taxation, Said Business School, Oxford University.

Dharmapala, Dhammika, C. Fritz Foley, and Kristin J. Forbes. 2009. Watch What I Do, Not What I Say: The Unintended Consequences of the Homeland Investment Act. National Bureau of Economic Research Working Paper 15023.

Diamond, Peter, and James Mirrlees. 1971. Optimal Taxation and Public Production I: Production Efficiency. 61 American Economic Review 8–27.

Drawbaugh, Kevin, and Andy Sullivan. 2013. How Treasury's Tax Loophole Mistake Saves Companies Billions Each Year. Reuters, May 30. Available online at http://www.reuters.com/article/2013/05/31/us-usa-tax-checkthebox-insight-idUSBRE94T17K20130531

Duhigg, Charles, and David Kocieniewski. 2012. How Apple Sidesteps Billions in Taxes. New York Times, April 29.

Durst, Michael. 2007. A Statutory Proposal For U.S. Transfer Pricing Reform, 115 Tax Notes 1047.

Faeth, Isabel. 2006. Consequences of FDI in Australia—Causal Links Between FDI, Domestic Investment, Economic Growth, and Trade. University of Melbourne Department of Economics, Research Paper Number 977.

Feenstra, Robert C., and Gordon H. Hanson. 2001. Global Production Sharing and Rising Inequality: A Survey of Trade and Wages. National Bureau of Economic Research Working Paper No. 8372.

Fleming, Clifton J., Robert J. Peroni, and Stephen E. Shay. 2001. Fairness in International Taxation: The Ability-to-Pay Case for Taxing Worldwide Income. 5 Fla. Tax Rev. 299–354.

Fleming, Clifton J., Robert J. Peroni, and Stephen E. Shay. 2009. Worse Than Exemption. 59 Emory Law Journal 79–149.

Flynn, Finbarr, and Dara Doyle. 2013. Apple No Ghost in Ireland Where Cork Frets Senate Hearing. Bloomberg News, May 31. Available online at http://www.bloomberg.com/news/2013-05-31/apple-no-ghost-in-ireland-where-cork-frets-senate-hearing-taxes.html

Freedman, Samuel G. 2010. A Long Road from "Come by here" to "Kumbaya." New York Times, November 16.

Funk, William M. 2010. On and Over the Horizon: Emerging Issues in U.S. Taxation of Investments. 10 Houston Business and Tax Journal 1.

Garland, David. 2010. Peculiar Institution: America's Death Penalty in an Age of Abolition. Cambridge, MA: Belknap Press.

Giovannini, Alberto. 1989. Capital Taxation. 4 Economic Policy 346–386.

Gordon, Roger H., and A. Lans Bovenberg. 1996. Why Is Capital So Immobile Internationally? Possible Explanations and Implications for Capital Income Taxation. 86 American Economic Review 1057.

Graetz, Michael J. 1977. Legal Transitions: The Case of Retroactivity in Income Tax Revision. 126 University of Pennsylvania Law Review 47.

Graetz, Michael J. 2000. Taxing International Income: Inadequate Principles, Outdated Concepts, and Unsatisfactory Policies. 54 Tax Law Review 261–336.

Graetz, Michael J. 2008. A Multilateral Solution for the Income Tax Treatment of Interest Expenses. Yale Law School, John M. Olin Center for Studies in Law, Economics, and Public Policy, Research Paper No. 371.

Graetz, Michael J., and Itai Grinberg. 2003. Taxing International Portfolio Income. 56 Tax Law Review 537–586.

Graetz, Michael J., and Michael M. O'Hear. 1997. The "Original Intent" of U.S. International Taxation. 46 Duke Law Journal 1021–1109.

Graetz, Michael J., and Paul W. Oosterhuis. 2001. Structuring an Exemption System for Foreign Income of U.S. Corporations. 54 National Tax Journal 771–786.

Graham, John R., Michelle Hanlon, and Terry Shevlin. 2011. Real Effects of Accounting Rules: Evidence from Multinational Firms' Investment Location and Profit Repatriation Decisions. 49 Journal of Accounting Research 137–185.

Gravelle, Jane G. 2009. International Corporate Income Tax Reform: Issues and Proposals. 9 Florida Tax Review 469–496.

Grinberg, Itai. 2012. Beyond FATCA: An Evolutionary Moment for the International Tax System. Available on-line at http://scholarship.law.georgetown.edu/fwps_papers/160.

Gruber, Jonathan. 2011. Public Finance and Public Policy (3rd edition). New York: Worth Publishers.

Grubert, Harry. 2009a. MNC Dividends, Tax Holidays, and the Burden of the Repatriation Tax: Recent Evidence. Oxford University Centre for Business Taxation Working Paper 09/27. Available on-line at http://www.sbs.ox.ac.uk/centres/tax/Documents/working_papers/WP0927.pdf.

Grubert, Harry. 2009b. Foreign Taxes, Domestic Income, and the Jump in the Share of Multinational Company Income Abroad. Oxford University Centre for Business Taxation Working Paper 09/27. Available on-line at http://www.sbs.ox.ac.uk/centres/tax/Documents/working_papers/WP0926.pdf.

Grubert, Harry, and Rosanne Altshuler. 2008. Corporate Taxes in the World Economy: Reforming the Taxation of Cross-Border Income. In John W. Diamond and George R. Zodrow (eds.), Fundamental Tax Reform: Issues and Implications. Cambridge, MA: MIT Press, 319–354.

Hall, Robert E., and Alvin Rabushka. 1995. The Flat Tax. Stanford, CA: Hoover Institution Press.

Harberger, Arnold C. 1962. The Incidence of the Corporation Income Tax. 70 Journal of Political Economy 215–240.

Harrison, Ann, and Margaret McMillan. 2008. Offshoring Jobs? Multinationals and U.S. Manufacturing Employment. Unpublished manuscript.

Hartman, David G. 1985. Tax Policy and Foreign Direct Investment. 26 Journal of Public Economics 107.

Hejazi, Walid, and Peter Pauly. 2003. Motivations for FDI and Domestic Capital Formation. 34 Journal of International Business Studies 282–289.

Hellerstein, Jerome R. 1963. Taxes, Loopholes, and Morals. New York: McGraw Hill.

Her Majesty's Treasury. 2007. Taxation of Companies' Foreign Profits: Discussion Document.

Hines, James R. 2008. Foreign Income and Domestic Deductions. 61 National Tax Journal 461–475.

Hines, James R. 2009. Reconsidering the Taxation of Foreign Source Income. 62 Tax Law Review 269–298.

Hines, James R., and Lawrence H. Summers. 2009. How Globalization Affects Tax Design. In Jeffrey R. Brown and James M. Poterba (eds.), Tax Policy and the Economy (vol. 23). Cambridge, MA and Chicago, IL: NBER and the University of Chicago Press, 123–157.

Horst, Thomas. 1980. A Note on the Optimal Taxation of International Investment Income. 94 Quarterly Journal of Economics 793–798.

House Ways and Means Committee. 2011. Technical Explanation of the Ways and Means Discussion Draft Provisions to Establish a Participation Exemption System for the Taxation of Foreign Income. October 26.

Hufbauer, Gary Clyde. 1992. U.S. Taxation of International Income: Blueprint for Reform. Washington DC: Peterson Institute for International Economics.

Hufbauer, Gary Clyde, and Ariel Assa. 2007. U.S. Taxation of Foreign Income. Washington, DC: Peterson Institute for International Economics.

Huizinga, Harry P., and Johannes Voget. 2009. International Taxation and the Direction and Volume of Cross-Border M&As, 64 Journal of Finance 1217.

Isenbergh, Joseph. 2004. International Taxation: U.S. Taxation of Foreign Persons and Foreign Income (3rd edition). New York: Aspen Publishers.

Isenbergh, Joseph. 2006. International Taxation (2nd edition). New York: Foundation Press.

James, Vaughn E. 2002. Twenty-First Century Pirates of the Caribbean: How the Organization for Economic Cooperation and Development Robbed Fourteen Caricom Countries of Their Tax and Economic Policy Sovereignty. 34 University of Miami Inter-American Law Review 1–50.

Kane, Mitchell A. 2006. Ownership Neutrality, Ownership Distortions, and International Tax Welfare Benchmarks. 26 Virginia Tax Review 53–79.

Kane, Mitchell A. 2012. Bootstraps and Poverty Traps: Tax Treaties as Novel Tools for Development Finance. 29 Yale Journal on Regulation 256–305.

Kane, Mitchell A. 2009. Considering "Reconsidering the Taxation of Foreign Income." 62 Tax Law Review 299–315.

Kane, Mitchell A., and Edward B. Rock. 2008. Corporate Taxation and International Charter Competition. 106 Michigan Law Review 1229–1283.

Kaplow, Louis. 1995. Recovery of Pre-Enactment Basis Under a Consumption Tax: The USA Tax System. 68 Tax Notes 1109.

Kaplow, Louis. 2008. The Theory of Taxation and Public Economics. Princeton, NJ: Princeton University Press.

Kaplow, Louis, and Steven Shavell. 2002a. Fairness Versus Welfare. Cambridge, MA: Harvard University Press.

Kaplow, Louis, and Steven Shavell. 2002b. Human Nature and the Best Consequentialist Moral System. Cambridge, MA: Harvard Law School Discussion Paper No. 349.

Keen, Michael. 1993. The Welfare Economics of Tax Co-ordination in the European Community: A Survey. 14 Fiscal Studies 15–36.

Kingson, Charles I. 1981. The Coherence of International Taxation. 81 Columbia Law Review 1151–1289.

Kleinbard, Edward D. 1991. Equity Derivative Products: Financial Innovation's Newest Challenge to the Tax System. 69 Texas Law Review 1319–1368.

Kleinbard, Edward D. 2001. The Theory and Practice of Subpart F as Applied to Financial Services Firms. Unpublished manuscript, on file with the author.

Kleinbard, Edward D. 2007. Throw Territorial Taxation from the Train. 114 Tax Notes 547.

Kleinbard, Edward D. 2010. An American Dual Income Tax: Nordic Precedents. 5 Northwestern Journal of Law and Policy 41–86.

Kleinbard, Edward D. 2011a. Stateless Income's Challenge to Tax Policy. 132 Tax Notes 1021–1042.

Kleinbard, Edward D. 2011b. Stateless Income. 11 Florida Tax Review 699.

Kleinbard, Edward D. 2011c. The Lessons of Stateless Income. 65 Tax Law Review 99.

Kleinbard, Edward D., and Patrick Driessen. 2008. A Revenue Estimate Case Study: The Repatriation Holiday Revisited. 120 Tax Notes 1191.

Kleinert, Jorn, and Farid Toubal. 2009. The Impact of Locating Production Abroad on Activities at Home: Evidence From German Firm-Level Data. Review of World Economics (forthcoming).

Knoll, Michael S. 2010. The Corporate Income Tax and the Competitiveness of U.S. Industries. 63 Tax Law Review 771–795.

Kocieniewski, David. 2008. The Congressman, the Donor, and the Tax Break. New York Times, November 25, page A-1.

Krugman, Paul. 1984. The U.S. Response to Foreign Industrial Targeting. 1 Brookings Papers on Economic Activity 79.

Kuntz, Joel D., and Robert J. Peroni. 2013. U.S. International Taxation. Valhalla, NY: Warren, Gorham & Lamont.

Linebaugh, Kate. 2013. Firms Keep Stockpiles of "Foreign" Cash in U.S. Wall Street Journal, January 23, page A-1.

Lohman, Judith. Corporate Income Tax Apportionment Formulas. OLR Research Report 2012-R-0414. Available online at http://www.cga.ct.gov/2012/rpt/2012-R-0414.htm

Margalioth, Yoram. 2003. Tax Competition, Foreign Direct Investments and Growth: Using the Tax System to Promote Developing Countries. 23 Virginia Tax Review 161–204.

McAdams, Richard H. 1997. The Origin, Development, and Regulation of Norms. 96 Michigan Law Review 338–433.

McDaniel, Paul R. 2001. Trade and Taxation. 26 Brooklyn Journal of International Law 1621–1640.

McGuire, Kelly. 2010. China Moves to Build Smart Grid, GE, Siemens Feel Competition. Available online at http://smart-grid.tmcnet.com/topics/smart-grid/articles/86212-china-moves-build-smart-grid-ge-siemens-feel.htm

McLure, Charles E. 1981. The Elusive Incidence of the Corporate Income Tax: The State Case. 9 Public Finance Quarterly 395–413.

McLure, Charles E. 1997. The U.S. Debate on Consumption-Based Taxes: Implications for the Americas. 29 U. Miami Inter-American Law Review 143–196.

Mirrlees, James, Stuart Adam, Timothy Besley, Richard Blundell, Stephen Bond, Robert Chote, Malcolm Gammie, Paul Johnson, Gareth Myles, and James Poterba (eds). 2010. Dimensions of Tax Design: the Mirrlees Review. Oxford: Oxford University Press.

Morse, Susan C. 2013. A Corporate Offshore Profits Transition Tax. 91 North Carolina Law Review 101–153.

Musgrave, Peggy B. 1969. United States Taxation of Foreign Investment Income: Issues and Arguments. Cambridge, MA: Harvard Law School.

Musgrave, Peggy B. 2000. Interjurisdictional Equity in Company Taxation: Principles and Applications to the European Union. In Sijbren Cnossen (ed.), Taxing Capital Income in the European Union: Issues and Options for Reform. New York: Oxford University Press, 46–77.

New York State Bar Association. 2002. Report on Outbound Inversion Transactions. May 2002.

Nozick, Robert. 1974. Anarchy, State, and Utopia. New York: Basic Books.

Obstfeld, Maurice, and Kenneth Rogoff. 2000. The Six Major Puzzles in International Macroeconomics: Is There a Common Cause? National Bureau of Economic Research Working Paper 7777.

Office of Tax Policy, Department of the Treasury. 2000. The Deferral of Income Earned Through U.S. Controlled Foreign Corporations: A Policy Study.

Organisation for Economic Cooperation and Development. 1998. Harmful Tax Competition: An Emerging Global Issue. Paris, France: OECD Publications.

Organisation for Economic Cooperation and Development. 1998a. Tax Sparing: A Reconsideration. Paris, France: OECD Publications.

Organisation for Economic Cooperation and Development. 2013a. Addressing Base Erosion and Profit-Shifting. Available online at http://dx.doi.org/10.1787/9789264192744-en

Organisation for Economic Cooperation and Development. 2013b. Meeting of the OECD Council at Ministerial Level. Available online at http://www.oecd.org/mcm/C-MIN(2013)22-FINAL-ENG.pdf

e, James M., James A. Duncan, and Sarah L. Berman. 2008. Overbroad FTC Antiarbitrage Regulations Enter Into Force. 120 Tax Notes 495–502.

Peroni, Robert J. 2001. The Proper Approach for Taxing the Income of Foreign Controlled Corporations. 26 Brooklyn Journal of International Law 1579–1593.

President's Economic Recovery Advisory Board. 2010. The Report on Tax Reform Options: Simplification, Compliance, and Corporate Taxation.

Ramsey, Frank P. 1927. A Contribution to the Theory of Taxation. 37 Economic Journal 47–61.

Rawls, John. 1971. A Theory of Justice. Cambridge, MA: The Belknap Press of Harvard University Press.

Redmiles, Melissa. 2008. The One-Time Dividends Received Deduction. IRS Statistics of Income Bulletin, vol. 27, number 4 (spring), 102–114.

Ribstein, Larry E., and Erin Ann O'Hara. 2008. Corporations and the Market for Law. 2008 University of Illinois Law Review 661.

Richman, Peggy Brewer. 1963. Taxation of Foreign Investment Income: An Economic Analysis. Baltimore, MD: Johns Hopkins Press.

Robinson, Joan. 1947. Essays in the Theory of Employment. Oxford: Blackwell Publishing.

Rosen, Harvey S. and Ted Gayer. 2009. Public Finance (9th ed.). New York: McGraw-Hill.

Rosenbloom, H. David. 1994. What's Trade Got to Do With It? 49 Tax Law Review 593–598.

Sanders, Laura. 2011. The IRS Targets Income Tricks. Wall Street Journal, January 22. Available online at http://online.wsj.com/article/SB10001424052748703951704576092371207903438.html?mod=WSJ_PersonalFinance_PF5#articleTabs%3Darticle

Schmidt, Wilson E. 1975. U.S. Capital Export Policy: Backdoor Mercantilism. In U.S. Taxation of American Business Abroad. Washington, DC: American Enterprise Institute.

Shaheen, Fadi. 2013. The GAAP Lock-Out Effect and the Investment Behavior of Multinational Firms. Available on-line at http://papers.ssrn.com/sol3/papers.cfm?abstract_id=2271403.

Shaviro, Daniel N. 1989. Risk and Accrual: The Tax Treatment of Nonrecourse Debt. 44 Tax Law Review 401.

Shaviro, Daniel N. 1992. An Economic and Political Look at Federalism in Taxation. 90 Michigan Law Review 895–991.

Shaviro, Daniel N. 2000a. When Rules Change: An Economic and Political Analysis of Transition Relief and Retroactivity. Chicago: University of Chicago Press.

Shaviro, Daniel N. 2000b. Economic Substance, Corporate Tax Shelters, and the *Compaq* Case. 88 Tax Notes 221.

Shaviro, Daniel N. 2001. Does More Sophisticated Mean Better? A Critique of Alternative Approaches to Sourcing the Interest Expense of American Multinationals. 54 Tax Law Review 353–420.

Shaviro, Daniel N. 2002. Endowment and Inequality. In Joseph Thorndike and Dennis Ventry (eds.), Tax Justice Reconsidered: The Moral and Ethical Bases of Taxation. Washington, DC: Urban Institute Press, 123–148.

Shaviro, Daniel N. 2004. Replacing the Income Tax with a Progressive Consumption Tax. 103 Tax Notes 91–113.

Shaviro, Daniel N. 2007. Why Worldwide Welfare as a Normative Standard in U.S. Tax Policy? 60 Tax Law Review 155–178.

Shaviro, Daniel N. 2008. Simplifying Assumptions: How Might the Politics of Consumption Tax Reform Affect (Impair) the End Product? In John W. Diamond and George R. Zodrow (eds.), Fundamental Tax Reform: Issues and Implications. Cambridge, MA: MIT Press, 75–124.

Shaviro, Daniel N. 2009a. Decoding the Corporate Tax. Washington, DC: Urban Institute Press.

Shaviro, Daniel N. 2009b. Suggestions for the Volcker Tax Reform Panel. [From June Tax Notes.]

Shaviro, Daniel N. 2009c. The Obama Administration's Tax Reform Proposals Concerning Controlled Foreign Corporations. 4 British Tax Review 331–339.

Shaviro, Daniel N. 2009d. The Optimal Relationship Between Taxable Income and Financial Accounting Income: Analysis and a Proposal. 97 Georgetown Law Journal 423–484.

Shaviro, Daniel N. 2009e. The 2008–09 Financial Crisis: Implications for Income Tax Reform. New York University Working Paper No. 09-35. New York: New York University.

Shaviro, Daniel N. 2010. Rethinking Foreign Tax Creditability. 63 National Tax Journal 709–721.

Shaviro, Daniel N. 2011a. The Case Against Foreign Tax Credits. 3 Journal of Legal Analysis 65–100.

Shaviro, Daniel N. 2011b. The Rising Tax-Electivity of U.S. Corporate Residence. 64 Tax Law Review 377–430.

Shaviro, Daniel N. 2012. The Financial Transactions Tax vs. (?) the Financial Activities Tax. [to be published in Tax Notes]

Shaviro, Daniel N., and David A. Weisbach. 2002. The Fifth Circuit Gets It Wrong in *Compaq v. Commissioner*. 94 Tax Notes 1359.

Shay, Stephen E., J. Clifton Fleming, Jr., and Robert J. Peroni. 2002. "What's Source Got to Do With It?" Source Rules and U.S. International Taxation. 56 Tax Law Review 81–155.

Sheppard, Lee. 2006. More Questions for Inversion Regulations. 110 Tax Notes 1273.

Sheppard, Lee. 2013. Delta Dawn: No Escape from Dividend Withholding? 138 Tax Notes 143–148.

Simpson, Helen. 2008. How Do Firms' Outward FDI Strategies Relate to Their Activity at Home? Empirical Evidence for the U.K. Working Paper, Centre for Market and Public Organisation, Bristol University of Public Affairs.

Slemrod, Joel. 1995. Free Trade Taxation and Protectionist Taxation. 2 International Tax and Public Finance 471–489.

Slemrod, Joel, and Shlomo Yitzhaki, 1996. The Costs of Taxation and the Marginal Efficiency Cost of Funds. IMF Staff Papers, Volume 43, No. 1.

Soubbotina, Tatyana P., and Katherine A. Sheram. 2001. Beyond Economic Growth. Washington, DC: World Bank Publications.

Steinberg, Lewis. 2010. Reverse Endowment Effect. 88 Taxes 79–82.

Stevens, Orrie P. 1962. A Current Appraisal of Foreign "Base Companies." 40 Taxes 117–120.

Sullivan, Martin A. 2008a. Reported Effective Corporate Tax Rates Down Since Late 1990s. 118 Tax Notes 882.

Sullivan, Martin A. 2008b. Why Reported Effective Corporate Tax Rates Are Falling. 118 Tax Notes 977.

Sullivan, Martin A. 2008c. U.S. Multinationals Shifting Profits Out of the United States. 118 Tax Notes 1078.

Sullivan, Martin A. 2009. A Simple Overview of the Obama International Tax Proposals. 123 Tax Notes 1301.

Sullivan, Martin A. 2010. Cisco CEO Seeks Relief for Profits Shifted Overseas. 129 Tax Notes 951–955 (November 29).

Sullivan, Martin A. 2011a. Foreign Tax Profile of Top 50 U.S. Companies. 132 Tax Notes 330–333.

Sullivan, Martin A. 2011b. Apple's High Effective Tax Rate Obscures Foreign Tax Benefits. 132 Tax Notes 459.

Sullivan, Martin A. 2012. Apple Reports High Rate But Saves Billions on Taxes. 134 Tax Notes 777.

Suranovic, Steven. 2010a. International Trade: Theory and Policy. Published online at http://www.flatworldknowledge.com/printed-book/205113 by Flat World Knowledge

Suranovic, Steven. 2010b. A Moderate Compromise: Economic Policy Choice in an Era of Globalization. New York: Palgrave Macmillan.

Surrey, Stanley S. 1956. Current Issues in the Taxation of Corporate Foreign Investment. 56 Columbia Law Review 815–859.

Surrey, Stanley S. 1958. The United States Taxation of Foreign Income. 1 Journal of Law and Economics 72–96.

Sykes, Alan O. 1991. Protectionism as a "Safeguard": A Positive Analysis of the GATT "Escape Clause" with Normative Speculations. 58 University of Chicago Law Review 255–305.

Tesar, Linda L., and Ingrid M. Werner. 1995. Home Bias and High Turnover. 14 Journal of International Money and Finance 467.

Tiebout, Charles. 1956. A Pure Theory of Local Expenditures. 64 Journal of Political Economy 416–424.

Tillinghast, David R. 1984. A Matter of Definition: "Foreign" and "Domestic" Taxpayers. 2 International Tax and Business Lawyer 239–272.

United States Department of the Treasury. 2006. United States Model Income Tax Convention of November 15, 2006.

United States Government Accountability Office. 2008a. Comparison of the Reported Tax Liabilities of Foreign- and U.S.-Controlled Corporations, 1998–2005. GAO-08-957 (July).

United States Government Accountability Office. 2008b. U.S. Multinational Corporations: Effective Tax Rates Are Correlated with Where Income Is Reported. GAO-08-950 (August).

VanderWolk, Jefferson P. 2010. Inversions Under Section 7874 of the Internal Revenue Code: Flawed Legislation, Flawed Guidance. 30 Northwestern Journal of International Law and Business 699–719.

Vann, Richard J. 2010. Taxing International Business Income: Hard-Boiled Wonderland and the End of the World. Available on-line at http://www.sbs.ox.ac.uk/centres/tax/conferences/Documents/INTR%202010/Vann.pdf.

Voget, Johannes. 2011. Relocation of Headquarters and International Taxation. 95 Journal of Public Economics 1067–1081.

Walker, Andrew. 2009. Exceptions in Search of a Rule: The Source and Taxability of "None of the Above" Income. The Tax Club, New York City, May 18.

Warren, Alvin C. 1995. The Proposal for an "Unlimited Savings Allowance." 68 Tax Notes 1103.

Warren, Alvin C., Jr. 2001. Income Tax Discrimination Against International Commerce. 54 Tax Law Review 131–169.

Weiner, Joann M. 2006. Company Tax Reform in the European Union: Guidance from the United States on Implementing Formulary Apportionment in the EU. New York: Springer.

Weiner, Joann M. 2007. Redirecting the Debate on Formulary Apportionment. 115 Tax Notes 1164.

Weisbach, David A. 1999. Line-Drawing, Doctrine, and Efficiency in the Tax Law. 84 Cornell Law Review 1627–1681.

Weisbach, David A. 2003. Does the X-Tax Mark the Spot? 56 SMU Law Review 201.

Weisbach, David A. 2008. Implementing Income and Consumption Taxes. In Alan J. Auerbach and Danel Shaviro (eds.), Institutional Foundations of Public Finance. Cambridge, MA: Harvard University Press, 59–93.

Wells, Bret. 2012. Cant and the Inconvenient Truth About Corporate Inversions. 136 Tax Notes 429–439.

Wetzler, James. 1995. Should the U.S. Adopt Formulary Apportionment?, 48 National Tax Journal 357–362.

White House, Office of the Press Secretary. 2009. Leveling the Playing Field: Curbing Tax Havens and Removing Tax Incentives for Shifting Jobs Overseas (May 4). Available online at http://www.whitehouse.gov/the_press_office/leveling-the-playing-field-curbing-tax-havens-and-removing-tax-incentives-for-shifting-jobs-overseas.

Woodward, Bob. 2012. The Price of Politics. NewYork: Simon & Schuster.

Young, Sam. 2007. JCT Chief Discusses Thorny Issues on Hill Agenda. 117 Tax Notes 1110.

Index